PAN-AFRICANISM *AND* CROSS-CULTURAL UNDERSTANDING: *A READER*

Edited by
François N. Muyumba and Esther Atcherson
Indiana State University

GINN PRESS

Printed in the United States of America

10 9 8 7 6 5 4 3 2 1

ISBN 0-536-58486-9
BA 5178

GINN PRESS

160 Gould Street/Needham Heights, MA 02194
Simon & Schuster Higher Education Publishing Group

PAN-AFRICANISM AND CROSS-CULTURAL UNDERSTANDING: A READER

TABLE OF CONTENTS

PREFACE

Numerous works in African and African-American Studies are designed to introduce students to the discipline. Some are thematic, with chapters devoted uniquely to major topics such as "Racial Identification", "Black Philosophy and Ideology of Nationalism", "History and Social Change", "Religions and Black Leadership", "Africans in America", and so on. Other works are encyclopedic in nature, a veritable "Who's Who" in the field providing brief summaries of writers and approaches from ancient times to the present. Each approach has its merits, place and significance and both serve higher purposes.

This book takes a different approach. We make no claim to have covered every aspect of the scope of Pan-African Studies, much less every writer or scholarly contributor. We do, however, propose to: (1) discuss the underlying assumptions and trends that influence scholarly work in Pan-African studies and research - the emerging philosophical constructs or images labeled Afrocentric Dimensions of Pan-Africanism which are inherent values defining Pan-Africanism; (2) provide in the chapters and readings representative samples of contemporary theoretical works and analyses that can help a student master and internalize the meanings of Pan-Africanism; (3) introduce undergraduate and graduate students to key concepts used by scholars in their study of Pan-Africanism; and (4) encourage students to scrutinize critically works dealing with Pan-African relations and challenges.

The fourth purpose is of particular importance to us especially as the perspectives of Africans and the image of Africa and its dispersed sons and daughters seem to be distorted and neglected. If a student leaves the classroom better prepared to analyze everyday events, to ask the difficult questions, to recognize underlying assumptions of writers' works by academics, government officials, and journalists, this achievement would transcend any others such as memorizing which author is associated with what theory. We have attempted to make the subject understandable and to not overwhelm the reader with details in reports of the major Congresses. Particular events and authors are mentioned when it is necessary to highlight a critical concept, debate, issue, trend, or theory. Topical headings in each chapter call attention to key concepts and factors.

We fully recognize the problem of generating a particular image of Pan-Africanism when there are varying perspectives. We have thus discussed levels of perceptions and contexts of interactions that make Pan-Africanism understandable and which provide the learner with less associative difficulty.

We trust that this volume of original articles will add a powerful vision to the Pan-African Studies Movement; it represents a concentrated effort to help students become acquainted with cross-cultural features and dimensions of Pan-Africanism. The manuscript for the book could not have been prepared without the many participants in annual Pan-African conferences at Indiana State University, the contributions and suggestions of colleagues, and the excellent secretarial assistance of Shannon Long and Shirley Herrington. We also wish to acknowledge grants from the Presbyterian Church (USA) and the Lilly Endowment which have helped make this volume possible.

Dr. François N. Muyumba and Esther Atcherson
June, 1993

ABOUT THE EDITORS AND AUTHORS

Benjamin Asare, Ph.D., Temple University. Dr. Asare is Assistant Professor of Political Science at Indiana University Southwest.

Esther Atcherson, M.S.W., University of Iowa. Ms. Atcherson is Assistant to the President for Affirmative Action and Adjunct Assistant Professor of Social Work, Indiana State University. She has edited and authored papers and publications on minority and gender research, medical and social issues, and on interdisciplinary curricula.

Augustin Ainamon, Ph.D., Dr. Ainamon is Professor of English Language and Literature at the Université Nationale du Bénin, Cotonou, and was a Fulbright scholar in 1988-1989.

Assefaw Bariagaber, Ph.D., University of Southern Illinois, Carbondale. Dr. Bariagaber is Assistant Professor in the Department of Political Science, University of Nebraska-Kearney.

Harban S. Bhola, Ph.D., Ohio State University. Dr. Bhola is Professor of International Comparative Education and Educational Media at Indiana University. Dr. Bhola has authored numerous publications, and his research interests include adult literacy, history and foundations of education, and communication and education. Dr. Bhola has served as UNESCO consultant for several years and has been directly involved in the development of literacy programs in Africa, Iran, and India.

Donald F. Bobb, Ph.D., University of Texas, Houston. Dr. Bobb is Pastor of a Presbyterian Church in Austin, Texas. He formerly served as the Director of Islamic - Christian Center in West Africa. Dr. Bobb has a specialty in Global Christian Ministry and in the Christian Youth Movement. He spent twenty years or more in Africa.

Edward Boyle, Ph.D. candidate, Department of Geography at the University of Illinois, Champaign -Urbana, Illinois.

Marie-Josée Cérol, Ph.D., Sorbonne, France, Department of Linguistics. Dr. Cérol is an Assistant Professor in African-American Studies at Temple University. She has taught at the University of Texas in Austin, Texas and at Pennsylvania State University, University Park, Pennsylvania. Her research interests include language and culture in the Caribbean, sociolinguistics, and literature and language as tools for both oppression and liberation.

Andrew Conteh, Ph.D., Kiev State University in the former USSR, Political Science. Dr. Conteh is Professor of Political Science at Moorhead State University. Currently, his research interests include international relations and international law, emerging countries of the former USSR, international economics, and relationships of Africa's Afro-Marxist states, the Russian Federation and the United States.

Arun Elhance, Ph.D., Boston University. Dr. Elhance is Assistant Professor of Geography, University of Illinois, Urbana-Champaign. His research interests are economics, geography, and regional science.

Father Carroll Houle, has spent over thirty years in East Africa and specifically in Tanzania as a missionary with the Maryknoll Missionary Society. He toured the United States in 1986 to inform Americans about causes of famine and crises that have affected Africa. He is the Director of the African Area within the Maryknoll Father's Organization.

Anthonia C. Kalu, Ph.D. University of Wisconsin. Dr. Kalu is Associate Professor and Chairperson, Department of African-American Studies, Northern Colorado University. Her research interests include African women's studies, African-American literature, African language and literature, African culture and Pan-African studies.

Edmond J. Keller, Ph.D., University of Wisconsin, Madison. Dr. Keller is a Professor of Political Science and Dean of Graduate Studies at the University of California, Santa Barbara. His specialty is African politics and public policy. Dr. Keller is the author of publications on Africa, Afro-American Politics, and Education including *Education, Manpower and Development: The Impact of Educational Policy in Kenya, Revolutionary Ethiopia, Afro-Marxist Regimes* (co-edited with Donald Rothchild). Dr. Keller has worked extensively in Ethiopia and Kenya.

Safro Kwame, Ph.D. degrees in Philosophy from the University of Ghana in 1982and the University of Cincinnati in 1989. Dr. Kwame is an AssistantProfessor of Philosophy at Lincoln University. His research interests include: metaphysics and moral/political philosophy, epistemology, philosophy of mind and philosophy of education. He has articles in *Contemporary Philosophy, Journal of Business Ethics,* and *Personalist Forum.*

Mbella Ngomba-Maija, Ph.D., Howard University, Mass Communication and Media Research. Dr. Mbella is an Assistant Professor of Communication at Indiana State University. His research interests include media studies, international communication and development.

Yeno Mansoni Matuka, Ph.D., Ball State University, English and Applied Linguistics. Dr. Matuka is an Assistant Professor of English and French at Ball State University. A graduate of the Zairian Institut Pedagogique National (I.P.N.) in Kinshasa, Dr. Matuka's research interests include language and culture, sociolinguistic research, communication for conflict resolution, psycholinguistics and its applications in pedagogy, and methodology of language teaching.

Ali Mazrui, Ph.D., Oxford University in England (B.A., Manchester University, England; M.A. , Columbia University, New York). Dr. Mazrui is a Distinguished Professor of Political Science and African and African-American Studies at the State University of New York at Binghamton. Dr.

Mazui is a prolific scholar-teacher whose publications and other writings are well known worldwide. His video series, "The Africans: A Triple Heritage," (jointly produced by the BBC and Public Broadcasting Service in association with the Nigerian Television Authority) has been widely viewed by audiences throughout the world. Dr. Mazrui was formerly Chair of the Department of Political Science and Dean of the Faculty of Social Sciences at Makerere University in Kampala, Uganda.

François N. Muyumba, Ph.D., Indiana University, English Education and Curriculum, M.A., Linguistics. Dr. Muyumba is Associate Professor of African-American Studies at Indiana State University. He has authored publications, reviews, and articles and was co-editor of *From Third World to One World: the Pan-African Perspective* and *North-South Dialogue: New Directions.* Dr. Muyumba is the founding director and convener of the Annual Pan-African Studies Conferences at Indiana State University. His research interests include language and culture, sociolinguistics, Pan-Africanism and political education, interdisciplinary approaches to global development, African-American studies, and African oral traditions and culture. Dr. Muyumba was born in Zaïre, has lived and worked in Zambia and Cameroon.

Georges N. Nzongola, Ph.D., University of Wisconsin, Madison, Political Science. Dr. Nzongola is a Distinguished Professor of Political Science and African Studies at Howard University. His speciality is African politics and public policy. Born in Zaire, Dr. Nzongola has served for the past fifteen years as Executive Director of Cerez (Center for Research on Zaire). He is the author of numerous publications on Africa, the political economy, and crises that affect Africa. He has served as President of the African Studies Association (USA) and as a Consultant to African University. He has lived and worked in Nigeria and visited many countries in Africa, including Zimbabwe, Djibouti, Eritria, and Ethiopia.

Bamidele A. Ojo, Ph.D., Nottingham University, England (B.S., University of Ife, Nigeria). Dr. Ojo is an Assistant Professor of Political Science and African

Studies, Department of History, Social Sciences and International Studies at Fairleigh Dickinson University.

Diana F. Ryan, Ph.D. candidate, Department of Instructional Systems Technology, School of Education, Indiana University. Ms. Ryan has lived and worked in Kenya and her research interests include mass media, mass communication and socio-political integration.

Vincent Simiyu, Ph.D., University of Nairobi, Kenya. Dr. Simiyu is an Assistant Professor at the University of Nairobi and has been a Fulbright visiting scholar.

Clifford Staten, Ph.D., Northern Texas University, Political Science. Dr. Staten is an Assistant Professor of Political Science at Indiana University Southeast. His research interests include the international political economy and African and Third World development theories and applications.

Wendell Stills, graduate student in doctoral program, Department of Geography, University of Illinois, Urbana-Champaign, and a co-author with Arun Elhance and Edward Boyle.

Ezabele Wa Yasak, Ph.D. candidate, Michigan State University, Sociology. Mr. Yasak is an USAID Fellow. He has served as an Assistant Professor at theUniversity of Kisanagani, Zaïre, and his research interests include social work, sociology and the farming communities, institutional violence and socio-political integration.

Kwasi Yirenkyi, Ph.D., University of Pittsburgh (M.A., Pittsburgh Seminary). Dr. Yirenkyi is an Associate Professor and Acting Chair of the Departmentof Philosophy and Religious Studies at Indiana University of Pennsylvania. His research interests include religions and political development in Africa and in the Diaspora, Christianity and social ethics, religion and traditional culture, and sociology of religion.

INTRODUCTION

How can the image of a modern Africa reconcile with its past and prepare for its future? Scholars are attempting to retrace the history of the entire African continent and to establish links based on cultural heritage, linguistic relationship, and historical connections between peoples. There is a vast heritage in which to take pride, a heritage which attests to the strength and resilience of African people. Yet it is evident, according to Cheikh Anta Diop (and others), that there has indeed been a decline in Africa, especially at the level of the masses, a decline due to colonization.

In recent decades, at least from the 1920's onward, there have been conflicts and competitions with special meanings for Africa. Many African countries like the Belgian Congo/Zaire have been tarnished by colonialist domination and by political crises and economic decline. African dictators such as Mobutu in Zaire have received public recognition and praise from leaders in the United States and the former Soviet Union even though the well-being of African people under their dictatorial leadership has remained tragically at a very low priority among the order of issues influencing the superpowers' foreign policies.

The U.S. involvement in Africa in the 1960's and 1970's was characterized by a refusal to offend allies in Western Europe through appearing to be overly interested in their colonies in Africa. Such fear receded by 1975 when Mozambiqueans and Angolans overthrew the Portuguese colonialists where the U.S. had found new interests. The success of Afro-Marxist regimes in these two countries (Keller et al, 1987) made it clear that superpowers' clashes would be spreading throughout the continent. Zambia, Zaire and South Africa benefited a great deal and their political value increased not only because of abundant natural resources (copper, uranium, diamonds and other rare minerals) but also because of the utility of their geopolitical location.

The dilemma in Pan-African relations has been defined both politically and economically. In the first place, for over 400 years the Diaspora has been kept in perpetual dependency if not in a state of slavery whereby African identity, self-esteem, and self-determination have been made to appear as impossible dreams! Dreams of equality and humanhood have all been deferred by the overwhelming and disarming white supremacist ideals, behaviors and socio-political and economic policies - the incarnation of White Power in the American hemisphere. From Harlem to Rio de Janeiro to Capetown, Africans have exhibited the dualistic effect of enslavement. They have resented being who they were and have earnestly striven to become what they were not. They have wanted to pass as if they were Whites, hence, the growth of self-hate and rejection of things culturally African.

Even though many educators and Afrocentric writers since the 1920's have called for a return to things African, the transformation from Afro-saxons to Afrocentricity, from "boys" and "girls" to "men" and "women" has indeed constituted a long struggle for the Diaspora. During the 1960's, for example, there were incidences in which individuals at Virginia Union University in Richmond, Virginia, fought with those who called them Black, or Africans. They clearly preferred being called 'Negroes' because a Negro was neither Black nor African (and might even be half white)! More affinity was claimed with White oppressors and more connection with White American's skin. This social distortion of reality reflected a psychological lack of knowledge of self and the Tarzan-mentality imposed systematically upon the Diaspora.

Both powerlessness and ignorance retarded the fulfillment of Pan-Africanist ideals and desires to become actively involved in the liberation of the African community. How could non-Africans envision sacrificing themselves for supposedly 'backward' and often misrepresented Africans? By the 1970's, the political environment had changed as the Soviet Union appeared to have concluded they had a role to play in selected national liberation movements on the African continent and, if necessary, in the American hemisphere. Certain African leaders had always wrongly assumed that the Soviet Union was an active opponent of neo-colonialism while inherently Western Europe and the U. S. were inclined to imperialism. We know better now. The super powers fed on each other's fears and misconceptions to define themselves. They indeed were not different in their intention to dominate the global economy. Their continuing power provides explanations why the initial political strides of the Pan-African movement had limited success.

This book of original essays is divided into six different sections. Each section represents a collection of related ideas that reflect contemporary perceptions, approaches and understanding. In Section I, the authors have concentrated on the history, scope and meaning of Pan-Africanism. They catalogue its chronological evolution and trace a new direction for what has become a Pan-Africanist scholarly and cultural movement. Dr. François Muyumba examines the Afrocentric properties of Pan-Africanism. He views Pan-Africanism as a grand old ideology that includes inherent Afrocentric dimensions of humanity suggesting an advanced, progressive march toward the realization of a world community founded on principles of equity, justice, and respect for all people. Pan-Africanism engenders a multi-dimensional view of a holistic 'world in the making' in which there is an ongoing struggle to develop mutual concord among people and their governments. Dr. Muyumba also envisions Pan-Africanism as a philosophical construct having both impact and influence to affect positively the quality of education needed to produce new types of world citizens. Those world citizens who are Africa's sons and daughters can be rightfully proud of African ancestry and, using lessons drawn from their African heritage, can work toward humanizing world affairs by their contributions to the enhancement of others' lives. The dimensions of Pan-Africanism thus include qualitative Afrocentric ideals which provide guidelines for our participation in community, regional, national, and international leadership.

In the second chapter of Section I, Dr. Ali A. Mazrui questions African dependence on the North. He notes African's reliance on foreign languages has caused not just linguistic dependency but also scientific and technological dependency. Dr. Mazrui proposes that African nations "stop watching Europe and America" and instead look at what is happening in Asia. As for the force of gender in Africa, Dr. Mazrui notes that disproportionate burdens are put on women in African society and asserts a way must be found to combine freedom with significance. Dr. Mazrui concludes that the relationship between a developed world and Africa is a global experience which cannot be regarded simply as a case of political economy. It also represents a political culture which clearly touches upon religion, language, education and gender as well as the wider ideology that dominates our universe.

In the next chapter, Dr. Andrew Conteh retraces the evolution of the Pan-

African movement from the Diaspora to Africa through the contributions of Henry Sylvester Williams, W. E. B. DuBois, George Padmore, Amy Ashwood Garvey, and Marcus Garvey. It was W. E. B. DuBois' vision of Pan-Africanism as part of oppressed peoples' global struggle for freedom and justice that produced the dimensions outlined elsewhere in this book. Dr. Conteh provides an overview of the historiography of transition from ideological orientation to institutionalization of these ideals in the African continent through the efforts of President Kwame Nkrumah of Ghana, Milton Obote of Uganda, Jomo Kenyatta of Kenya, Mwalimu Julius Nyerere of Kenya, and others, culminating in the founding of the Organization of African Unity. The search for African unity is both a global endeavor and a regional undertaking. The meaning of Pan-Africanism is important at all levels of interactions and discourse.

Section II deals with the issue of media, language and liberation. There has been considerable research by scholars examining the role of language in communication and especially in cultural domination. In Chapter 4, Dr. Marie-Josée Cérol writes about the power of language in liberating African people from oppression. She proposes that effective knowledge and masterful usage of language is liberating, especially via expression of one's own creative cultural ideas. In Chapter 5, Dr. Augustin Ainamon discusses the relationship between language and literature in the learning process. He questions the relevance of using English, French, or other languages from colonialization as media for communications and instruments of national education. In Chapter 6, Dr. H. S. Bhola examines the importance of adult literacy in the fulfillment of the goals and purposes of Pan-Africanism. He asserts that cultures exist in communication and that literacy provides another means for Africans to speak with each other, listen to each other, and develop commonalities even though there are at least 1000 different African languages.

In Chapters 7 and 8, Diana F. Ryan and Dr. Mbella Ngomba-Maija examine respectively the problems related to communication in printed media as well as on radio and television. Ms. Ryan contends that the African press has the power and potential to identify and promote values that link urban and educated people to rural uneducated people. In line with Pan-African thinking, Ryan argues that, rather than maintaining and promoting differentiation between the urban elite and rural poor, the press can and should contribute to unity by promoting values that both groups identify with, whether in development projects or on other matters. Dr. Mbella Ngomba Maija concentrates on the overwhelming dominance of Western media systems in Third World nations generally and more particularly in Africa (after all, few countries have the financial ability to gather international news). Dr. Mbella notes that the four largest Western news agencies - AP (U.S.), UPI (U.S.), AFP (France), and Reuters (U.K.) - have largely shaped the presentation of news in developing countries and defined news values for their mass media. He furthermore observes that the quality and quantity of news coverage is not determined by media philosophies; rather it is due to economic factors.

The third Section focuses the attention of the reader on the development of military systems of government at the expense of socioeconomic systems. In Chapter 9, Drs. Asare and Staten examine the success and failure of the structural adjustment measures adopted by the Republic of Ghana under Rawlings in the 1980's and their impact on overall development. According to the authors, Ghana is regarded as a model for structural adjustment among developing states of the world primarily because Ghana agreed to stabilize its economy through devaluation of its currency (cedi), liberalization of import policies, curtailing of domestic deficit financing, income policy, tax reform, and other measures. Despite these structural adjustments, Asare and Staten illustrate that overall economic development came to a standstill in 1982. They conclude that the semi-feudal land tenure system and lack of farmers' accessibility to the world market call for a change in focus from short term growth to long range development.

In Chapter 10, Ezabele Wa Yasak examines the violence directed against the farmers in Zaire by the authoritarian regime of Mobutu. Mr. Wasak asks whether farmers are consulted by the state and international organizations about social and economic policies that affect them. Given their low income, how can farmers afford fertilizer or seed at the government ordained prices? Zaire has served as a convenient battle ground for cold war rivalries between the superpowers, and has, through the authoritarian policies of Mobutu, engaged in luxury consumption and unproductive investments and expenditures. In Chapter 11, Dr. Safro Kwame provides a stinging criticism of Pan-Africanism as conceived and developed by both W. E. B. DuBois and Kwame Nkrumah whom he claims are race focused. He suggests that Africans better learn from the recent developments in Somalia which involved Black-on-Black violence. He doesn't believe Africa has the capability to wage a successful struggle for unity on grounds that its people are biologically of the same stock. Rather, all African thinkers should 'return to the drawing board' to produce a new plan of action aimed at building a system of accountability and efficiency that acknowledges human imperfections while building an efficient and sensitive system capable of responding to the needs of Africa's hungry, poor, and sick people.

The scholars in Section IV turn their attention to the role of religion in building socio-psychological, cultural, and spiritual bases for solidarity. Pan-Africanism as an ideology encourages the coming together of people not because they believe in similar things but because they are able to celebrate their diversity. In Chapter 12, Dr. Donald Bobb outlines the role of Moslems and Christians, two major religious organizations, in the development of Africa. Dr. Bobb suggests that Moslems and Christians in Africa are called to become critical caretakers and servants in West Africa today, and that much of the future direction and influence of both faiths will depend on their relevance to socio-economic and political development within the cultural milieu of the African people.

Dr. Kwasi Yirenkyi writes in Chapter 13 about the ethics which enable a society to determine the rules governing the distribution of available wealth and about the moral dimensions of the repression and dehumanization of Africans as illustrated in Ghana. Some political scientists state that African pre-colonial political institutions were stable because they were widely accepted by people and allowed for participation of the citizenry in political affairs. Dr. Yirenkyi maintains that the traditional moral and spiritual basis of law and its relationship with the people have been ignored by African law makers. Africans should never forget the exploitation of land and people that has accompanied Western industrialization. In pursuing development along Western models, Africans should be reminded that the search for harmony is the essence of development.

In Chapter 14, Father Carroll Houle examines the tragic impact of warfare and violence in Africa. He asks how can countries develop their agriculture and industries in war zones? Father Houle says that U. S. foreign policy may be the cause of violence in the forms of war and hunger, especially in places like Angola and Mozambique; he proposes a concentrated and unified effort to change U.S. Foreign policy for Africa's betterment.

The fifth Section includes a range of approaches and interpretation directed toward analyzing the relationship between African-Americans and Africa. In Chapter 15, Dr. Edmond J. Keller introduces a critical review of the misunderstandings that characterize African-Americans' perception of Frantz Fanon's work. He points out that the defining conditions of the Diaspora make it difficult to apply what Fanon says to America. Dr. Keller explains that although Fanon was admired by members of the radical Black Power movements in the late 1960's and early 1970's, advocates of Black Power and Black intellectuals of the 1980's have not fully comprehended Fanon's message. Keller concludes that "while national liberation in the sense that Fanon meant it for Africa is beyond the reach of Black America, meaningful political empowerment is a realistic goal for many Black communities."

In Chapter 16, Dr. Vincent G. Simiyu tackles the topic of commonalities that bind Africans and African-Americans historically, culturally and socially. Dr. Simiyu states that the preservation of culture through oral tradition as well as material culture is one of the most fascinating common themes. He finds commonality in African and African-American peoples' contributions to the rise of the North American economic system and that of the entire Western hemisphere. Africans and African-Americans shared a common experience of having been exploited through European colonialism and slavery. Dr. Simiyu concludes that African-Americans are part and parcel of the African cultural experience.

In Chapter 17, Dr. Yeno Mansoni Matuka introduces the reader to a system of conflict resolution known as the 'palaver' practiced in the Central Bantu region of Africa. For Dr. Matuka, the palaver reflects African intuition and a propensity to address issues, find a consensus, and preserve the peace. The issues become Maambu, "affairs or conflicts", when they are not dealt with promptly and correctly. The palaver must be able to resolve publicly these disputes by bringing the disputants and the public audience to a consensus, seeking the collective welfare more than personal interests.

In Chapter 18, Dr. Anthonia Kalu proposes that Pan-Africanist scholarship, social relations and dialogue should be aimed at the creation of a new Diaspora. For Dr. Kalu, the contemporary denial of Africa's rich culture and history is rooted in both Eurocentric and irresponsible African attitudes and scholarship, in the continent and in the Diaspora, which distorted and sometimes mis-analyzed African realities. For her, this denial has facilitated internationalization of an inferiority doctrine dating back to the time of Africans' subjugation. Dr. Kalu observes that Africa has produced a formidable number of excellent thinkers, often unrecognized and called to spend their energies initiating strategies and maintaining processes for liberation from bondage. In order to fight misrepresentations and avoid this denial, Dr. Kalu concludes that we need to create a new Diaspora, a set of new vibrant, active, visible, courageous and dynamic communities rooted in African perceptions of the world and its rich presence in it. For Dr. Kalu, the acceptance and internationalization of the inferiority doctrines in both colonial and slavery time is understandable, but a continued adherence to those ideas during the final days of the century is indeed inexcusable.

The sixth Section is an overview of present and future conditions that impact on Pan-African scholarship. The challenges include the status of the Organization of African Unity (OAU) in the context of democracy movements in Eastern Europe, the Russian Federation, and in Africa. In Chapter 19, Dr. Bamidele Ojo provides an analysis of Africa in the context of world affairs. He claims that contemporary African leaders and governments, in their relationship with major game players in the world, demonstrate the boyish attributes of Peter-Pan. They do not want to accept responsibilities for their domestic and foreign policies. By blaming anybody rather than themselves, they have failed to display any sense of self-determination and sovereignty. For Dr. Ojo, this irresponsible behavior has resulted in Africa becoming too dependent on external forces and sources of power and, accordingly, becoming a nation-state where a sense of the leaderships' accountability is absent. Dr. Ojo stresses the fact that competent political leadership has the capacity to translate far sighted policies into political realities. "Leaders should not only have the national interest at heart, but must also have the ability to turn good intentions into good programs and must be able to seek and obtain public support for proposed programs and policies." As Dr. Ojo concludes, quality and competence of political leadership is crucial to ensuring the sustainability of African economic growth.

Dr. Assefaw Bariagaber examines a decade of challenges for the Organization of African Unity (OAU) in Chapter 20. He stresses the fact that this regional organization was established to promote the unity, independence, and well-being of African people. Dr. Bariagaber forecasts that the OAU will gradually emerge as a resource to resolve conflicts and problems, especially as it becomes recognized as a central authority and storehouse of Pan-African affairs. The OAU's broad capacity for leadership and competence in settling problems rising between regional organizations will give a much needed dynamism to the process of changing Africa.

In Chapter 21, Dr. G. Nzongola outlines the status of democratic movements in Africa. Drawing from his long involvement with African politics, he provides insights about both positive and negative developments. He believes that the major sources and determinants of democratic movements in Africa today are peoples' longstanding aspiration for political and economic participation. This aspiration has manifested itself in (1) indigenous precolonial democratic traditions such as democratic principles of governance in African societies and the palaver; (2) the anticolonial struggle all over the continent, beginning with ANC of South Africa in 1912; and (3) secondary independence movements (Zaire, Chad, Uganda). The presence of oppressive military dictatorships has challenged peoples' humanity and attempted to subjugate them even in their own lands. Dr. Nzongola identifies, among other positive dynamics, the National Conferences and national multiparty elections emerging as political institutions and/or mechanisms through which political changes are expected to take place. While international solidarity with our brothers and sisters engaged in the struggle is necessary (and it is particularly important for U. S. citizens to support them), the current struggle for democracy will be won by the people waging it on African soil.

In Chapter 22, Edward Boyle, Wendell Stills and Arun Elhance examine the readiness of African nation-states, in their present 'soft state' status, to assume the important role of effecting change and setting the pace and foundation for a new world order. They propose viewing Pan-Africanism as a philosophy or ideology which can provide African nation-states with a critical mass of thought and direction for the 21st century. In addition to its being a philosophy of Africanism, Pan-Africanism has the potential to become a force with an economic development agenda, but an agenda which encourages greater interdependency between African states as opposed to the types of unions actively being proposed between former colonies and their colonizer. Africa has new and significant roles to play in the post cold war world which will require considerable collective efforts.

Contemporary African Political Map

SECTION I

PHILOSOPHY OF PAN-AFRICANISM: HISTORIOGRAPHY AND SCOPE

CHAPTER 1

AFROCENTRIC DIMENSIONS OF PAN-AFRICANISM

François N. Muyumba

Pan-Africanism as a socio-cultural and political ideology rises from an African philosophy of life. As with humans in other places, Africans have dealt with the ultimate questions of life and death, and they have come up with a systematic way of life in response. Tempels (1959) points out, for instance, that human beings everywhere particularly return to their God when crises and sicknesses affect them. Otherwise, many in Europe and America may deliberately refuse to be faithful to their religion until some shocking event leads to seeking a divine intervention.

Africans act in the same way even in relationship to Christianity. When stricken with serious illness, for example, they may receive appropriate medical treatment and follow their religion; however, if there is not an immediate, sufficient and satisfactory cure, they will also seek the help of the African 'Nganga' and an explanation of why things have happened the way they have. The Nganga or diviner is the connecting link to the traditional and cultural way of life. He/she interacts with the spiritual and physical spheres and obtains positive results because of familiarity with a basic philosophy of life in which one needs to be cured both physically and spiritually. African ontology governs the African way of thinking and dealing with the universe. In this realm, one is bound to maintain good relationships with living humans, with departed relatives who become ancestors, and with the Supreme Being.

In the Bantu's philosophy, all persons are the incarnation of both spiritual and physical realms, the points of contact between the visible and invisible worlds. Among the Bantu, the concept, "Nvidia-Mukulu Mawej'a Nangila, Nkayenda Mudifuka, Diba Katangidi tshishiki, wa kutangila wabuela Nsesa," expresses the idea of "The Wise and Loving Eternal God, who created Himself, who, like the sun, cannot be seen by the naked eye; anyone who dares look at Him will be blinded." The bond between God, ancestors, and living humans is maintained by a code of conduct which Tempels (1959) and Yirenkyi (1993) refer to as ethics. Ethics in Bantu culture are taboos or laws that govern harmony, insure the stability of family life, and regulate relationships. All forms of family relationships are defined and dictated by these ontological principles.

Afrocentricity as a philosophy of social change and psychological liberation requires discussion of the *vital force* that grounds it in African philosophy. Born out of African cultural and political thought and given impetus by struggles for self-definition, Pan-Africanism and Afrocentricity mutually support one another in bringing back the African personhood. The Pan-African movement toward unity at all levels of interactions and Afrocentricity's focus on an African philosophy of life are extensions and projections of the same creative force or 'Nommo.' They emerge as the collective responses of African peoples in the continent and Diaspora to the historical and psychological challenges that have characterized their presence and contributions (Muyumba 1989).

Some argue that Pan-Africanism is a political movement created, developed and used by Africans in the Diaspora as opposed to those in the continent. However, the notion of African unity and collective destiny is profoundly embedded within the central core of African civilizations and cultures.

Pan-Africanism has been a socio-political movement dating back to the 1800's which has advocated and concretely sought to bring African people in the continent and in the Diaspora together. I will argue that Pan-Africanism as a cultural movement and philosophy is deeply rooted in the African way of life. It has acquired broad dimensions and conceptualizations which reflect the original oral and written ideas and ideals. These sources help articulate Pan-Africanism. The ideological origins of African-American nationalism are certainly not confined to the *Ethiopian Manifesto* by Robert Young and/or by Walker's *Appeal*, both of which are more Pan-Africanist than slogans of the 1900's to 1970's. What is important is the fact that these quests for freedom originated in the peoples' thoughts and had been part of the oral tradition. Both Walker and Young, like Nat Turner, appealed to oppressed and suffering Africans to rise up and work on their own behalf, a call to action in preparation for the day when a Messiah and/or liberator would emerge among them. These two abolitionists illustrated Pan-Africanism as an ideology of liberation defined by values and dimensions extending far beyond the boundaries of our geopolitical vision. It is essentially a set of concepts containing social, cultural, political, economic, material and spiritual aspirations for mutual respect, collective responsibility, economic cooperation, and self-determination.

PAN-AFRICANISM AND PERSONHOOD

The term 'Pan' means 'open,' 'without borders' or 'all.' It gives global scope to the term Africanism and distinguishes Africans by assigning an African identity to everyone instead of a racial nationality. As Lemelle (1992) observes, this idea and movement grew out of Black people's desire to rediscover and recover their individuality and heritage and their desire to fight for their liberation from colonialism and racism (Lemelle, 1992 p.12). Beyond belonging to a segment of the world community characterized by the dehumanizing denial of personhood, Pan-Africanism conveys a sense of being grounded in a shared cultural philosophy of life. As the Bantu often say, it assigns to each person an African 'bumuntu' or a sense and a right to be a human. The absence of 'bumuntu' or the less 'bumuntu' one has, the less 'muntu' or human being one becomes.

In African philosophy a person can be accused of having caused someone's illness and/or even death simply because of a dispute or an insult. In most Western settings such accusations would not be considered to have any foundation. In Africa, however, a traditional court known as 'Tshikos'a Bilumbu' or palaver breaker would have to convene and render judgment which the accused would have to accept. The accused may have to pay, without argument, the damages claimed even if the accused has been tried in a civil court and found to be not guilty (Tempels, 1959: 28-30).

With Africans coming to the Americas today and African-Americans traveling to different parts of Africa, the ongoing Atlantic cross-currents are diluting the enshrined impact of slave trade with its forced immigration and misinformation, and they are leading toward the creation of a new Diaspora. In this diaspora, an emphasis is placed on the revitalization of Africanity, the Afrocentric family and Pan-African solidarity. A kind of revival is taking place in which African ontology brings an underlying spiritual reasoning to bear. The human hardships that have occurred during slavery, colonialization, and in recent dictatorships by the neo-colonial African states have probably not only affected individuals but have disturbed the ancestors and God to the point that the life-force, the essence of beings and bond of relationship, is broken and there is disharmony. As Pan-Africanism broadens from being a link between dispersed, disorganized, undisciplined and confused Africans to becoming a community of disciplined, well informed Africans, it gives back to Africans the courage and hope to work for fundamental changes wherever they live.

RELIGIOUS DIMENSIONS OF PAN-AFRICANISM

In the African way of life, religion, medicine, and metaphysical events are thought to be connected in the central core of life force or 'Mpokodi wa muoyo' rather than being separate. In African philosophy 'to be' is to possess life force. While human beings are not thought to possess the power to affect other human beings by either increasing or decreasing another person's life force, God affects everything because He is considered to be the 'Mpokodi' or source and all things emanate from the source. Metaphysically speaking, every existing thing draws life force from the *vital force* when its relationships to the *vital force*, relatives, and ancestors is in equilibrium. When those relationships are not balanced, there is cause for fear because things expected and unexpected begin to happen.

The origins of Pan-Africanism are embedded in the African way of life. The kidnapping, enslavement, forced immigration and transplantation of Africans into Europe and the New World opened a door for external oppression of captives which continued for 400 years. But these events alone did not constitute the start of African aspirations for unity and nationalism. Africans were motivated to build such visible monumental civilizations as in the states of Ghana, Mali, and Songhay, or in the Kush, Ethiopia, Nubia, Egypt and others. It is accurate to expect the search for freedom, personhood and equality would have been present in a culture where notions of collective destiny, collective responsibility, cooperation and a commonality existed. The diverse civilizations of Zimbabwe, Kush, Western Sudanic States, and/ or the Central Bantu states of Luba, Lunda, Kongo, Chokwe and Ovambo would not have emerged without the presence of strong bonding sentiments of oneness, togetherness and cooperation, distinctive features of an African ontology.

AFRICAN UNITY IN AFROCENTRIC PERSPECTIVES

Pan-Africanism promotes holistic approaches to the study and analysis of the historical conditions that have engendered the present state of the African people. It claims that no one person can be free when some or all of one's neighbors are still in bondage. This philosophy was reflected in many of Kwame Nkrumah's speeches and writings and in Patrice Lumumba's statements in the early days of Congolese/Zaïrean independence. During the inaugural speech for independence on June 30, 1960, Lumumba, spoke in the following terms:.

> The republic of the Congo has been proclaimed, and our beloved country is now in the hands of its sons and daughters. Together, my brothers and sisters, we are going to start a new struggle, a sublime struggle, which will lead our country to peace, prosperity, and greatness. Together we are going to establish social justice and ensure for each man [and woman] just remuneration for just work. We are going to show the world what a Black man can do when he works in freedom, and we are going to make the Congo the hub of all Africa. We are going to be vigilant that the lands of our nation truly profit our nation's children (Clark, 1970, p. 45).

The independence of Congo/Zaïre represented a victory and Lumumba himself became in life and death a symbol of the success of the Pan-African movement because of his nationalist ideas and Afrocentric vision. For Lumumba, free African people had a mission, defined by Frantz Fanon, to struggle for the creation of a renewed personhood after long centuries of enslavement and colonization. "We are going to show the world what [African] man [and woman] can do when he works in freedom,..."(Clark, 1970, p.43-44). These nationalistic aspirations questioned the colonizer's behaviors and values reflected in religion, psychology, ethics, economics, culture and politics, and sought to challenge them by a return to and reliance on values found in a traditional way of life. Pan-Africanism includes an intent to foster a society grounded in equity and justice in which citizens are consciously aware of their worth and work in order to live in harmony with others while rejecting isolationism, individualism, negative emotions, and tensions. This philosophy of life encourages a communal way of reflection by restraining individual desires while allowing individual persons the necessary latitudes for pursuing individual family goals. Pan-Africanism which does not promote the creation, establishment, and sustenance of solid, stable and productive families fails the test of Afrocentricity.

The African culture recognizes the fragility of the family as an institution, explained in part by the functions of taboos and other intense family constraints which regulate, sustain and safeguard it. The culture finds its significance and values in such proverbial expressions as 'charity begins at home'. Whether in a patriarchal or matriarchal family system, the presence of both mother and father is recognized as an essential and integral criterion for an effective family. There are certainly occasions and latitudes whereby role exchanges between male and female are tolerated and sanctioned, but the culture and ontology of governance of these relationships does not allow confusion. In the matriarchal family, for example, in which a female emerges as a head of her lineage, the family wealth and children logically become the responsibility of the mother; however, the female's role in the household vis à vis her husband is not different from that of a wife in the patriarchal family. The family is recognized as the most fundamental unit of society; it provides a mirror-image of that society and society is reflected in it. Contemporary failure to uphold the taboos (laws that govern family relationships) seems to emanate from confusion created by the presence of two conflicting mores - the Eurocentric individualist model versus the Afrocentric groupness model. As one is taught to love one's parents, brothers, sisters, cousins, aunts, uncles, nephews, and nieces by regarding them as members of one family, one cultivates the habit and propensity of loving lavishly one's spouse, of exuding human warmth, of compassion and of giving and helping others. Once so conditioned, one would indeed behave in this manner not only toward one's family but also toward the clan, the ethnic group, the community, the nation, and toward humanity as a whole.

Pan-African intellectuals, wherever they may be, must strive to promote the cultivation and sustenance of effective family units grounded in the African philosophy of life. The family in this context is a microcosm of, and foundation for society. As observed by Robert Williams (1972), Billingsley (1968) and Karenga (1980), the African-American family which ceases to be grounded in the *vital force* becomes dysfunctional. An Afrocentric family is strengthened by the following philosophical ideals and cultural values inherent in the African worldview, a set of values that define and guide African people:

(1) **Groupness:** This concept describes the propensity of African people to be group-oriented. It accounts for the intense sentiments toward the unification of Africa's sons and daughters expressed through Pan-Africanism, and it is reflected in African peoples' communal way of life. For example, African games and pastimes call for group involvement. Party dances demand drummers, singers, dancers and the audience. Game hunting is done in parties. Even the telling of tales, fables and stories calls for a group of listeners. Draw-net fishing or female fishing known as 'Kutuwa' (drawing water) requires a party of many women to erect a barrier which cuts off the flow of a stream; the women then go down the stream and collect fish on the dried up riverbed! Even in official propositions of marriage, one is supposed to do it in groups and be represented by important others who know him, who testify to his real identity, and who can speak in his behalf. As Yirenkyi (1993) in this volume observes, it means that "I am because we are ". One's full identity is confirmed by the entire community.

(2). **Commonality:** Commonalities are properties of shared traits that distinguish a particular cultural group. For example, whenever a mother has given birth, the significant others (especially the grandparents) are the first to look for common traits and characteristics that do not make the baby so unique that his/her origins are placed in doubt. It is very important to be said to resemble a relative, even if it is a distant one. In some parts of Africa this has been so important that we are still able to find practices where common tattoos and other body markings are done to facilitate recognition.

(3). **Sameness:** The third feature is the property of *sameness* in which efforts are made to conform to the identity of the group in language, customs, expression, and so on as opposed to seeking to be perceived as an outsider amongst one's significant others.

(4). **Cooperation:** Grounded in the collective nature of the African way of life, cooperativeness is the quality of being available and disposed to lend a hand to others in need, and the expectation that when one's needs for help rise, the other will be disposed and ready to do the same. African villages continue to rely heavily on cooperation to accomplish what one individual cannot easily achieve such as building a large house, burying one's dead relative, or resolving disputes in palaver court as well as in the civil court system.

(5). **Generosity:** African ethics and codes of conduct dictate that one take delight in generosity, kindness, and forgiveness. It has been accurately said that few Africans will ever become rich because most Africans tend to be too generous. When African Kings agreed to give acres of land in the Congo to Stanley in the name of King Leopold II of Belgium, and/or when the Kongo and Ovambo Kings in Portuguese colonies gave theirs to the Portuguese, they were not prompted by bribes or stupidity but by this African habit of generosity. It should not be astonishing that African nations have generally maintained good to excellent relationships with their former colonizers. One would venture to claim that this is due in part to the cultural habit of forgiving and forgetting all this ingratitude. Generosity in an African setting demands reciprocity and is an excellent foundation upon which to build caring communities and sustained development. In some parts of Africa such as in Cameroon, female members of the community have institutionalized this practice into collective financial institutions where money is collected by individuals each month and is given to one member to assist in launching a business. In a limited way, men are also engaged in this manner now.

(6). **Collective responsibility:** This concept refers to the practice whereby members of the community assume responsibility for altruistic things and engage in collective endeavors which benefit the whole community. Examples might be building a dwelling place for the Chief or simply doing public projects that bring satisfaction to everyone like building a school, providing scholarships for poor children, and/or defending the community. But this may also take on augmented forms such as playing a parental role when other adults, or elder members of the community are absent or incapacitated. As Spike Lee would say "Do the right thing" by acting as a parent for a child who has no parents present! If a child is misbehaving, the adult who is present at that moment will not have to wait for the parent to return. Rather, the adult assumes responsibility for correcting and disciplining the child and then tells the absent parent later. This is the origin of the saying, "it takes an entire village to raise a child." It is the responsibility of all adults to make sure that the younger generation is properly raised.

(7) **Survivability and continuity of the group:** The survival of the group as opposed to the survival of an individual (Eurocentric model) is one of the

principal concerns of African people. The African philosophy of life praises the sacrificial contributions of an individual to the survival of the entire community, an idea embedded in collective responsibility in which the survival of one or survival of a group is the business of the entire community. Whenever there are famines, droughts or other tragedies, those who are physically fit and able are expected to provide for those who are helpless.

The above seven values are embedded in the Afrocentric philosophy of life which undergirds the ideology of Pan-Africanism and reflects a particular way of life. From its inception in 1900, the Pan-African movement has sought political liberation of African peoples and of African lands, and it has also emerged as an expression of cultural unity - a testimony to multiple undertakings by Africans that project their collective way of life as an alternative contribution to the development of an equitably just and prosperous global community.

GEOPOLITICAL DIMENSIONS OF PAN-AFRICANISM

Pan-Africanism's holistic approach and equalitarian dimensions capture the meaning of human liberation; not a single individual, society, or nation is truly free if one or more of its members remains oppressed and is denied basic freedom. Both as a cultural movement and ideology, Pan-Africanism calls upon Africans to organize themselves in order to deal with their realities and free both themselves and their oppressors. There is an ethical link between Pan-Africanism and the universal struggle for the creation of a humane, peaceful, and harmonious global community. As Karenga observed, "History is the struggle and record of humans in the process of humanizing their world" (Karenga, 1982, p. 43).

From W. E. B. DuBois to Kwame Nkrumah, calls for political unity have appeared under several guises as an expression of the collective will of Africans. The geopolitical levels of National, Continental, Trans-Atlantic, and Global Pan-Africanism represent and recognize the complexity of the challenge facing Pan-Africanists. How can the dream of a united Africa be realized when Africa's daughters and sons are so dispersed? If the dream and potential of cultural unity is realized, the dream of political and economic unity will become definable. Consider the four different types of Pan-African relations:

National Pan-Africanism: Pan-Africanism rejects all forms of prejudice and discrimination based on narrow ethnic and kinship ties. It also rejects those forms of leadership (such as in South Africa) in which ethnic and racial nationalism have led to separation of races (apartheid) as a mechanism to weaken the majority while imposing a minority government. The majority of African states can be regarded as having adopted National Pan-Africanism insofar as they promote the creation of pluralistic nations with pluralistic political structures oriented toward the coexistence and harmony of multilingual and multicultural ethnic groupings of people.

Continental Pan-Africanism: Continental Pan-Africanism proposes the unification of all African states organically under one government. The concept of political unification of Africa has been attributed to President Kwame Nkrumah of Ghana. In his view, "No single part of Africa can be safe or free to develop fully and independently while any part remains unliberated, or while Africa's vast economic resources continue to be exploited by imperialistic and neo-colonialist interests" (Nkrumah, 1963, p. v).

The Organization of African Unity (OAU) has symbolized the movement toward political unification of Africa. Since 1964, the OAU has been headquartered in Addis Ababa, Ethiopia, where it has functioned as a central authority in African affairs. The OAU is headed by a Secretary whose political authority and decisions are subordinated to a Council of Ministers under a Council of Presidents. There are not yet elected officials nor a vocal assembly of delegates to represent the interests of Africa's people as a whole. Despite these limitations, the OAU represents an advanced stage in the institutionalization of Pan-African unity at the continental level and in the diaspora. However, the concept of continental government has been difficult to realize. The size and complexity of the continent and its languages, geographies, climactic conditions, and other natural barriers create problems that have not yet been bridged in terms of communication and mobilization.

Trans-Atlantic Pan-Africanism: Pan-Africanism has emerged as a trans-Atlantic concept unifying African people in the New World and the African continent. There has been renewed interest in cultural ties and historical roots linking African-Americans to Africa. Africa, itself, was part of the so-called 'New World' even before Columbus was born or travelled to North America.

Africans mingled with the native people in Northern America and left visibly significant marks in the Olmec civilization. By the sixteenth century arrival of newly transplanted Africans, previously settled Africans had been assimilated, and their monuments could be found in Olmec languages, culture, architecture, and so on (Van Sertima, 1976, p. 142-179).

Trans-Atlantic Pan-Africanism in the early twentieth century centered around a limited but significant role played by intellectuals in the Americas. This role was most apparent in protests against colonialism in Africa and the Caribbean. These intellectuals sought to educate, sensitize, and mobilize Europeans toward granting gradual emancipation and the control of their own affairs to Africans. Pan-African sentiments were often visible in the literature and art of African-Americans and in their responses toward the wars that, from time to time, involved innocent African territories (e.g. the occupation of Ethiopia by Italy in the early 1900's). Under the leadership of Randall Robinson, President of the Trans-African Organization, trans-Atlantic Pan-Africanism has recently captured the limelight with its organized protest by African-Americans and others against apartheid in South Africa and its lobbying influence in the U. S. Congress.

Global Pan-Africanism: Pan-Africanism has raised the issue of a global community and the global unity of humans; the struggle for human freedom from oppression in one part of the world becomes the concern of free men and women everywhere. The universal struggle for human rights is at the same time a struggle to guarantee that human liberation from domination by other humans and from the chains of racism, sexism and any other idiosyncratic bondage could be realized in peace. Global Pan-Africanism calls for working to free Africans and other oppressed people from neocolonialism and authoritarianism; to abolish racism everywhere; and to plant the seeds of peace, justice, and equality in the socioeconomic and political systems of their societies. Pan-Africanists become involved in a continuous struggle to correct the distortions - in image, achievements, and world view - found in world history concerning Africa and its sons and daughters. The authentic historical experiences of all humankind, dating from the African roots of humanity's very beginnings, must be studied in regard to both their liberating and oppressive aspects. As both Armah (1974) and Asante (1980) conceptualize it, Pan-

Africanism becomes the "Njia" or "Way" and is founded in the traditions of Africans as "the spirit of humanity meant to be an expressive symbol for the survival of African essence" (1980, p. 26-27).

PAN-AFRICANISM AND POLITICAL LIBERATION

The quest for historic and cultural identity requires a knowledge of African history - one is obligated to know the past in order to understand the present in which we find ourselves. It is a matter of history that, for a number of centuries, many considered Egypt to be geographically and socially detached from Africa. European writers and scholars spoke of Egypt as if she were a part of Europe. Yet, black nationalists in Africa and the Diaspora have taken pride in the old civilizations of Africa - the ancient civilization of Egypt and the uninterrupted history of Ethiopia as a sovereign African nation. (In the 1930's, for example, thousands of African-Americans enlisted and fought for the liberation of Ethiopia from Italian occupancy.) African history teaches that long before the thirteenth century, Africans established contacts with people in other countries and in the 'New World'.

A careful examination of African historical records exposes sociocultural and psychological struggles to correct deliberately distorted information concerning the status and contributions of Africans worldwide. To some degree, African history is dominated by quests for identity, equality and personhood especially throughout the Diaspora. The significance of slavery in the 'New World' can be demonstrated by its economic value and by its overwhelming penchant to socially, physically, and psychologically treat Africans as nonhumans. Slavery represented a vicious effort to dehumanize and de-Africanize both people of African origin and their historical record. In African-American history, the quest for freedom was most directly related to slaves' yearning for liberty and their undying struggle to regain their total humanity and self-esteem. Enslaved Africans passed on to each succeeding generation the mental stamina and determination to survive, to seek freedom, to internalize the struggle and to keep it alive throughout two hundred years of bondage. The Emancipation Proclamation finally came (1863) and it institutionalized those aspirations. The Emancipation Proclamation did not, however, alter Africans' determination to continue to look for ways and strategies to enhance their freedom by improving the quality of their personhood, social standings and lives. As Andrew Young, former Ambassador to the United Nations and former Mayor of the city of Atlanta (Georgia) pointed out, most major socio-political changes that have permanently changed the rights and privileges of the majority of all American citizenry have originated from the African-American struggle.

In continental African history, the struggle for political independence and national sovereignty symbolized the same aspirations for freedom. The demand for independence from the colonizers began as a reaction to European and American literature that characterized Africans as 'Sambos' and 'Makkaks' or monkeys. As Asante said, "Nothing transforms one's self-concept like authentic confrontation with what one is not" (Asante, 1980, p. 52). Pan-Africanism as the collective response to inequality was advocated by such prominent leaders as David Walker, Robert Young, Frederick Douglass, and Sojourner Truth, all of whom denounced racism and called on Africans everywhere to organize and work on their own behalf. Among other leaders involved in Pan-Africanism have been Mary Church Terrell, W. E. B. DuBois, Sylvester Edwards, George Padmore, Marcus Garvey, Kwame Nkrumah, Julius Nyerere, Angela Davis, Malcolm X and Martin Luther King, Jr. In Africa itself, Frantz Fanon, Patrice Lumumba and others called for the creation of 'New' men and women different from those Europe and America generated during the 400 years of slavery and colonization.

In the second half of the twentieth century, Gamal Abdul Nasser of Egypt and Haile Selassie I of Ethiopia inaugurated the re-Africanization of these important African countries, and with them came Algeria, Morocco, Libya, Tunisia, and Mauritania. In 1963, the Arab North and sub-Sahara were unified within a framework of periodic meetings of African heads of states and governments. The transfer of the OAU headquarters from Accra in Ghana to Addis Ababa in Ethiopia (1964) was a very significant event in the re-unification and re-Africanization of the northernmost countries with the rest of Africa.

To date, the Organization of African Unity (OAU) stands as an outstanding accomplishment of the Pan-African Movement, especially in those aspects that lend credit to Dr. Kwame Nkrumah (former president of Ghana) and his friends and advisors, Dr. W. E. B. DuBois and George Padmore. The three men encouraged reunification of African states under a continental leadership. Since its establishment, the OAU has spearheaded the struggle for liberation of Africa from the hand of the colonizers, including the colonial domains of Namibia and Azania. Pan-African sponsorship of liberation movements in Angola, Mozambique, Zimbabwe, and Djibuti has already yielded successful political victories. The remaining challenges in Namibia, Azania, and Polssario warrant our attention because those important African lands must be restored to African hands.

The Pan-African approach has always been and continues to be a collective struggle for the liberation of Africans from colonial domination as well as their liberation from racist capitalist policies in the New World. Culturally, liberation from colonial exploitation and from racist capitalism in the Americas can no longer be separated. By promoting Pan-Africanism, DuBois' intention was to internationalize the African-American struggle for human rights and to show its connectedness to the conditions that prevailed in colonized Africa. Struggling for the attainment of African-Americans' civil rights in America has been a part of the same struggle that Africans have had to wage. As Malcolm X said "as long as Africa is not free, Black men anywhere will not be respected."

Liberation movements are indicative of Pan-Africanism's legacy to this generation. Pan-Africanists are called to rise above racism, to recognize the importance of human beings' common characteristics as opposed to such differences as skin color. As Paulo Freire observed, "...concern for humanization leads at once to the recognition of dehumanization, not only as an ontological possibility but as an historical reality. As man perceives the extent of dehumanization, he asks himself if humanization is a viable possibility" (Freire, 1974, p. 24). The historic task of liberation may well be in the hands of the oppressed. As Freire states, "the oppressors who oppress, exploit and rape by virtue of their power, cannot find in this power the strength to liberate either the oppressed or themselves" (Freire, 1974, p. 28). Pan-Africanists have an obligation to identify the false leaders of the people and to expose their inability to liberate those who are oppressed or themselves.

PAN-AFRICAN VALUES , EDUCATION, AND DEVELOPMENT

Pan-Africanism promotes the unified, holistic, global approach toward analysis of human problems. As Makidi-Ku-Ntima has stated, Pan-African values require the development of educational foundations with the capability to generate a sufficient number of people, each of whom must qualify as:

> ...a social critic, a person whose concern is to identify, to analyze and in this way to help overcome the obstacles barring the way to the attainment of a better, more humane, and more rational social order. As such, he/she becomes the conscience of society and the spokesperson of such progressive forces as it contains in any given period of history. And as such, he/she is inevitably considered a 'troublemaker' and a nuisance by the ruling class seeking to preserve the status quo, as well as by the workers in its service who accuse the intellectual of being utopian or metaphysical at best, subversive or seditious at worst (Baran. 1965, p. 10).

Pan-African education must be characterized by its focus on politico-economic development and cultural socialization most likely to be significant to the education of the oppressed. As James Coleman has stated:

> Political development can be regarded as the acquisition by a political system of a consciously sought and qualitatively new and enhanced political capacity as manifested in the successful institutionalization of (1) new patterns of integration regulating and containing the tensions and conflicts produced by increased differentiation, and (2) new patterns of participation and resource distribution adequately responsive to the demands generated by imperatives of equity (Coleman, 1965, p. 15).

Africans have not evolved a racist ideology that could be comparable to the one created and practiced by Caucasians in their dealing with non-Caucasian groups. Despite their long and broad contacts with Europeans and Asians, there is no African equivalent to the practice of 'apartheid' in South Africa or the centuries of racism in the United States. All Africans have belonged and continue to claim nationality in specific nations based on their ethnic lineages or a collectivity of lineages. These nations have been defined by kinship ties or blood relations, history, or well defined geographical boundaries and culture. One was never confused about identity or whether a person was Ashanti, Azande, Ibo, Kongo, Luba, Mande, Mongo, Shona, Zulu, and Yoruba or not. The national identity was characterized by people's names, speech, value systems, and the ruling lineages of the kingdom. Each of the traditional nations of Africa represented a political system. Some of these nations have substantial population size:

Ibo of Nigeria, 6-8 million people;
Luba of Zaire, 5-7 million people;
Mongo of Zaire, 2-4 million people;
Shona of Zimbabwe, 1-2 million people;
Wolof of Senegal, 850,000 - 1 million people;
Zulu of Azania, 5-7 million people;
Yoruba of Nigeria, 14-19 million people;

(By comparison, the state of Israel, with all its dominance in world news and its Zionism, has approximately 3 million people.)

As Wade Nobels has said, "Black psychology is not derived from the negative aspects of being black in white America, but rather from the positive features of basic African philosophy which dictates values, customs, attitudes, and behavior of Africans" (Karenga, 1982: 336-338). Yet, through liberation movements Africans have developed a strong sense of cultural unity or 'Africanity' which Macquet describes in the following terms:

> The struggle of one people for its national independence strengthened the struggle of all the others and was strengthened by them. Colonial rule has had to be fought by united action, not piecemeal. Negritude (the intellectual stand) and Pan-Africanism (the political stand) converged in that they both affirmed (l) that all Africans (in the continent and in the diaspora) have a common civilization and (2) that all Africans must stand together (Macquet, 1972, p. 8).

From both the pedagogical and liberal education viewpoints, a fully educated person today should be familiar with the multicultural, multilinguistic, and multiclass systems of our world. Pan-African educators have an obligation to inform African people worldwide that they are among the most oppressed masses. Slavery, colonialism, neo-colonialism, and military authoritarian rules under which Africans have lived have common philosophical grounds. The African people must become capable of uniting to seek political, socioeconomic, and cultural change; education can provide the missing links between people. As noted by Louis Farakhan on the Donahue Show in 1985:

> It is high time black intellectuals, educators, politicians, artists, and the hosts of others get together, forget their personal conflict and address the problems of the (African) people of this world, instead of blaming the whites or surrendering the problems to them to solve it for us. Only (African) people can solve their problems and the only mode to do it is by uniting together as a group (March 28, 1985).

The Civil Rights movement in the 1960's offered 'field experience' that allowed students to make crucial decisions regarding their roles, places, and chances within the total societal scheme. The struggle for independence in Africa and the Caribbean provided continuing practical experience for the youth. Whether at the individual level, family level, community level, or societal level, the remediation of historical oppression and dependence may require education that offers students firsthand experiences in change and development designed to solve a particular cultural, socioeconomic or political problem. Today, summer internships, opportunities to travel to other countries as exchange students, and service in the Peace Corps and Crossroads Africa are just a few of the avenues that students might pursue to gain these important firsthand experiences in human problem-solving.

Pan-African education must take full advantage of the communication revolution to enable people everywhere to see and hear one another. It must promote the study of African languages as a means for international understanding and self-esteem. It must also increase scientific study and research that seek to improve methods of production of food crops most generally consumed by Africans. The inequitable distribution of resources, wealth, and power threaten many with massive starvation, and this cannot be hidden in a high-tech information era. Pan-African education must expose the behavior of oppressors wherever it exists. It must denounce the ominous trends toward multi-national corporations and increasing possibilities for super powers to make satellite states out of sovereign nations via corporate investment and military assistance, all in the name of socioeconomic development. It is reasonable to question whether these capitalist ventures serve the majority of people.

Over the past thirty years we have generated African Studies and Black Studies Departments within academe. The importance of cultural understanding requires educators to familiarize themselves with interdisciplinary social sciences and supporting subject matter. These faculty members are the very vanguard of Pan-Africanism within higher education today as they teach about African contributions in the sciences, arts, and humanities. Yet, historically black institutions of higher education in the United States, departments and centers for African or African-American Studies in predominantly white institutions, and colleges and universities in the Caribbean and Africa are experiencing a chronic crisis in collegiality, cooperation, collective research, mutual promotion and respect. Even if these are reflections of our historical experiences as oppressed people and of the state of crisis in which we find ourselves, Pan-African educators must continually re-examine their contributions to each other and to the different sectors of the African-American community who need change and development.

Pan-African educators strive to assist in the transfer of culture, technology, science, and other skills wherever they might be needed. They are challenged to serve as catalysts in the development of research and methodologies that will contribute to the greater good. There is a need to re-assess the qualitative values inherent in our 'Njia' or 'collective will' so that they can become integral components of Pan-African education which, in turn, should be able to generate "capacitation operations that do not try so much to define and control the future as to establish present conditions or capacities that will move a given society to meet its problems in the future" (Makidi, 1985, p.6). Education of this kind will be designed to promote skills that enhance the chances for institutionalization of such Afrocentric, humanistic values as the promotion of equitable distribution of resources and wealth, enhanced civil and human rights, peaceful resolution of conflicts, justice, equality, respect for human life, and international and intercultural understanding.

We need to focus attention on preparing a new generation of leaders who may be able to contribute not only in acquisition of power but also in management of power and its use for the benefit of all people.

MALE-FEMALE ROLES AND PAN-AFRICANISM

The gap between traditional male and female roles and opportunities for self-determination reflects sexism in human societies. Women have been victimized by attitudes that have assigned an inferior status while, at the same time, more than their share of work in homes, fields and elsewhere has been expected. By virtue of their sexual identity, women have suffered from inequalities that extend far beyond their expected contribution to the family welfare.

In order to promote the development of respectful attitudes between men and women, women's roles and functions at different levels of relationships and their importance to the struggle for total liberation of humanity must be recognized. Generating female Pan-Africanists will be accomplished only through the creation of more opportunities for equitable democracy in our societies.

It must be made clear that the position and social status of women in Africa, in the Diaspora, and in the world at large contradicts the highest ideals of liberalism and progressive social order; it threatens the development and institutionalization of civil liberties and the very promise of democracy. Increased access to the centers of decision making by women is one of the most fundamental preconditions for a successful conclusion of the struggle for liberation. Pan-Africanism must create media through which the oppressed can express their views on major issues confronting them at individual, family, community, national and global levels. From such cultural practices as circumcision of women in some parts of Africa to the pornographic illustrations and depictions of women as sexual objects in Europe, America, and Asia. Pan-Africanists are called to involve themselves in women's struggles to acquire human rights and civil rights in their respective societies. Accordingly, values that do not promote the search for and adoption of new technological advances reducing human dependency on sheer physical strength will not contribute to the liberation of women. Technological advances that become accessible to poor people are among the more important and creative responses for combating traditional and contemporary gender inequalities. Pan-Africanism should continue to encourage women to organize relevant political and economic activities that would empower them and allow them to become effective partners with men in development.

Pan-African education must become as Friere says "a struggle for meaning and a struggle over power relations. Its dynamic is forced in dialectical relations between individuals and groups who live out their lives with historical conditions and structural constraints, on the one hand, and those cultural forms and ideologies that give rise to contradictions and struggles that define the lived realities of various societies, on the other" (Friere, 1985, p.xiii). A true Pan-African education must seek to generate healthy debate toward the identification and definition of values inherent in women's rights, and present them as factors in the process of building a global community. The gap between the sexes has generally retarded the arrival of women within the centers of decision making in their communities and particularly in Africa and the African diaspora. Increased respect for women's rights is important. After all, women constitute a crucial and integral part without which our humanity has neither a future nor the power to realize its global destiny.

SUMMARY AND CONCLUSION

This chapter has outlined and discussed the Afrocentric dimensions of Pan-africanism which are described as underlying cultural values inherent in the ontology of African life. While Pan-Africanism has been promoted and recognized as a politico-economic movement toward the unification of African people's aspirations worldwide, this movement is an extraordinarily difficult challenge due to the long history of dispersal of Africa's sons and daughters and the rigid, oppressive systems which have engendered their present conditions. The quality of being African is not defined by race but by the relationship one maintains with the *Creative Force* recognized as the source of everything. All visions of reality, personhood, family, community, nation, and the world are therefore reflected in the fundamental cultural values without which one ceases to be truly African. The values that define and guide African people are groupness, commonality, sameness, cooperativeness, generosity collective responsibility, and survivability of the group. These values are reflected at different levels of relationships within and without the African universe, and they are called into action every time there is need to respond to challenges confronting them.

At the ethnic level, as in the case of Zulu and Ndebele, strong Pan-African values should resolve any animosities and replace them with enlightened, cooperative and mutually interdependent political and socioeconomic relationships. This was illustrated by the 1993 agreement between Nelson Mandela of the ANC and Kwa Zulu Chief Bothelezi to stop bloodshed between the ANC members and Kwa Zulu people by working and appearing together. The message here is that greater loyalty is entirely possible and can be accommodated by the African philosophy of life. At a broader level, the direct linkage between Africa and its dispersed sons and daughters in Asia, the Caribbean, Central and South America, Canada, Europe, and the United States must be encouraged, especially if Africa is to occupy its rightful place in the world.

Pan-Africanism's new role is to facilitate the global dissemination of information about the culture of Africa and the Diaspora. One form may be via education of Africans in the continent so that they may cultivate an awareness of black contributions to the sciences, arts, and humanities. In the New World, black cultural centers can offer continuing education for lay leaders about the fundamental changes that have been occurring during the process toward full independence of all nations in Africa.

One can easily argue that the Pan-Africanism movement has provided impetus for redefining the notions that are crucially instrumental to increasing appreciation for African nationalism, its culture and its humanistic worldview. Without continuing strides toward an Afrocentric search for meaning and identity, one might find it difficult to challenge the status quo, to seek new creative ways to recognize the oppressive systems for what they are, and to seek ways to change them.

The challenge today is whether or not African-American intellectuals living in a superpower nation with advanced participatory democratic traditions and technological innovations will accept responsibility for leadership in problem-solving that Africa is not likely to receive from those living anywhere else. The same applies to African intellectuals from the continents who, in turn, are in a position to provide an excellent cultural foundation and enriching examples that can be useful in cultural change and re-linkage. Pan-Africanism demands a higher loyalty from everyone than any other ideology at this moment in our history. The concept might be in the terminology identified by Macquet as Africanity; by Asante as Afrocentricity; by Armah and Tempels as the 'Njia' or 'Way of life;' or as the Luba have called it 'Mpokolo Wa Muoyo' or 'Source of life.' It is a unifying and grounding concept that one can maintain while remaining loyal to one nation.

The important ideas outlined above are central to education for liberation of those who have been oppressed for centuries. Pan-Africanism must provide an education that informs, enriches, and motivates the soul toward greater development. The promotion of group solidarity with an emphasis on justice, equity, and increased understanding of one another are important aspects of Pan-African values and its humanizing dimensions. The quality of our collective destiny will be determined by our willingness to work collectively for the greater good.

Pan-Africanism is an abstract concept that has begun to be translated into Afrocentric programs of education, strategies for liberation, and actions for development. It reflects the persistence and resilience of the *vital force* which guides and directs the African philosophy of life, and it illustrates Africans' resolve to move decidedly toward the creation of an equitable world where everyone will share justice, resources, and power.

A key challenge to social scientists and Pan-Africanist scholars is to search for new ways of collecting, organizing and presenting knowledge on a broad scale. How well one does that will determine the extent to which one will become an honest contributor to the process of humanizing as opposed to being part of the problem of dehumanizing. The global challenges await Pan-Africanists who are motivated to liberate people from the chains of ignorance, racism, injustice, and excessive abuses of power. Perhaps true Pan-Africanist scholars and activists may yet have an Afrocentric role to play; why not ? Margaret Walker was probably motivated by the *vital force* to poetically dream for her people:

"FOR MY PEOPLE "

Let a new earth rise.
Let another world be born.
Let a bloody peace be written in the sky.
Let a second generation full of courage issue forth:
Let a people loving freedom come to growth.
Let a beauty full of healing and strength of final clenching be the pulsing in our spirits and blood.
Let the martial songs be written,
Let the dirges disappear.
Let a race of men now rise and take control.
(Chapman, 1968, p. 460)

REFERENCES

Abdul, Alkalimat and Associates. *Introduction to Afro-American Studies: Peoples College,* 1984, University of Illinois at Urbana.

Asante, Molefi Kete. *Afrocentricity: The Theory of Social Change*, Amolefi Publishing Co., Buffalo, 1980.

Baran, Paul. "The Commitment of the Intellectual," *Monthly* Review, 16, March, 1965.

Billingsley, Andrew. *Black Families In White America.* Prentice Hall, Inc., Englewood Cliffs, 1968.

Chapman, Abraham (ed.). *Black Voices: An Anthology of Afro-American Literature,* Mentor Books, New York, 1968.

Clark, Leon E. The Rise of Nationalism: Freedom Regained. Unit V, Through African Eyes: Cultures in Change, Praeger Publishers, New York, 1970.

Coleman, James S. (ed.). *Education and Political Development.* Princeton, 1965.

Diop, Cheikh Anta, *The African Origin of Civilization: Myth Or Reality,* Translated and Edited by Mercer Cook. Lawrence Hill & Company, Westport,1974.

Franklin, John Hope. *From Slavery to Freedom: A History of Negro Americans.* Alfred A. Knopf, New York, 1947, 1974.

Freire, Paulo. *Pedagogy of the Oppressed.* Harder and Harder, New York, 1972.

__________ *The Politics of Education: Cultural Power and Liberation,* Bergin and Garvey Publishers, Inc., Mass., 1985.

Hall, Clyde W. *Black Vocational Technical and Industrial Arts Education: Development and History.* American Technical Society, Chicago, 1973.

Herskovits, Melville J. *The Human Factor in Changing Africa.* Vantage Books, New York 1958, 1962.

Hunt, Maurice P. *Foundations of Education: Social and Cultural Perspectives.* Holt, Rinehart, and Winston, New York, 1975.

Ianni, Francis A. J. and Edward Storey. *Cultural Relevance and Education Issues.* Reading in Anthropology and Education. Little, Brown and Co., Boston, 1973.

Kakonen, Jyurki (ed.). *The Mechanisms of Neo-Colonialism.* Proceedings of a Nordic Seminar, Finnish Peace Research Association, Manta, 1974.

Karenga, Maulana. *Introduction to Black Studies.* Kawaida Publications, Inglewood, 1993.

Karenga, Maulana R. *Essays on Struggle: Position and Analysis.* Kawaida, San Diego, 1978.

Keller, Edmond J. and Donald Rothchild, editors, *Afro-Marxist Regimes: Ideology and Public Policy.* Lynne Rienner Publishers, Boulder, 1987.

King, Kenneth. *Pan-Africanism and Education: A Study of* Race, Philanthrophy and Education in the Southern States of *America and East Africa.* Clarendon Press, Oxford, 1971.

Lemelle, Sid. *Pan-Africanism for Beginners.* Writers and Readers Documentary Comic Book, New York, 1992.

Macquet, Jacques. *Africanity: The Cultural Unity of Black Africa.* Oxford University Press, New York, 1972.

Makidi, Ku-Ntima."Pan-Africanism and Development," (Presentation at 3rd Pan-African Conference), Indiana State University, 1985.

Muyumba, François et. al. *From Third World to One World: The Pan-African Perspective.* Center for Afro-American Studies, Terre Haute, 1988.

Nkrumah, Kwame. *I Speak of Freedom.* PANAF, London, 1973.

____________ *Africa Must Unite.* international Publishers, New York, 1970.

Nyerere, Julius U. *Uhuru Na Ujamaa: Freedom and Socialism,* (Selections from the Writing of), Oxford University Press, London, 1968.

Perot, Ruth Turner. *Black Power: A Voice Within, Black Nationalism in America.* Edited by John H. Brecey, Jr., August Meier, and Elliott Rudwick, the Bobbs-Merrill Co., Inc., Indianapolis, Indiana, 1970, p. 465-470.

Robinson, Patricia W. *Black Quest for Identity.* Burgess Publishing Company, Minneapolis, 1978.

Tempels, Placide. *Bantu Philosophy.* Presence Africaine, Paris V$^{\underline{e}}$,1959.

Ubbelohde, Carl and Jack R. Fraenkel (ed.). *Values of the American Heritage: Challenges, Case Studies and Teaching Strategies.* National Council for Social Studies, 45th yearbook, 1976.

Van Sertima, Ivan. *They Came Before Columbus: The African Presence in Ancient America.* Random House, New York, 1985.

CHAPTER 2

CULTURAL POWER IN NORTH-SOUTH RELATIONS: PAN-AFRICAN PERSPECTIVES

Ali A. Mazrui

The theme of North-South Dialogue tends normally to be a theme of political economy. I propose to treat it as a theme of political culture and to relate it to Pan-Africanism and African aspirations. There are a number of issues that touch upon relations between the Northern Hemisphere and the Southern Hemisphere. Part of the subtitle of this paper refers to those feelings of solidarity which do bring people together, people of Africa and African ancestry, both in the continent and in the diaspora, in the dispersal of the sons and daughters of the continent. Among the areas of North-South dominance is the issue of language. African's reliance upon foreign languages has caused not just linguistic dependency but also scientific and technological dependency. And this in turn has affected the degree to which we are in command of our ecology.

Why should language affect science and technology? Well, because a society that conducts all its scientific thoughts primarily in foreign languages still has some way to go before establishing its credentials as a scientific society. African physicists sitting together to discuss physics have only European languages in which to conduct their discourse. There are no professional meetings of scientific subjects in the African continent that are conducted in African languages. Even in the social sciences, as in my own field of Political Science, we switch very rapidly to the use of a European language. I am suggesting that unless there is a significant assimilation of the scientific disciplines in the wider society through a language intelligible to a large proportion of the population, the society has a lot of trouble becoming fertile for scientific innovation. So, until we take the issue of language seriously, we are not taking the issue of science seriously.

Even in language and ideology, the reliance on foreign languages is disproportionate. I have not met a single African Marxist who is not at the same time substantially Westernized. It is a socio-linguistic impossibility for an African to be a sophisticated Marxist without being at the same time substantially Westernized. Why? Because linguistic access to the body of literature constituting Marxism is almost entirely through European languages. You must have been brought up into either English or French or Portuguese at school to then have the linguistic key within which to study the works of great Marxist thinkers and to be introduced to the literature that has been disseminated out of that body of thought. So we need to handle the issue of language, not just for its own sake, although that is important, not just for the sake of nation building, although that too is important, but also in terms of its essential prerequisite role in the dissemination of scientific knowledge within society as a whole. We need to render African tongues more scientific if we are to reduce that area of dependence in the North-South equation. Now, not very many countries do take the issue of language seriously in Africa. There is remarkable complacency about it. And, as you know, we all talk about English speaking Africa and French speaking Africa. Nobody talks about English speaking Asia and French speaking Asia. African countries still base their identity partly on the issue of inherited imperial language whereas Asian countries have their identities independently of the bequeathed language of the former imperial powers.

However, there is a country in my part of the continent that has attempted to deal with the issue of language more seriously than average and that is Tanzania. Tanzania embarked on two major revolutions. They were not equally successful but they were both attempted. One was a revolution in political economy predicated on socialism and one a cultural revolution based on the dissemination of the Swahili language and its escalating use in national business. So, on one side you have the political economy of socialism and, on the other, the political culture of the policy of Swahilization. The socialism and political economy was a strategy of reducing economic dependency. The Swahilization was an attempt to curtail cultural dependency. Socialism was an attempt to promote economic self reliance in Tanzania. The promotion of Swahili as a national language was a strategy of cultivating cultural self reliance.

The socialist experiment included a leadership code to reduce elitism so that leaders in the party and in government were not supposed to own extra houses or to serve on boards of directors of private companies. There was a built in assumption of conflict of interest if leaders in government and the party should have, at the same time, extensive economic interests. So the Arusha Declaration, as their guidance charter was called, was intended to reduce elitism. That is the political economy side. On the political culture side, the adoption of Swahili was also a crusade against elitism. When you don't require a leader to be fluent in the English language, you immediately broaden the area of political recruitment. You extend the boundaries where you can pick leaders because you don't require of them a command of a language learned only at school and essentially of foreign derivation.

So elitism was reduced through language policy as well as through the political economy of socialism. And then the political economy of socialism attempted to reduce luxuries imported for the elite. Luxuries for the elite could affect the issue of how much foreign exchange you have left when you haven't imported wine and scotch whiskey and special kinds of toothpaste as well as gadgets from Japan and so on. So, the anti-elitism had foreign exchange consequences. And the language policy also reduced imports including imports of books. Books written by Africans like me using a foreign language, English, have a harder time entering the country and they are often expensive. But, Tanzania has one of the most vigorous publishing enterprises in African languages. The game of producing publications in the Swahili language is pushed to a considerable extent.

The socialism they adopted de-linked itself from Karl Marx. It was socialism without Karl Marx. It was intended deliberately to link up with the collective value system of traditional society. Ironically, the language policy was not entirely Swahili without Shakespeare. While Socialism de-linked from Marx, the Swahili relinked with Shakespeare. How? By a deliberate policy to demonstrate that the Swahili language could sustain the high culture of other civilizations. So, no lesser person than the President of the country, Julius Nyerere, translated Shakespeare's Julius Caesar and later on translated Merchant of Venice while some of his compatriots were translating Machiavelli's The Prince. There was a feeling that for this language to be truly adequate, it must demonstrate a capability to deal with cultural trends outside itself. And by challenging the language to deal with major thinkers from external civilizations, it was a kind of re-linking with Shakespeare but in a bid to establish parity of eloquence.

The socialism of Tanzania was a form of ideological non-alignment, avoiding just falling into the capitalist package of priorities or the Marxist package of preferences, Instead, Tanzania was exploring a socialism that was independent of external stimulus, and, on the Swahili side, was exploring a quest for cultural universalism. Rather than applying Marx entirely in the domestic scene, Nyerere regarded the Marxist message as more relevant to the global scene, that the world itself was divided into haves and have nots, that there was a global class struggle. In his domestic scene, Nyerere assumed Marx was not relevant.

Nyerere also applied Shakespeare to the class struggle. The title of Merchant of Venice in Swahili translated to the Capitalist of Venice, a mobilization of concepts of exploitation applied not only to Shylock but to other characters in the play. Tanzania was one society which attempted both political economy of transformation through socialism and a political culture of transformation through language policy.

Tanzania's success story is in nation-building through language policy rather than in economic transformation through socialism. Tanzania attempted both policies but one policy, the political economy one, was too vulnerable to external factors and collapsed under the heavy burden of the ecology of development, ecology defined both literally in terms of the natural environment and ecology of development defined in terms of the political economy of the total world system. In reality its political economy policies have been far less successful than its political culture strategies. But Tanzania is still struggling, not abandoning socialism altogether. What is clear is that the Swahilization policy has made substantial progress and more progress than almost any other attempt elsewhere.

Religion is another area worth taking into account over and above language. Religion can be the basis of identity but it can be the basis of dependency as well. Both Christianity and Islam have spread quite fast in Africa, to some extent staggeringly fast, too fast almost. When you think about it, Asians were introduced to Christianity centuries before Africans were; yet, to the present day the only country in Asia that could be described as Christian is the

Philippines. There are individual Christians in Asia and sometimes large numbers of individual Christians. But, you don't have Christian countries in Asia the way you have Christian countries in Africa although Christianity came much later, sometimes centuries later than in some parts of Asia. In general, there was an African responsiveness to external religion which sometimes did us proud in the sense that we were prepared to listen to other messages and to alternative moral codes but sometimes created an unease as to whether we were responding too rapidly, giving up too rashly, abandoning local heritages too precipitately. All of these were factors we have to bear in mind.

Our own African culture in the religious field is relatively ecumenical. In fact, of the three traditions of religion in Africa - Christian, Moslem, and indigenous - the most tolerant is indigenous, partly because it is not competitive, it does not seek to convert the human species as a whole. The Yoruba don't attempt to convert their Ibo neighbors to the Yoruba religion. The Kikiyu don't feel that the Liyou ought to follow the Gods of the Kikiyu. The Banganda don't feel that it is time to convert the Banura to Banganda religion. So there is no idea that you cross cultures in religion or that one system of religious belief is for the whole of the human species. And you know the result? There is a basic ecumenical and tolerant tendency within the indigenous scene in Africa. Where else in the world would you have an overwhelmingly Moslem society that had a Roman Catholic President for twenty years? Where else but in Africa would that happen? But that happened in Sénégal. Sénégal is over 80% Moslem, and for twenty years it had Léopold Senghor as its President.

This country, America, has a Constitution which claims separation of church from state. In 1960 for the first time there was a chance to elect a non-Protestant within the Christian tradition, John F. Kennedy. To the present day we are not sure whether this society has ever elected a non-Protestant. We only know Kennedy became President. We don't know whether the society elected him because there was some hanky panky in Illinois and the margin was so narrow that he might not have gotten a majority, that Nixon was persuaded not to challenge the election for reasons of greater nationalism. But we are not even absolutely sure whether the society has ever elected a non-Protestant; we only know that a Catholic did enter the White House as President.

The Jews have excelled in most other domains but they deliberately avoid the White House. Wisely. I think a Jewish bid for the President of the United States could precipitate a wave of anti-Semitism and the Jews are not ready to risk that for the time being.

There may be as many Moslems as Jews in the United States. Yet, a Moslem President of the United States is unlikely to happen, not just in my lifetime but even in the lifetime of my children. And yet here is Sénégal out there on the West Coast of Africa, not just choosing a Moslem over another denomination from the dominant population but choosing somebody outside of the religion altogether. Sénégal had a Roman Catholic as a President when over 80% of the population were Moslem and had no riots in the streets against the President, and not just for two years, not just for five years, not just for ten years, but for twenty years. Now Sénégal has a Moslem President and you know what? The First Lady is Roman Catholic so the society continues this ecumenical tendency.

Where we get into trouble in Africa is when religion reinforces ethnicity, when there is another division and you add a religious division. For example, all the Hausa or almost all the Hausa are Moslem. Almost all Ibo are Christian. They have an 'Iboness' about them and the Hausa have a 'Hausaness' about them independently of their religion. When you add religion on top of cultural and linguistic differences, then you are sharpening differentiations that are already there. So religion in Africa becomes divisive when it reinforces the ethnic divide.

That also applies to Sudan. The distinction between North and South is not just between Moslem and non-Moslem. There is a whole range of additional cultural differences of language, way of life, orientation, and history between North and South. When, on top of that, you add the religious differences, then you could be in trouble. So we have had tensions. And yet, even in Sudan, if you take their two civil wars, they seem to be on their way toward a kind of ecumenicalism. The first Sudanese civil war from 1965 to 1972 was separatist and anti-ecumenical. The South saw itself as different, religiously, and the missionaries of the Western world reinforced that divide. That civil war ended in 1972.

Eleven years later another civil war began. It was not separatist. This civil war right now does not seek to tear the South out of Sudan. It does not seek to create a separate country. It seeks to democratize the Sudan as a whole and create a more equitable relationship between North and South. So the second civil war is closer to the ecumenical spirit of the African tradition than the first. Religion and language themselves continue to tempt toward either integration or division.

Wole Soyinka, our distinguished playwright from Nigeria and winner of the Nobel Prize for Literature in 1986, is an integrative force on the issue of language in Pan-African terms. He even supported the idea of having the Swahili language taught continent-wide so that you get the beginnings of regional language that is indigenous, regional in the sense of the whole of Africa. On the linguistic side, Soyinka has been integrative even in his work, in his written literature, because he combines Yoruba idiom, Yoruba imagery, Yoruba metaphor with the English language and produces a distinctively innovative approach to the literary discourse. And, in addition, he has a view about language policies in the continent, a view that is not guided by the parochialism of his country of origin.

But Wole Soyinka may be a divisive force on the issue of religion. For example, in a major speech he unjustifiably attacked my television series, "The Africans, A Triple Heritage", for treating Islam seriously. He distorted my position, almost portraying me as an instrument of Qaddafi in his African policy. And yet, Soyinka comes from a country which has more Moslems than any single Arab country. When people think about Islam they immediately think Arab, but Nigeria has more Moslems than any single Arab country. That part of the Nigerian population which is Moslem is larger than the Moslem population of Egypt, and it is the largest concentration of Moslems in any single African country. Nigeria has even been called the largest Moslem country in Africa, not because it is an Islamic state but because of the population of Moslems within it. And here is the first television series that treats Islam as a major part of the African phenomenon and our leading African playwright thinks this is playing mulla. Half the population of the continent is Moslem and he thinks that if I stray beyond the usual divide between the West and African culture I am playing Qaddafi's game. That is divisive.

Then, more recently, comes the Salmon Rushdie affair. Soyinka wrote a very vitriolic article in the Guardian, not the British Guardian but the Guardian in Nigeria. Originally, when he went to India and was asked whether India was justified in banning Rushdie's Satanic Verses, Soyinka said "yes" because of the likely impact on the Indian society. There he was sociological, a pragmatist, because he thought the book could disturb law and order in India, and over twenty people have died in the Indian subcontinent since the book was published as a direct result of the book.

But then the same Soyinka who was so sensitive about the Indian predicament turns out to be less than sensitive about Nigeria, even though he knows Nigeria and their emotions that sometimes come not quite all the way to those of India on religious issues but quite close. It is true that in India sometimes you can have a bloodbath because a cow has been killed outside a Hindu temple, or you can have riots because three pigs were deliberately led right across a Moslem mosque. You have emotions at work on issues of religion. The West is used to riots periodically over sports and the British, who used to pride themselves on the sporting spirit, now have rioting connected with sports every so often. But, in Africa and, of course, even more so in India, rioting for God is more common than rioting for football, and Soyinka should have known that. But, he wrote this vitriolic article, and there were, in fact, demonstrations against him, "Death to Soyinka." It was absurd, but it was happening. Fortunately, the threats weren't pursued. If the book were serialized in a Christian newspaper in Nigeria, lives might be lost. There could be riots. This raises a whole new dimension about writers in the North-South equation.

What is happening today is that writers can gain a lot of money because the reading constituency is much larger than anything in human history, in the history of letters. Rushdie was given an advance for his book of over 800,000 of what some say were dollars but the Guardian of England says were pounds, 800,000 pounds advanced for Islam-bashing. If it was an advance in pounds, that is over a million and a half dollars. Before the death sentence was passed on Rushdie, the author had this package of money given to him. The author was warned by advisers of the publishing company in India that this book could cause serious destabilization, and India is the country where he was born. The Indian government, which is not, of course, a Moslem government even though India has a large Moslem minority, decided to ban the book. Rushdie wrote to Rajiv Gandhi appealing against the ban, criticizing him for banning, to the applause of the Western world. Since then, Rushdie's life has also been compromised.

What he does not acknowledge as remotely having anything to do with him is that over twenty people of the subcontinent of his birth have died from rioting which was predictable from the beginning with advice given to the publishers before the book was published. So, question: Are we at such a stage now when on one side writers can gain more money than ever before, especially if they write in the right language? If you write in the right language (and English is the most right of the right languages), and you are lucky and you are good, you could have a reading constituency unprecedented in the history of letters. Does that give us additional responsibility to estimate the likely consequences of what we write if a book published in London can kill people in Karachi and Bombay, if a book published thousands of miles away can have fatal consequences thousands of miles elsewhere? It is something with which writers must reckon. The global village is also global in literary terms. It is not just a global village ecologically in the literal sense of the term. It is not just a global village in political economy. It is a global village in literature and the consequences of literature, and should we assume responsibility for that?

Now the issue of Rushdie raises the whole business of treason in North-South relations, and it is an issue important to Africans as well as elsewhere. In general, the West understands treason against the State. This is an established part of Western experience. The West also understands treason punishable by death if it is against the State. The United States executed Julius and Ethel Rosenberg in the 1950's for treason and espionage. These were Americans, but their loyalties were deemed to be to the Soviet Union and they were executed.

The West no longer understands treason to the faith or to the political fealty if it is defined in religious terms. Now, for people in Iran there is no distinction between loyalty to the State and loyalty to the religious community; someone like Rushdie is deemed to be guilty of cultural treason. If it was just someone who was never a Moslem, who had grown up in Daytona Beach and written a ferocious attack on Islam and the prophet Mohammad - so what else is new? There are dozens of such books. Every year they are published somewhere.

The difference with Rushdie is that he was a person born into the Islamic faith, brought up as a Moslem. Therefore, he qualifies as a cultural traitor. Rushdie's fate is deemed to be apostasy which is a religious form of treason and not just unbelief of someone who is not a Moslem in any case.

With Ethel and Julius Rosenberg, if they had been Soviet citizens and had done the same thing they did in the United States, they would have been locked up and in some deal between Moscow and Washington they would have been exchanged spies. But, they were executed because they were Americans betraying their country. They would not have been executed if they had been patriots of the Soviet Union caught in the United States spying for their country.

As Westerners understand treason against the State and Moslems understand treason against the religious community, many black people understand treason against the race, again the sociology of the situation. And, sometimes in South Africa where blacks are not in control, they take into their own hands the death penalty for those they regard as traitors. So they have this punishment which they call the 'necklace', a burning tire. It is dreadful, but it is the nearest thing to South Africa militance, the nearest thing to their equivalent of Rushdie's death sentence.

In Africa, continentally, we had a big traitor once. He was called Moise Tshombe. He was in the Congo as it was then called, now the Zaire. He wanted to pull out Katanga into a separate country, and he collaborated with the Belgians and other whites. He became the symbol of what constitutes treason to Africa. All over Africa, Tshombe became symbol number one of what constitutes continental treason. He also participated in the execution of Patrice Lumumba, who was widely regarded in Africa as a martyr to Western conspiracies.

What finally happened was Tshombe was abducted, taken to Algeria and, as far as we know, he is supposed to have died of natural causes in the area. But, whether it was natural causes or an abduction of a traitor or of someone who had betrayed a people, whether it was that or the other, his was a big case of treason.

What is often not remembered is that Africa now doesn't have either big heroes or big traitors, and in a way that is tough for Pan-Africanism. There are times when solidarity requires villainy on a grand scale or heroism on a grand scale. So our very successes in liberation, in de-colonization, have reduced the potentialities of villainy on a grand scale. One country after another has become independent, and we no longer have a traitor of the size of Tshombe really astride the African continent like a colossus. The cause of solidarity has suffered.

If you compare our predicament with that of the Jews and the Nazi atrocities, there were no heroes on a grand scale while the Jews were suffering. There were individual heroes but no heroes of the grand scale standing out, saying to Hitler, "Let my people go." There was nothing of Mosaic stature. But the villain was of the grandest scale ever. Could anything ostensibly human be more evil than Hitler? So you had an enormous villain, and what did it do to subsequent Jewish solidarity? It deepened it with a sense of martyrdom. It deepened it in spite of the absence of grand heroism during the period of suffering. There isn't anything of that equivalence with us and we have to find a way of compensating for it if the level of solidarity for us is to be comparable to that experience of the Jews.

Even our martyrdom of slavery is seldom invoked in the same manner. On the whole we forgive too easily. We have a short memory of hate in America. You can have somebody like Ian Smith, who declares something called independence for Rhodesia, rules, and hangs people for a couple of decades, and then you can have the country become independent. Ian Smith is not subjected to a Nuremberg trial. There is no accountability. Quite the contrary, he actually gets elected to the legislature and sits in Parliament abusing the African government of the day for a few more years before the constitutional order is changed. Now again, probably nowhere else in the world does that sort of thing happen, that degree of willing forgetfulness which is sometimes to our credit. Sometimes we just make it too easy for sinners to think that one day they will just be forgiven readily. It is something to bear in mind.

As for the force of gender in Africa and how it affects North-South relations and Pan-Africanism, traditionally in our African society women were entrusted with the custody of fire, the custody of water, and custody of earth-three elements constituting the ecology. God took charge of the fourth element, the custody of the omnipresent air.

Women were custodians of fire, symbol of heat and light. And what happened? Structurally, we put disproportionate burdens on women in African society. The source of energy in the rural countryside is very often firewood. Women become disproportionately accountable for making sure that firewood is available for the family, for the extended family, for the community; those of you who have been to Africa remember huge bundles that our women carry. Women were custodians of water, the symbol of life, survival, and cleanliness. Again, a disproportionate burden. Women traverse long distances carrying water. They work out immense balancing acts, holding one child here, a baby on the back, having water on their heads and carrying firewood with their other hand, a remarkable balancing act that only the miracle of African women could accomplish. Women are custodians of earth, the linkage to double fertility the fertility - of the womb, women as mothers, and the fertility of the soil, women as cultivators in our society.

Women have all these disproportionate roles. Men can fell trees so that women can collect firewood. Men can dig wells so that women can get water. In more recent times, men can go to the cities and to mines to earn the wages while women cultivate. But there is still a disproportionate role on the African woman.

Comes the role of the new culture and, unfortunately, there is a marginalization, the impact of North-South relations. When you see a farmer on bended knee tilling land for the family, the chances are it is a she. But when you see a tractor driving by and the driver waves "Hi", the chances are it is a he. So with the transition from traditional implements of cultivation to the tractor, it is a transition very often toward the male as the technology gets more advanced. And as the economy gets more international, it is the men who sit on the boards. So the internationalization of African economies increases disproportionately the tendency toward male dominance in our society.

The effect of Westernization is not always simply liberation of women, although sometimes it can have that effect. Even with the liberalization, there is a marginalization. The woman who ceases to be custodian of fire, water, and earth and becomes a typist filing in some man's office may be free by five o'clock. She is a freer woman, but she does things less fundamental to the society than what she was doing in the heartland of cultivation at the center of energy. She has become more free but less important in the role she plays. The balance is still wrong. We must find a way to combine freedom with significance.

In the political domain we have not caught up with Asia yet. It is our sister continent, and I do wish we would look at Asia much more often than we look at the West. We don't look at what is going on in Asia. There is a trend that is happening in Asia which is one route for women to the pinnacle of power. While not satisfactory, it is what I call female succession to male martyrdom, when a woman attains supreme authority after the demise of a male relative and then demonstrates new skills at the top.

It began in Sri Lanka, Ceylon, with Mrs. Sirima Bandaranaike. Her husband was assassinated. She then took over the Party, led the Party, became the Prime Minister, and she is still a tough woman in opposition today. Then we have had Mrs. Indira Gandhi. Her father, Jawaharial Nehru, was not assassinated but her succession was partly on the credentials of her enormously important father. Once in power she demonstrated toughness and ability. Thirdly, we have Mrs.Corazón Aquino. Her husband, Benigno Aquino, arriving from the United States, got killed descending from the plane. She was propelled into national prominence, gradually became a national figure, and now is President of the country. We don't know how tough Mrs. Aquino will remain. She is more fragile, it would seem, than Mrs. Gandhi was, although Mrs. Gandhi in the end paid with her life. And now we have had the first Moslem head of government who is a woman, Benazir Bhutto, in Pakistan. Again, her father, Zulfikar Ali Bhutto, was executed, and she ascended to the supreme pinnacle of political power in a Moslem society. The neighboring country, Bangladesh, has also potential female candidates who may in fact succeed to supreme authority.

There are things happening in Asia as one route toward ultimate power, initially on the credentials of a martyred male. These are opportunities that a woman can then transform to an avenue for power and control, setting the precedent for a future female independently of male martyrdom. We had a woman, Winnie Mandela, who stood a remote change of becoming a leader by that route. For a while she appeared to be a potential female successor to a male martyr. Her husband, Nelson Mandela, was in jail and she, herself, became increasingly prominent in the political process. Now she has been compromised, partly because of decisions that are controversial in her own society and partly because of things which are done by people in whom she believed. I haven't ruled her out altogether as yet. She may make a political comeback. If she doesn't, she will be in the running for what until now has been primarily an Asian phenomenon, a key to ultimate power for females through the political significance of male martyrdom.

Africa - stop watching Europe and America. Deign on the passing Asian to cast your eyes and pause a while from the West to be wise. Just deign to look at what is happening in Asia.

The relationship between the North and the South is a global experience. It is not just a case of political economy. It is a case of political culture which touches on religion, it touches on langauge, and it touches on gender as well as the wider ideology. We must learn to marry religion to the ecumenical spirit inherent in the indigenous faiths of our ancestors. We must marry ecology and its concerns to attain the ideology. We must make ethnicity a source of cultural enrichment instead of a destructive element in the political process. And, we must rely less on villainy and treason for our solidarity and, instead, produce the kind of heroes we had briefly in the last days of colonialism and the first years of independence. We must learn to change fundamentally and to create an Africa worthy of our sons and daughters and worthy of the identity of its people.

CHAPTER 3

THE SEARCH FOR AFRICAN UNITY

Andrew Conteh

A major period in the history of Africa is occupied by slavery and Colonialism. Colonialism in particular fettered the development of the enslaved people of the African continent. So as to facilitate Colonial exploitation, the West deliberately hampered economic and cultural progress in the colonies. It preserved and restored obsolete forms of social relations and fomented discord between nationalities and tribes. However, the drive for super-profits dictated the development of the extractive industry, plantations and capitalist farms, and the building of ports, railways and roads in the colonies. In consequence, social changes did take place in the colonies, irrespective of the will of the Colonialists. Feudal and semi-feudal relations were undermined and new social forces emerged.

Meanwhile, international law of this period refused to recognize any rights of the so-called "uncivilized" Colonial peoples. They were regarded as objects of the law of the "civilized" states. The Colonial powers could "lawfully" conquer, buy, sell, rob and kill the inhabitants of the colonies. The science of international law took great pains to justify Colonial conquests. There were references made to "pity for the poor natives", to the need to "convert natives to Christianity," to "civilize the barbarians", and so on. This monstrous treatment of the peoples of the colonies was further explained by Westerners by asserting that "the law of nations, as a law between states based on the common consent of the members of the family of nations, does not contain any rules concerning the intercourse with the treatment of such state as are outside that circle."[1] American jurist Charles Cheney Hyde, claiming that international law was "inapplicable" to the Colonial peoples, alleged that even if they had a statehood, they were "unfamiliar with the full requirements of civilization as tested by the standards prevailing in the international society."[2] F. List also pointed out that "no tributary state can repudiate protectorateship inasmuch as it has renounced its state sovereignty in favour of sovereign state. Such repudiation is "invalid as is, for instance, a colony's declaration of independence."[3]

Thus, Colonialism as a political-economic and social category was promoted through the utilization of international law. This enabled the Colonial powers to embark upon indiscriminate exploitation of the colonies. The rate of exploitation was so high that even Western economists are forced to accept this fact. The suppressed in Africa and other parts of the world were never satisfied with these practices. Although the suppressed kicked against the Colonial powers, the latter nevertheless succeeded in curbing every rebellion. This development reached its highest pitch after the Second World War. This war left a deep imprint on the minds of Africans, both those who directly took part in it and those who worked in the fields, mines and factories. Africa's tangible contribution to the victory over fascism thus helped it to become aware of its own strength. Millions of Africans regarded the liberation of the fascist-enslaved countries and peoples as a beginning of their own liberation. The collapse of the Nazi racialist ideas also signified to the African freedom fighters the collapse of racialism in general and the ideology of Colonialism based upon it.

Meanwhile, ideologists of the oppressed Africans clearly understood that a vital means in the struggle against colonialism is that Africans should be united. Two movements - Pan-Negroism and Pan-Africanism - developed in the West Indies and North America. Pan-Negroism was concerned with the dignity of all black peoples, while Pan-Africanism began both as a cultural and political movement to group together blacks in the diaspora and to mobilize blacks both in the diaspora and in Africa against white domination, oppression and racial discrimination. [4] In political terms it was a movement for a united black world. For continental Africa, Pan-Africanism nurtured the idea of African brotherhood and solidarity. It inspired the struggle for political independence and call for African Unity. Pan-Africanism laid the basis for African nationalism and was the mother of the concept of continental unity. [5] Pan-Africanism became an expression of the indigenous African quest for continental unity following the 1945 Manchester Congress. [6]

The Manchester Conference marked a turning point in the quest for African continental unity. While Pan-Africanism nurtured the idea of continental unity, the Manchester Congress betrayed the idea. Before 1945 sentiments among the Pan-Africanists leaned heavily towards a continental nation-state, but after the Manchester Congress attitudes began to shift away from the idea of an African state. The explanation for this development rests in the outcome of the 1945 Congress.

Firstly, the Manchester Congress did not draw up a concrete program of action to bring about continental unity. It failed to organize a continental political party. Instead, the Congress unleashed micro-nationalist forces upon the continent when it urged all Africans living in the diaspora to return to their respective colonial territories in order to fight for the independence of individual African colonies. 7 Local territorially based political activities quickly fell prey to the trappings of state nationalism and its accompanying inter-state power struggles.

Secondly, the emphasis of the Manchester Congress shifted. In 1947 the West African Secretariat organized the West African Congress. Both the Secretariat and the Congress pledged themselves to achieve self-government for West African territories, to create a federation of independent West African States and to use the West African federation to work towards African Unity. 8 Thirdly, the Manchester Congress injected into African international politics the concept of economic and social development by cooperation. 9 Thus, the Manchester Congress relegated continental political unity to the cause of regional unity. George Padmore, one of the fathers of Pan-Africanism, wrote in 1956 that "the Pan-Africanist perspective embraces the federation of regional self-governing countries and their eventual amalgamation into a United States of Africa." 10

Pan-Africanism has, however, remained very important to African international politics. Ever since the 1945 Manchester Congress African leaders have favoured some form of inter-African integration. Their views have varied from federalism to functionalism or neofunctionalism. But in the continuing search for African unity, federalism and neo-functionalism have been the dominant concepts.

Neo-functionalists approach the problem of international relations from the perspective of economic functionalism. They emphasize regional functional integration as a prerequisite for international integration. Neo-functionalism, associated mainly with Ernest Haas derives from the principle of economic determinism. [11] Its' basic proposition is that 'step-by-step' economic decisions are superior to crucial political choices. [12] Hence the first step to international integration is the achievement of regional functional integration. It argues further that functional regional institutions lead to increased regional exchanges. As these exchanges become intensified, greater pressure will be exerted on regional functional institutions. The center of economic activities will shift to the regional level, with entrepreneurs also transferring their allegiance from the nation-state to the regional organs. As a result, demands on the regional institutions would increase significantly and would warrant the establishment of regional political machinery capable of mediating conflicting interests at the regional level. The process eventually leads to the emergence of a dominant supra-national authority. Once regional integration has been achieved, a similar pattern of development should take place at the international level. [13]

Federalism refers to a political organization in which two or more states agree to form a union government with central authority, while retaining local autonomy. A federal system of government entails the writing of a constitution which spells out clearly the powers of the central government and of the constituent units. In the international system, federalism has been advocated by the proponents of world peace. Since the formation of the United States of America following the 1787 Philadelphia constitutional convention, federalists have looked to the United States as an example of how best people could unite to form a world government. Federalists thus call for a written constitution and the establishment of world political, legal and military institutions to take over the functions currently performed by national governments.

At a regional level federalism is the call for the coming together of independent nation-states to form a federal regional government. Federalists attach greater emphasis to political institutions than to economic and social factors which functionalists believe are essential in the gradual process of international integration.

Until 1965 the head of state most in favour of federalism was the late President Kwame Nkrumah of Ghana. But in his struggle for continental unity he stood alone against the majority of African leaders who tended to favour a neo-functionalist approach, because federalism involved constitutional or legal obligations while functional integration calls only for moral commitments.

In April 1958, the first ever conference of Independent African States convened in Accra, Ghana. It had been called by Kwame Nkrumah and it brought together all eight independent African States. The Union of South Africa was excluded. The conference considered the issue of African economic development, African unity, the questions of imperialism and colonialism and apartheid in South Africa. Kwame Nkrumah expected the Accra Conference to support the idea of a United States of Africa. But, guided by national interest, the independent states asserted the principle of the inviolability of national independence, sovereignty and territorial integrity. To guarantee the right of African states to exist, the countries pledged not to "interfere in the internal affairs of another country." 14

Nkrumah was not content with the conference's resolution endorsing African unity and solidarity without any commitment to a United States of Africa. Through his initiative, the first All African Peoples' Conference was convened in Accra in December, 1958, just eight months after the first Conference of Independent African States. Uninhibited by national interest considerations, the All African Peoples' Conference called for a Commonwealth of African States, a commonwealth without racial or tribal boundaries. Tom Mboya of Kenya, who had been elected chairman of the Conference, declared they had gathered in Accra to announce African unity and solidarity. The delegates went further and drafted a constitution with a provision for "United States of Africa."

Clearly the views taken by the two conferences diverged. African nationalists who had not yet won independence for their territories on the whole supported the idea of a United States of Africa in the hope that it would speed up the liberation of areas still under colonialism. Delegates representing independent national governments feared that such a development would destroy the nation-state.

The Second Conference of Independent African States, held in Addis Ababa, Ethiopia from June 15-24, 1960, highlighted the point. The conference revealed two diametrically opposed positions. The Ghanaian delegation took the position that the delegates should decide on the establishment of a 'Union of African States'. It proposed that the conference should recommend the establishment of 'a committee of experts with specific terms of reference to work out details of the Union of African States'.

According to the Ghanaian Foreign Minister, Ako Adjei, Nkrumah, Tubman and Sekou Toure had, at their meeting in Sanniquillie, Liberia on 19 July, 1959, agreed on the principles of a Union of African States. The leader of the Nigerian delegation, Y. M. Sule, objected. Having accepted Pan Africanism as 'the only solution to our problems in Africa', Sule observed that 'at the moment the idea of forming a Union of African States is premature'. The union should come gradually. Expressing the majority sentiment, Sule declared that "at the moment we in Nigeria cannot afford to form union by government with any African states by surrendering our sovereignty".

The Addis Ababa conference was another defeat for Nkrumah who had hoped to persuade African states that a union government was necessary. But Nkrumah received consolation from the second All African Peoples' Conference (Tunis, January 25-30, 1960). The conference amended the 1958 constitution but it retained the provision for 'a United States of Africa'. The third All African Peoples' Conference (Cairo, March 23-31, 1961) maintained the tempo by resolving to mobilize the African masses to work for the emergence of a union state. While the resolutions of the All African Peoples' Conferences implied mass interest in African unity, achievement of unity depended upon the nation-states themselves. But they were not ready to surrender their sovereignty. This fact explains why interest in federalism both at the regional and continental level failed to produce federal governments in Africa.

It seemed briefly that federalism might be more successful at the regional level. In the late 1940's leaders in the Maghreb began to discuss the possibility of forming a federation and by 1958, at a time when the newly independent states of Morocco and Tunisia were supporting Algeria's struggle for independence, enthusiasm for the federation was high. But in the end neither the Algerian war nor the later Arab-Israeli conflict were sufficient to overcome the differences within the Maghreb, and the federation was stillborn.

The Union of Nile States, formed by Egypt and Sudan and which anticipated the inclusion of Uganda, was motivated by the importance of the

River Nile to both Egypt and Sudan. The union collapsed in 1955, because Sudanese nationalists could not accept Egypt's interference in Sudan's internal affairs. The widely talked about East African Federation never materialized because of nationalism, particularly in Kenya. In the end, Kenya, Tanganyika (now Tanzania) and Uganda settled for functional integration in the form of the East African Community which lasted from 1967 to 1977.

The nearest any group of independent African states came to closer political integration was the establishment of the Ghana-Guinea union in November, 1958. Mali joined the union in December the following year. As conceived by Nkrumah and Sekou Toure, the union was to start as a confederation. Nkrumah and Sekou Toure declared in May 1959 that membership of the union would be open to all interested independent African states and that citizens of member states would be granted dual citizenship. The member states would jointly decide what elements of their national sovereignty to surrender to the union. National flags, anthems and mottos were to exist side by side with those of the union and each state in the union would maintain its national army and diplomatic representation.

When Mali joined the union in December, 1959, it looked as if the confederate arrangement might attract more membership. Given the determination of states to uphold their sovereignty and national identity, confederacy seemed the best political option that the federalists could offer in the hope of winning support for continental political integration. The Union of African States Charter drawn up in Accra on July 1, 1961 by Nkrumah, Sekou Toure and Modeibo Keita was a well tailored document which took into account both Nkrumah's enthusiasm for a tangible Union of African States and the concern of less enthusiastic confederalists for the preservation of national identity. Section I (Article II) of the charter stated that the Union of African States would serve 'as the nucleus of the United States of Africa'. It thus gave Nkrumah the hope that a confederal system would, in the future, develop into a federal system embracing the entire continent. Article V of the same section created 'the supreme organ of the Union of African States' made up of the heads of state of member countries.

Although Section I (Article IV) and Section 4 (Article VII) provided for a joint defense system, member-states maintained their respective national armies. The charter, on the whole, left national independence, sovereignty and territorial integrity intact. However, the Union of African States failed to attract any additional countries after Mali. The failure reflected widespread hostility to federalism on the continent.

Between 1960 and 1962 Africa became polarized into two political blocs known as the Brazzaville-Monrovia group on the one hand, and the Casablanca group, on the other. The division arose from many factors - ideological differences, personalities of the leaders, national interest considerations - and having just achieved independence, many leaders were reluctant to surrender any of their power to a newly created confederal authority.

The Brazzaville-Monrovia Group, which became the Lagos Group in 1962, consisted of twenty conservative and moderate African states. It had its origin in the December, 1960, Brazzaville Conference of twelve conservative former French colonies opposed to the support of African states for Patrice Lumumba's government in the former Belgian Congo. The Brazzaville twelve also opposed the political union of African states. They favoured functional integration. A larger group met in Monrovia in May, 1961. Like the Brazzaville twelve, it rejected the idea of a continental political union and endorsed inter-Africanfunctional co-operation. 15

The Casablanca Group arose in response to the Brazzaville twelve whose opposition to Lumumba's government, recognition of Mauritania to which Morocco laid claim, failure to recognize the Algerian Liberation Front and rejection of a contemplated union of African states antagonized a section of African states. The group consisting of seven countries with diverse interests met in Casablanca in January, 1961. Morocco wanted support for its opposition to Mauritania's independence and admission to the United Nations. Nasser saw the group as a chance of increasing Egyptian influence in Africa and to gain the support of African states against Israel. For Sekou Toure the enlarged group provided badly needed political support against France and the former French colonies that had ostracized him for refusing to remain within France's sphere of influence. To Modiebo Keita and Nkrumah the group offered a forum for projecting a collective African view on the Congo crisis and for advancing the idea of a union of African states. 16

The Casablanca Conference decided to reject the idea of drawing up a constitution for an African Union. A constitution is a legally binding document and its provisions are enforced by a court of law. Wade and Philips have defined a constitution as "the rules which regulate the structure of the principal organs of government and their relationship to each other and which determine their principal functions." [17] Professor Dicey adds that a constitution defines "the rules of a country which determine the form of its government, the respective rights and duties of the government towards its citizens, and the citizen towards the government." [18]

The Casablanca invariably understood the implications of a binding constitution. It would create a new political system of government which stood above the existing nation-states. It was consequently felt to be unacceptable. Instead, the Conference participants drew up a charter which they called 'The African Charter of Casablanca'. The African Charter of Casablanca established an association of African states willing voluntarily to preserve and consolidate their identity of views and unity in international affairs, to safeguard hard won independence, the sovereignty and territorial integrity of the states, and to reinforce peace in the world by adopting a policy of non-alignment. On African unity, the charter provided for the establishment of an African consultative assembly, but only when conditions permitted. In the meantime, the charter created a political committee to coordinate foreign policies, an economic committee to promote economic cooperation, a cultural committee and a joint African High Command to coordinate defense.

During the months following the signing of the charter and especially after the heads of state approved the protocol for the implementation of the provisions of the charter in June, 1961, the Casablanca states attempted to make the three committees and the Joint High Command operational. However, the actual operation of these organs remained at conference and diplomatic representation levels only. [19]

The importance of the African Charter of Casablanca is two- fold. First, in the quest for African unity, it provided a political and industrial framework. Ingrained in the charter was Nkrumah's belief that political unity should come first, as the necessary prelude to the creation of an extended field for which integrated economic and social development plans could be worked out. Nkrumah maintained this approach at the May, 1963 Addis Ababa summit meeting (Cervenka, 1969: 139-40, 80-1). Second, it introduced the charter system into inter-African politics. The Casablanca Charter was the precursor of the Monrovia Charter (May 12, 1961), the Lagos Charter (January 30, 1962) and the Organization of African Unity Charter (May 26, 1963). The document which came out of the Monrovia conference was only a draft charter, but it laid the basis for the Organization of African Unity. It expressed the views of all those opposed to a political union. First and foremost, the Monrovia draft charter emphasized the absolute equality and sovereignty of African states. Without mentioning names it cautioned Ghana and Morocco against attempting to annex other states. (Ghana had laid claim to Togo on the grounds that the colonial boundaries dividing the Ewe between Ghana and Togo were illegitimate while Morocco had claimed Mauritania on historical grounds and religious affinity). The draft charter further stressed the principle of non-interference in the internal affairs of sister states and prohibited the harboring of dissidents from other African states. The document registered strong opposition to racial policies in Southern Africa and it pledged support for African liberation movements. The Monrovia draft charter, unlike the African Charter of Casablanca, laid out a functionalist and non-political approach to African unity. It proposed that "the unity aimed to be achieved at the moment is not the political integration of sovereign African states, but unity of aspirations and actions considered from the point of view of African social solidarity and political identity. [20] The Monrovia document moved toward inter-African functional integration by calling for economic, educational, cultural, scientific and technical cooperation.

The Monrovia Conference had only produced a draft charter. Its ratification, however, had to await the proposed Lagos Conference which the Monrovia group hoped would be attended by the Casablanca powers. But when the Lagos Conference convened on January 25, 1962, all the Casablanca states declined the invitation to attend. Of the twenty countries present all had belonged to the Brazzaville-Monrovia group, except Tanganyika (Tanzania) and Congo (Zaire). Thus at the close of this conference on January 30, the twenty countries agreed to ratify the Monrovia draft charter in principle only and gave it the title 'The Charter of Inter-African States and Malagasy Organization'. The charter left the door open for other African states to suggest changes and to sign it. One thing that should be noted about the Lagos Charter is the fact that it omitted African unity. The reason for this is contained in Article III of the Charter which, among other matters, emphasized the principle of 'the sovereign equality of the African and Malagasy states, whatever may be the size of their territory, the density of their population or values of their possession.

There were two main innovative features of the Lagos Charter - the creation of a general secretariat to act as the central administrative organ of the Inter-African States and Malagasy Organization and consideration of Mechanisms for resolving inter-African disputes. Both features were to find their way into the OAU Charter.

Despite all the divisions between the various African blocs the cause of African unity had made considerable progress since the Manchester Congress. First, and most importantly, by 1963 the majority of African states had become independent. Second, there was widespread agreement on the need for some form of continental unity, although, as we have seen, radicals such as Nkrumah were isolated in their wish for a Pan-African government. Third, there was universal condemnation of the racist apartheid regime of South Africa. Lastly, all the conferences held between 1958 and 1963 passed resolutions in support of national liberation struggles on the continent. All these sentiments were neatly expressed in the final declaration of the 1958 Conference of Independent African States:

> We resolve to preserve unity of purpose and action in international affairs; safeguard our hard won independence, sovereignty and territorial integrity; and to preserve among ourselves the fundamental unity of outlook on foreign policy so that a distinct African personality will play its part in cooperation with other peace-loving nations to further the cause of peace.

THE ESTABLISHMENT OF THE ORGANIZATION OF AFRICAN UNITY

Early in March, 1963, the idea of holding a summit meeting of African heads of state and government from May 23 -26, 1963 was largely accepted. A conference of foreign ministers convened May 15 in Addis Ababa to work out the agenda. Four divergent approaches to African unity emerged. 1) Africa needed only a single all-African states charter which would replace the African

Charter of Casablanca and the Monrovia-Lagos Charters. Its proponents envisaged a charter which would lay out a "Declaration of Principles" of inter-African conduct, a position held by Libya and Sudan. All African states would be expected to subscribe to these principles without surrendering any of their sovereignty. 21

The second proposal added to the idea of a declaration of principles the concept of "a loose association of African States' which would be set up within the framework of an all-African Organization". Its leading advocate was Liberia, along with other states which felt that the Organization of American States pro - vided the best model for African conditions.

The third view was a mixture of functionalist and regional federalist views. Nigeria ruled out the possibility of an organic unity of African states. Nigeria favoured inter-African economic cooperation and thought that efforts toward organic unity should be a step-by-step process starting with regional co-operation and finally extending to the whole continent. This posture was held also by Ethiopia, the Brazzaville Group and Tanganyika which advocated the federation of East African states.

Finally, there was the view, held mainly by Ghana, that the Addis Ababa summit meeting should produce a Union of African States, with a Union Government, an African Civil Service, an African High Command and a Court of Justice. Nkrumah went to Addis Ababa determined to persuade the assembled heads of state and government to accept his proposal for an All-African Union Government. Tafawa Balewa of Nigeria had already become fully convinced that political integration was completely unacceptable. What had formerly been thought different views on the concept of African unity were reduced to a subtle political duel between Ghana on the one hand and Nigeria on the other. 22

What was behind this political duel between Ghana and Nigeria? *First,* most African heads of state and government did not want a political unification of Africa, and Nigeria assumed the role of leadership of the group opposed to an African federation. *Second*, the United States government had succeeded in convincing key African leaders, among them Tafawa Balewa, William Tubman and Haile Selassie, that a United African government would be led by the socialist and pro-Soviet Nkrumah and Nasser. The United States suggested instead a regionalist approach to inter-African integration. [23]

Third, on the eve of the summit meeting, there was a concerted international effort to depict Nkrumah as a ruthless and power-thirsty Pan-Africanist who would use any means (including political assassination) to achieve his goal. This image of Nkrumah was accepted by many West African leaders, and it set the stage for confrontation at the founding of the Organization of African Unity. [24]

On May 24th, Nkrumah submitted to the conference that African unity can only be gained by political means and put before the assembled heads of state and government his proposal for a political and institutional approach to African unity. (In his book, *Africa Must Unite*, Nkrumah had warned that the choice before African states lay between unity and survival on the one hand and disunity and collapse on the other. [25]) Nkrumah's proposals called for establishing three commissions to draft a constitution, prepare an economic and industrial plan, and work out a common foreign policy. With only Milton Obote as a supporter, the proposals were not adopted by the conference. This stalemate threatened the creation of the OAU, a fear expressed by Haile Selassie. [26] But, African heads of state and government buried their differences and united on the issue of decolonization. [27]

On May 25th, 1963, a draft charter with a few corrections was adopted by the delegates, and the first Continental Organization of Africa was established. The leaders of independent African states and governments realized the importance of African unity to solve the complex problems of nation-building. At the Addis Ababa Conference:

(a) The founding of the Organization was a compromise which is usually how large groups of states set up international organizations;

(b) African leaders in 1963 felt that the OAU would promote unity and solidarity of African states;

(c) Those concerned with the rights of individual states saw in the OAU the best organ for establishing legitimacy among members;

(d) In addition to legitimization of the nation-state, the OAU was expected to partly increase the bargaining power of African states in vital economic, financial and commercial areas;

(e) The formation of the Organization reflected the international legal personality of the independent Africa states;

(f) The Organization however meant different things to the thirty-one heads of state and government who founded it;

(g) The OAU Charter was designed to cater for most of the diverse views mentioned above reflecting the politics of compromise.

AIMS AND PRINCIPLES OF THE ORGANIZATION OF AFRICAN UNITY

The Charter of the Organization of African Unity in itself is an international treaty known as the Constituent Act of the Organization. Usually the constituent act of an organization constitutes an aggregate of norms governing the structure, the procedure of the performance of functions and the relations between the internal sub-divisions of the organization. The norms contained in the constituent act are legally binding upon the member states, and they form part of public international law as well as part of private international law.

The founding fathers are said to have devoted almost half of their time to discussing the preamble of the OAU Charter which outlines the aims and principles of the Organization. 28 This was because of their desire to accommodate most of the divergent views prevailing in Addis Ababa in order to enable unanimous agreement. Five of the preamble's twelve paragraphs dealt with fundamental human rights such as the inalienable right of all peoples to self-determination, the recognition of historical demands by African peoples to freedom, equality, justice and human dignity and acceptance of the United Nations Declaration of Human Rights as forming the basis for international peace. In the minds of African leaders, the elimination of colonialism was associated with peace and security. The aims of the Organization are outlined in Article II of the Charter as follows:

1) To promote unity and solidarity of African States;
2) To co-ordinate and intensify their co-operation and efforts to achieve a better life for the peoples of Africa;
3) To defend their sovereignty, territorial integrity and independence;
4) To eradicate all forms of colonialism from Africa, and
5) To promote international co-operation, having due regard to the

Charter of the United Nations and Universal Declaration of Human Rights.

At a glance, one can divide these aims into two distinct, though inter-related categories. The first category constitutes the aims of local and regional significance and the second category comprises aims that extend beyond the frontiers of the African continent. Paragraph II, of this Article goes farther to state that, to these ends, the member states shall co-ordinate and harmonize their general policies, especially in the following fields:

1) Political and diplomatic co-operation;
2) Economic co-operation, including transport and communications;
3) Educational and cultural co-operations;
4) Health, Sanitation and Nutritional co-operation;
5) Scientific and technical co-operation; and
6) Co-operation for defence and security.

Member-states, therefore, decided to co-operate either on bilateral or multilateral bases with an aim to achieving the goals of the organization - to cement, safeguard, and consolidate the hard-won political independence, sovereignty, and territorial integrity of member states and to fight against neo-colonialism in all its forms and manifestations.

In pursuit of the aims stated in Article II, Member-states solemnly affirmed and declared their adherence to the following principles (Article III):

1) The sovereign equality of all member states;
2) Non-interference in the internal affairs of states;
3) Respect for sovereignty and territorial integrity of each state and for its inalienable right to independent existence;
4) Peaceful settlement of disputes by negotiation, mediation, conciliation or arbitration;
5) Unreserved condemnation, in all its forms, of political assassination as well as of subversive activities on the part of neighboring states or any other states;
6) Absolute dedication to the total emancipation of the African territories which are still dependent;
7) Affirmation of a policy of non-alignment with regard to all blocs.

The first four principles of the Charter are not new to international law.

[29] These principles form an integral part of the *jus cogens*, which are recognized by contemporary international law as binding upon all subjects of international law. These principles have found their legal expressions in multilateral and bi-lateral treaties. On the other hand, principles 5, 6 and 7 are of a specific nature. They can only be traced in this particular charter. Thus, the principles of the organization are divided into the generally accepted principles of international law and specific or regional principles known only by this Charter.

ORGANIZATION OF AFRICAN UNITY AND AFRICAN ECONOMIC DEVELOPMENT

A set of measures meant to promote the objective of expanding intra-African cooperation in interrelated economic and social spheres was recommended in the resolutions of the 3rd Assembly of Heads of State and Government convened in Addis Ababa in 1966 and the 9th, 11th and 12th sessions of the OAU Council of Ministers which were held in Addis Ababa in 1967 and 1969 and in Algeria in 1968. Even though none of these economic decisions were translated into life, the discussion of these problems, formulation of approaches to their solution and elaboration of the relevant recommendations are important in themselves. Indicative in this sense is the Memorandum on the Responsibilities and Role of the OAU in the Economic and Social Fields adopted in August 1970 by the 15th session of the OAU Council of Ministers in Addis Ababa. [33] This detailed document states that the OAU should primarily play a coordinating role and become an organization outlining and regulating activities aimed at facilitating the continent's economic and social development.

During the period between 1963-1973, the Organization was able to develop a sense of awareness of the continent's economic problems and a sense of urgency in seeking solutions to them. The Organization pushed the idea of an Inter-African Cooperation. With the co-operation of the ECA, the Organization was able to work out a comprehensive Pan-African Telecommunications network. Also with the assistance of the ECA, a network of road communication was worked out to link up all parts of Africa and facilitate movements of goods and contact between her peoples. Very successful campaigns were launched and executed by the Organization against rinderpest and bovine pleuropneumonia saving the lives of millions of cattle throughout Africa. Many seminars were organized by the Organization in the fields of human health, in the disciplines of viral, bacterial and parasitic diseases, in trypanosoriuasis and schistosoriuasis. The Organization also promoted a continental approach to the exploitation and utilization of the continent's natural resources, as well as the cultivation and distribution of the continents' basic staple foods such as rice and millet.

A ministerial conference held in Dakar in 1972 deliberated on the development of trade and on Africa's monetary and financial problems. Also quite important was the convening in February 1979, on OAU initiative, of a colloquium in Monrovia (capitol of Liberia) at which the prospects for Africa's development through 2000 were discussed in detail. This workshop was attended by about 40 experts from several African countries - specialists not only in economic problems but also in social affairs (labour, health, etc.). It is significant that many of the economic measures elaborated were done in collaboration with the ECA and other specialized agencies of the U.N.

Nonetheless, rather than improvement in the economic situation of the continent, successive strategies made the continent stagnate and become more susceptible than other regions to the economic and social crises suffered by the industrialized countries. Thus, Africa was unable to point to any significant growth rate or satisfactory index of general well-being of its people.

MONROVIA STRATEGY FOR ECONOMIC DEVELOPMENT IN AFRICA

Following the adoption by the Council of Ministers in Monrovia in 1979 of the "Monrovia strategy for the Economic Development in Africa," the Heads of State and Government meeting also in Monrovia committed themselves to promoting economic and social development and integration of economics with a view to achieving an increasing measure of self-sufficiency and self sustainment. They committed themselves individually and collectively on behalf of governments and peoples to start to eliminate illiteracy, to achieve self-sufficiency in food production and supply, to cooperate in the field of natural resources control, exploration, extraction and use for economic development, and to cooperate in the preservation, protection, and improvement of the natural environment. Resolving to give special attention to the discussion of economic issues at each annual Session of the Assembly, they called on the Secretary General in collaboration with the Executive Secretary of the United Nations Economic Commission for Africa to draw up annually specific programs and measures for economic cooperation on a sub-regional, regional and continental basis in Africa.

Despite all efforts made by its leaders, Africa remains the least developed continent with 20 of the 31 least developed countries of the world. Africa is susceptible to the disastrous effects of natural and endemic diseases of the cruelest type, and it is a victim of settler exploitation arising from colonialism, racism and apartheid. In the 20 years from 1960 - 1980, the average rate of growth continent wide has been no more than 4.8%; a figure which hides divergent realities ranging from 7% growth rate for the oil exporting countries down to 2.9% for the least developed countries. Furthermore the second oil shock of 1979 had a devastating effect on the economies of the African States.

Africa's underdevelopment is not inevitable. Indeed, it is a paradox when one bears in mind the immense human and natural resources of the continent. In addition to its reservoir of human resources, this continent has 97% of world reserves of chrome, 85% of world reserves of uranium and 13% of world reserves of copper (without mentioning bauxite, nickel and lead); 20% of world hydro-electrical potential; 20% of traded oil in the world; 70% of world cocoa production; 50% of palm produce and so on. African leaders have expressed their conviction that the same determination which had virtually brought an end to political domination was required for the economic liberation of the continent.

LAGOS PLAN OF ACTION AND LAGOS FINAL ACT

The central principle of the Lagos Plan is that the worth of economic development is measured only by the well-being of the people. Africa's central objective, therefore, is alleviation of poverty and general improvement in the living standards of the people. Achieving this principle requires increased production through expanded and diversified productive capacities that can be sustained over a long period of time and which will not unduly suffer the shocks of outside events. Self-reliance - both national and collective - is a goal to be achieved by creating strong national economies and a dynamic African regional economy through regional and continent-wide economic cooperation and integration.

The Lagos Plan also stated importance should be accorded to the development of the agricultural base in order to achieve not only self-sufficiency in food production but also production of adequate surpluses. For the 1980s emphasis was to be given to the development of agriculture and agro-based industries even though the overall strategy put industrialization first. Increased aid levels were still the bottom line as African states declared they were owed a massive and appropriate contribution by the developed countries.

One major problem identified is the inability to follow up in the implementation of political decisions. There are two reasons - lack of financial and material support and lack of political support. There already are more multinational African institutions than the governments can support. Therefore, views about reducing their number have been coming from different sub-regions of the continent. The other problem is lack of political support to the institutions. Why was there a lack of political support or will?

On the side of speculation, several reasons could be suggested for the lack of political will, the first perhaps being sociopolitical instability. At the time when the Lagos Plan was adopted, there were countries, particularly in Southern Africa, that were still fighting liberation wars. There are also countries fighting civil wars or wars among themselves. This was the case in Uganda until recently and still is the case in Sudan, Somalia, Liberia and Ethiopia. Of the remaining African countries, most have one type of instability or another arising from a variety of internal factors such as religion, ethnicity, gaps in income, and access to wealth.

One could also speculate about concern with development issues and power struggles among political factions or interest groups. The latter phenomenon, like the one of political instability, tends to reflect the fragility of African politics. This is where the question of the struggle for power comes in.

Power confers the capability to deploy resources; it also confers fame, prestige, and privileges. Consequently, those who are in power are loath to relinquish it, while there are those who are ceaselessly struggling to attain it. And at a slightly lower level, there are those who fight at all costs to maintain the positions they have acquired even if they are not fit for them. They want to do so for the same reasons, namely power, fame, prestige, and privileges. In addition, power confers a good living standard comparable with the industrialized countries. Those in such positions fear to lose their privileges. They also fear having their ego hurt if they lose power, hence the fierce struggle to defend their positions stoutly against those who are fighting their way up. Perhaps this attitude is explained by poverty and the lack of realization that one can contribute to society in an infinite number of ways. If there is a realization that one could contribute to society in different ways without having power (as educators, religious leaders, and charity workers often do, for example) and that such a contribution can finally reward one with fame and prestige, then the struggle for power may abate.

IMPLEMENTING THE LAGOS PLAN

Adherence to the aims and tasks of the Lagos Plan of Action and the Lagos Act is the essence of the economic strategy worked out by the Organization of African Unity. The 1984 Session of the Assembly stressed the necessity of lessening the dependence of African countries' economies on external factors, as well as the need for collective self-reliance. In this connection, Julius Nyerere stated in his address to the 20th Assembly: "In the face of this response to world problems on the part of economically powerful nations, we in Africa have no choice but to increase our own endeavours to be self-reliant, both on a regional and on a national basis. Separately we are all very weak - all of us. Together, we could make Africa just a little less weak". 34 Acting OAU Secretary-General Peter Onu also directly and unequivocally said: "A collective determined effort on the basis of self-reliance is the only sure way out for Africa. This calls for dedication, sacrifice and realistic internal readjustment in economies". 35 The determination of OAU member-states is to put into practice the principles of self-reliance, 36 stressing the need for large-scale development of cooperation and integration as a permanent backbone of the continents' major sub-regional organizations: the Economic Community of West African States (ECOWAS) founded in 1975; the West African Economic Community (WAEC), which came into existence in 1974, consisting of seven francophone states and one francophone observer-country; the Southern African Development Coordination Committee (SADCC), a nine nation-state organization founded in 1979; the Preferential Trade Area for Eastern and Southern Africa, the agreement on which was signed by 15 states in 1981.

Resistance to the idea of agriculture as the engine of production died hard. However, African Ministers of agriculture and livestock and rural development assembled in Harare from July 16-25, 1984, and made a declaration on Africa's economic problems and their intention to tackle them resolutely. The Harare Declaration stressed four areas of effort: self-reliance, food and agricultural production, food security, and the focus on Africa by the FAO and other organizations with respect to self-reliance.

The question of self-reliance has been echoed many times in different forums. But it is noteworthy that any declaration of self-reliance is usually accompanied by solicitation of assistance from the international community. If both aspects of self-reliance and assistance from donors are stressed equally, then there is a conflict. One only hopes that self-reliance is stressed far more than assistance from outside: no self-reliance is feasible while Africa is always looking to the outside world for help. The recent trend, even in multilateral organizations, should awaken Africa. Contributions to these institutions are being cut and hence aid resources are becoming scarcer than ever before. Donors are also cutting back their direct contributions to Africa and are beginning to lose interest. For self-reliance to come about, both the will and the capacity for development must be present. Capacity exists in terms of resources, but it needs to be activated by the will, and it is this that is lacking. Otherwise, the capacity would have been applied. What happens is that the will is directed outward toward aid which it is thought, will accelerate development. Aid might help, but that depends on the type as well as utilization by the recipient country. There is no free aid, no matter how one thinks about it.

THE AFRICAN ECONOMIC SUMMIT - 1985

At the mid-July, 1985, Continental Summit on Africa's Economic Problems and Prospects, the palpable economic crisis in both Ethiopia and other areas within Africa combined with the renewed relevance (let alone fifth anniversary) of the continents' Lagos Plan of Action injected urgency into the proceedings. The half-decade since Lagos was marked by an intensification of the continental crisis as indicated in the ECA-ADB Economic Report on Africa - 1985. There were not only droughts and famines but also relentless recession and regression as the mix of exponential declines in terms of trade and exchange rates and increases in debt and population impacted on Africa's already vulnerable economies and ecologies.

Bayo Adedeji, Director of the Economic Commission for Africa, called for national and regional implementation of the Lagos Plan, criticizing inordinate delays in effecting Pan-African schemes for trans-continental highways and centres. He also lamented the decline in inter-African trade and the rise in African military expenditure. The Heads of State and Government in their common platform for action among member states of the OAU re-affirmed in "Africa's Priority Programme for Economic Recovery 1986-1990" that economic integration through sub-regional, regional and continental cooperation was a top priority to enable the economies of the African countries to be viable within a system of international relations characterized by inequality in the balance of power. This cooperation was to be intensified and extended in the following priority areas: agriculture and food; transport and communications; industry, trade and finance; science and technology and human resources.

UNITED NATIONS PROGRAM OF ACTION FOR AFRICAN ECONOMIC RECOVERY AND DEVELOPMENT (1986-1990)

Despite all the efforts by African Heads of State and Government the economic situation on the continent has shown no signs of improvement. Drought has been sweeping through the savanna, deserts and coastlines of all parts of Africa, and food shortages are rampant throughout at least half of all African countries, affecting millions of Africans. Hundreds of thousands of cattle have died from lack of feed and epidemics of cattle plague. Rivers and streams have vanished and wells have dried up. At least 150 million persons are faced with starvation in the 24 most seriously affected countries: Angola, Benin, Botswana, Cape Verde, Central African Republic, Chad, Ethiopia, Gambia, Ghana, Guinea, Guinea-Bissau, Lesotho, Mali, Mauritania, Mozambique, Saa

Tome and Principe, Senegal, Somalia, Swaziland, Togo, United Republic of Tanzania, Zambia and Zimbabwe.

Because of the food crises, the Heads of State and Government of the OAU requested a special session of the U. N. General Assembly in order to mobilize additional international resources for the continents recovery and rehabilitation following the continents devastation by its worst drought and famine in memory. The U. N.'s special session on the critical economic situation in Africa (1986) adopted a program of action for 1986-1990 to counter the continents continuing economic deterioration. The international community agreed to support fresh initiatives being undertaken by African States to promote food production, build up agricultural industries and related infrastructure, reverse the effects of drought and deslertification, and develop human resources through radical changes in the education systems. Elimination of protectionism, higher prices for agricultural commodities, greater balance of payments support and consideration of ways to lighten the debt burden are among the measures cited as important.

Even with these articulated intentions, the international community did not respond as expected, a warning to Africa. If Africa has not learned the lesson that externally derived and oriented solutions are no solutions and only encourage dependence, then it should learn it now. African leaders should long ago have grasped that the onus for developing Africa rests squarely on Africans themselves and that the starting point is unity.

At the February, 1987, meeting of the French West African Monetary Union, Côte d'Ivoire, Senegal, Mali, Burkina Faso, Benin, Niger and Togo launched a collective attack on the International Monetary Fund's structural adjustment reforms. Echoing the revolt of the major Latin American debtors, they argued that the IMF program and debt service together are strangling their economies. African hostility to painful, frequently hastily conceived, and often externally imposed, programs should come as no shock. Because they are the weakest, African countries are more vulnerable to international pressures than any other set of debtors.

In their search for new answers, many African governments were turning their politics into laboratories for the new Western development theories. Africa's main financial institution, the African Development Bank, led the way, pushing structural adjustment energetically from the early 1980's. The triple-A -rated bank, which expanded its lending by 42 percent in 1986 and tripled its capital in 1987, recently has put a large chunk of its money into agriculture and has set aside 60 percent of its resources for Africa's poorest states. In addition to farming, the ADB President, Baba - car N'Diaye recently laid out as priorities policy reforms and policy dialogue; inter-African trade; the promotion of the private sector; the insertion of women into economic development; and the problem of the environment.

AFRICAN COMMON POSITION ON AFRICA'S EXTERNAL DEBT CRISIS

In response to the serious debt situation facing the continent, African leaders took radical measures aimed at reducing their balance of payments deficits, including drastic cuts in imports and efforts to substantially increase the continents' exports. Despite these drastic measures the continent's debt service ratio continued to rise. The greater part of this debt was simply the result of fluctuations in exchange rates and increase in interest rates based on decisions in which African countries did not participate and over which they had no control.

Alarmed at the debt situation, in 1987 the Heads of States and Government of the OAU expressed their commitment to deal with the external debt crisis by organizing training workshops, courses and seminars on management of external debt for African countries; by increasing use of domestic resources; and by continuing efforts to reduce inflation and improve efficiency in economic and financial management. To promote further cooperation as envisaged in the Lagos Plan of Action, African countries with net surpluses were asked to invest part of these surplus funds in Africa and to help develop sub-regional capital markets needed as an effective mechanism for tapping African surplus funds currently invested abroad.

THE AFRICAN ECONOMIC COMMUNITY

The treaty establishing the African Economic Community wa adopted by the OAU Heads of State and Government in Abuja, Nigeria, in 1991. The objectives of the Community are to promote economic, social and cultural development and the integration of African economies in order to increase economic self-reliance and indigenous and self-sustained development; to establish on a continental scale, a framework for development, mobilization and utilization of human and material resources of Africa in order to achieve self-reliance; to promote cooperation in all fields of human endeavour with the goal of raising the standard of living of African peoples; and to coordinate and harmonise policies among existing economic communities. In addition to integration of national markets and cooperation in production, the States joining the Community also undertake to cooperate with each other in social, political, financial and monetary matters. One especially important way through which the objectives of the Treaty are to be achieved is by gradual removal from member States of obstacles to the free movement of persons, goods, services, and capital and the right of residence and establishment.

Another important non-tariff barrier to intra-African trade that the African Economic Community must confront is the present significantly diverse legal systems that exist in Africa. The membership of the Community represents at least four main legal systems, namely those of common law, Roman-Dutch law, Islamic law and civil law origin. Each, in turn comprises many different systems of law, especially including traditional customary laws, and every country has its own legal traditions, its own system of legal thought, its own method of law- making and its own process of judicial determination of disputes.

MODALITIES FOR THE ESTABLISHMENT OF THE COMMUNITY

Article 6 of the Treaty sets out six stages for the establishment of the Community over a period of 34 years. The *first stage* will be devoted to the strengthening of existing regional economic communities such as the PTA a ECOWAS, and to establishing similar economic communities in those regions where none exist. The *second stage* will be to stabiliz tariff and non-tariff barriers, custom duties and internal taxes. The *third stage* is the establishment of a free trade area. During this period a common external tariff is expected to be adopted and a customs union created. The *fourth stage* will aim at the furtherance of a customs union; *the fifth* is devoted to the establishment of the African Common Market; while the *sixth and final stage* will be devoted to consolidation and strengthening of the African Common Market. There is provision for the Assembly of Heads of State and Government to determine at the end of each stage (and time period) whether expectations have been sufficiently fulfilled.

The Treaty sets up a Court of Justice to ensure adherence to the law. However, the diversity of the legal systems in Africa requires that careful attention will have to be paid to the evolution of legal procedures that will be acceptable to all member States. There is also the problem of enforcement of the orders of the Court. Historically, African States have openly resisted any resort to binding court procedures. There will therefore be a need for African States to cultivate respect for court decisions. The Court will also have to be adequately financed and sufficiently independent to render decisions without fear.

OBSTACLES TO AFRICAN ECONOMIC INTEGRATION

Economic integration is perceived by many African leaders and governments as a promising vehicle for enhancing economic and social development in their respective countries. Regional cooperation can help to promote a more complementary and sustained development of African countries, through the reinforcement of the regional infrastructure, a more efficient system of pay ment, greater access to credit, a more interrelated institutional system, a greater mutual awareness among economic agents operating in the different countries and, above all, through a growing technical complementarity.

There are currently several African integration schemes including the West African Economic Community (CEAO), the Preferential Trade Area for Eastern and Southern African States (PTA), the Economic Community of West African States (ECOWAS), the Southern African Development Community (SADC), the Central African Customs and Economic Union (EDEAC), the African and Mauritian Common Organisation (OCAM); the Comit Permanent Consultatif du Maghreb (CPCM); the Economic Community of the Great Lakes Countries (CEPGL), and one may add the South African Customs Union (SACU).

The traditional explanation of the failure of integration schemes in Africa to date is that there is a *lack of necessary political will* to see integration succeed, expressed in the chronic non-observance of commitments undertaken within the respective agreements and in the insufficient use of instruments set up by those agreements. Many countries seem to go into economic integration agreements without any intention of parting with some measure of national sovereignty. African states have to accept that membership in an economic community has serious long-term implications for the States involved. It entails very close cooperation with one's neighbors; very often adherence to traditional rivalry and differences impede the integration process. Differences in linguistic, political, legal and administrative systems have to be overcome.

Another key factor is that the economic infrastructure is not yet adequate to support economic integration systems. Also, the existence of border conflicts and linguistic rivalries (especially between English and French) compounded by racial suspicion on the continent between Black Africans and Arab Africans can hamper economic integration.

No matter how good the arguments and intentions to integrate may look on paper, the political environment for their implementation and preservation must be right for the effort to succeed. Economic cooperation and integration flourish better in an environment that is politically peaceful and stable. The examples of successful economic integration drawn from history clearly illustrate that they are predicated primarily upon a common outlook to political affairs among the community members.

It is a happy development that the winds of democratization and of political reform now blowing across several regions and the world have not excluded Africa. Democracy is the ultimate guarantor of freedom of movement of goods and capital. Mutual respect and trust are expected to be fully restored between these newly emerging democratic leaderships and this will no doubt contribute to the advancement of regional co-operation and eventual economic integration. If the ambitious goal of creating an African Economic Community is going to be achieved, bolder efforts than have hitherto been made will be needed to deal with the problems outlined above to create an enabling environment for an economic community to flourish.

THE OAU AND INTERNATIONAL POLITICS

The OAU is the African body responsible for seeking the larger unity of African states. This aspect of unity has been exampled in the more or less unanimous resolve to help liberate the whole continent from colonialism. The legacy of colonialism was such that neighboring countries that were colonies of different colonial powers had little contact with each other. The lack of personal contacts between leaders and officials of the new countries further complicated the situation in the early years of independence. Also, the barrier of language, especially between Anglophone and Francophone, created a deep gulf.

The OAU has served as the channel for inter-African relations and has provided a framework for problem solving. The debate over whether to preserve the colonial boundaries in the interest of the integrity of the state or to make adjustments in the interest of uniting people raged in Africa even before any formal granting of independence. 37 Fear of the possible chaos likely to follow claims for border adjustments must have been decisive in the decision of the OAU to maintain the status quo. The ad hoc arrangements by the OAU have succeeded in either resolving or rendering manageable most territorial disputes so that no border has been changed since attainment of independence by African countries.

However, the OAU has often been criticized for its inability, some would say unwillingness, to intervene in conflicts either within individual countries or between member states since its' creation in May 1963. The list of such conflicts has been lengthening throughout the existence of the organization. In the last few years, the conflicts in Liberia, Somalia, Rwanda, among others and now the renewed fighting in Angola have all cried out for some sort of OAU initiative beyond the issuing of tons of declarations, which are mere recommendations with no legal binding force. The truth, however, is that the OAU lacks the appropriate mechanism for such intervention, especially as the principle of non-interference in the affairs of member states has been enshrined in the Charter of the Organization.

At the up-coming Summit of Heads of State and Government this June (1993) in Cairo, they will be asked to approve of the creation of a mechanism for dealing with conflicts within and between member states. All but one of the 29

Cabinet Ministers attending the Council of Ministers meeting in February, 1993, spoke in favor of the Secretary-General's proposals for an "OAU Mechanism for Conflict Prevention and Resolution". Sudan, itself gripped by civil war and the object of UN criticism for widespread human rights abuses, was the lone opponent.

Several diplomats and observers say that the U.S. action in Somalia accounts in part for Africa's new willingness to confront challenges. African leaders have been noticeably concerned at a situation which forces the continent to accept military expeditions by Western powers. Salim Salim appears to have swayed African governments with his argument that if Africa is to achieve meaningful independence, it will have to save itself. "If we have a mechanism in the OAU", he says, "it will be possible in many of these crises that the first course of intervention will be from Africa itself, rather than from the outside."

Discussions about an African intervention force have as long a history as the OAU itself. The idea was not popular with those African leaders who were against centralization within the pan-African movement. However, with the outbreak of conflict in so many parts of the continent the idea may have begun to take on a life of his own. 38 In fact, the OAU has of late even undertaken the observation of elections in a number of member states at their own request, an action which could most certainly have been considered interference in the past.

If intervention is no longer a taboo subject, it is still not a subject taken lightly either. All the demands and fears will have to be finely balanced. But beyond that is the claim that there has to be an African way of bridging the gap between the demands of total sovereignty and the 'right to intervene'. Again, from the secretariat in Dakar: "Given that every African is his brother's keeper, and that our borders are at best artificial, we in Africa need to use our own cultural and social relationships to interpret the principle of non-interference in such a way that we are enabled to apply it to our advantage in conflict prevention and resolution."

While there is almost unanimous agreement on the need for the OAU to be involved in peace-making, the issue of peace-keeping which is at the heart of the question of intervention has not been fully resolved; yet that is that issue on which most attention will be focused. There are many reasons why some African leaders might want to defer any action on peace-keeping but timing cannot be one of them. The fact that for the past three years this once-taboo subject has been on top of the agenda means there is a certain recognition that its' time has come. Much credit however goes to the current Secretary-General, Salim A. Salim, who has noted that we in Africa need to use our own cultural and social relationships to interpret the principle of non-interference in such a way that we are enabled to apply it to our own advantage in conflict prevention and resolution.

The OAU proposals are compatible with the UN's peace-keeping mission. and the UN is well placed to assist in building up the OAU peace-keeping capacity. But there is the bottom-line consideration of financing. One can expect a peace-keeping plan of some sort to emerge from the June meeting of the OAU. The second battle will be implementation. One of the major problems of the continent has been the tremendous hiatus between declarations of intentions and implementation.

THE OAU AND HUMAN RIGHTS

From its inception the Organization of African Unity has been accused by critics of mindlessly protecting the status quo. Increased repression, denial of political choice, restrictions on the freedom of association, and like events were met with rare murmurs of dissent from within the OAU. With regard to breaches of human rights, even of a grave nature such as genocide, the OAU, in short, historically considered human rights largely in the guise of self-determination, through ending alien or settler rule. Those African leaders who broke the conspiracy of silence about flagrant, widespread human right abuses in member states had little positive impact - at least initially. Politically sanctioned repression and murder in Uganda, the Central African "Empire", and Equatorial Guinea besmirched the Organizations' reputation and its overall credibility in criticizing human rights abuses in other countries. The break came in 1979 with the dramatic ousters of the tyrants Idi Amin, Jean Bedel Bokassa, and Marcias Nguema which evoked strong statements by African leaders about the importance of protecting human rights within member states. The human rights debate has broadened considerably of late. Growth models can no longer be designed along purely economic lines but must be linked to models of society too. People are gradually waking up to the fact that economic reforms are heavily dependent for their success on certain social structures, democratic ones especially, existing at the same time. Individuals cannot be expected to be productive unless they actually have the possibility of guiding and controlling, to some degree, the way benefits of their work are used. Therefore, human rights and democratic principles are not just an aim in themselves; they are a sine qua non of balanced, effective development designed to meet the basic needs of the people.

Switching to democracy means respecting fundamental rights, opening a political dialogue and running free elections to really guarantee a pluralist society. And if democratic systems are to be set up in the African countries, it must be primarily as a result of internal initiatives, for democracy cannot be imposed from the outside.

THE OAU AND THE POLICY OF NON-ALIGNMENT

Although the OAU Charter commits African states to the policy of non-alignment with regard to the great powers, more and more of its members have become entangled with the great powers. Since 1960, the USA, Belgium and France have maintained Mobutu in power. They are aware that his regime is an authoritarian one in addition to being one of the most corrupt governments in Africa. However, Mobutu is a dependable pro-West leader in Africa and he can be counted on as a protector of massive Western investment in Zaire.

The former USSR and the USA came to the assistance of African states in order to further their own interests and win client states. The departure of the colonialists left a power vacuum, and Africa was used by the superpowers to consolidate their position of global power. The former Soviet Union and the USA have both had economic and strategic interests in Africa. It is surrounded by major international waterways all of which have been considered crucial to global strategic and military calculations of the then super powers.

Until the 1970's, the West held key strategic points in and around the continent. France had, and continues to have, military bases in Djibouti in the Horn of Africa, Mayotte and Comoro in the Indian Ocean and on several islands in the Mozambiquean straits. In West Africa France has bases in Ivory Coast, Gabon and Senegal. Britain signed a secret military treaty with Kenya in 1963.

Britain also had a naval base on Diego Garcia on the Indian Ocean but after 1968 it was leased to the United States. The Portuguese controlled both Angola and Mozambique. South Africa falls informally within the NATO defence system.

Early Soviet attempts to acquire naval and air bases in Africa failed. The Soviet Union obtained its first major military base in Africa in the early 1970's when Somalia granted the Soviet Union a naval and air base at Berbera, which was held by the Soviet Union until 1977. Berbera provided a strategic base at the center of East Africa and the Horn of Africa. The importance of Berbera was elevated by the Soviet acquisition of another coastal base in Aden, South Yemen. The two bases are directly opposite and overlook each other with the Port of Aden lying at the point where the Indian Ocean and the Red Sea meet. The presence of the former Soviet Union in Ethiopia may also be explained by the desire to gain access to Massawa on the Red Sea. The Soviet Union had also entered into treaties of friendship and cooperation with Angola and Mozambique. Although it was not granted any military bases in Libya, the Soviet Union has maintained close relationships with Libya since 1969. Finally, Soviet interest in Guinea has not waned in spite of the rebuffs in the 1960's.

Since 1977 the United States has moved to forge military alliances with African states within the Horn of Africa. It has replaced the Soviet Union at the Berbera base. In 1980 it obtained military and naval facilities at Mombasa in Kenya, and signed a military agreement with Sudan. In the South the United States has increased contacts at an official level with the South African authorities. Egyptian military bases, like those of Sudan, Kenya and Somalia, are available for use by the recently created Rapid Deployment Force (RDF) attached to the Fifth Fleet. The objective of the RDF is to move quickly and intervene anywhere in the Middle East, the Persian Gulf or Africa if internal or regional developments appear to threaten vested Western interests. The most important of the American military bases is on Diego Garcia, and the African bases are seen as supplementary to it.

In spite of the OAU's policy of non-alignment, the following conclusions can be made:

1) African states have been involved with the superpowers in pursuit of what African policy makers viewed as vital national interest;
2) American and former Soviet policy-makers, like their African counter-

parts, are neither moralists nor idealists. They are realists guided in their interactions by considerations of national interest;

3) The nature of the relationship between the superpowers has also been a cause of conflict within Africa itself and between Africa and the superpowers.

SUPPORT FROM AMERICANS

If Africa is no longer considered to be of geopolitical importance, there is a danger that the world will not take seriously some of the problems of the continent. For example, except for Somalia, reporting on Africa lags behind coverage of Cambodia and Yugoslavia in major newspapers and network newscasts for January and February 1993. A bank for reconstruction has been formed with more than $10 billion in initial capital to assist the countries of what used to be called Eastern Europe, but very little new assistance has been forthcoming for Africa. Debt relief can be an example of how Americans who care about Africa can be most helpful.

The United States must demonstrate a stronger commitment to strengthening continental and sub-regional Pan-African institutions. One option in this regard would be for the U.S. to consult with African leaders on the appropriateness of the U.S. being accorded observer or associate membership status of the OAU accompanied by the appointment of a U.S. ambassador to that body. Closer diplomatic involvement by the U.S. in the OAU system would demonstrate America's commitment to supporting Pan-African institution-building within the framework of a new, U.N. - centered world order. An OAU ambassadorial post would help to consolidate and give coherence to U.S. diplomacy in much the same manner as the posting of a U.S. ambassador to the OAS facilitates hemispheric diplomacy. Further, it would firm up the U.S.-African relationship grounded in this country's African heritage, and place the U.S. in a better position to coordinate its response to African crises in consultation with Africans. This, in turn, would strengthen African confidence in the level of importance that Washington attaches to African concerns.

CONCLUSIONS

1) Today, as in 1963, the OAU represents Africa's determination to attain peace and security, freedom and justice, economic and social development through common efforts among African states'. The Organization is expected to provide the basis for African cooperation in order to promote the economic and social development of the continent.

2) Political stability and economic development need an authoritative agency, equipped with all the necessary legal means (including the use of legitimate force) to mediate, arbitrate and control conflicting interests with the society. The OAU lacks this quality.

3) It is a voluntary association whose authority lies in moral suasion and consensus of opinion. The member-states have yet to recognize that the benefits to be derived from inter-African integration should outweigh their determination to preserve the individual sovereignty of each state.

4) Although, the OAU represents Africans desire to speak with a single voice, Africa continues to be divided by ideological and personality differences and by the pursuit of conflicting national interests.

5) The OAU commits African states to complete the decolonization of the continent. However, efforts have been borne largely by nationalists. African states have often been divided over the question of collective military action against colonial regimes and White supremacy. Even on the issue of material support, where there is a general consensus, very few African states cooperate and contribute to the liberation fund.

6) The OAU has not been able to maintain inter-African peace. For example, when the OAU failed to mediate the territorial dispute between Uganda and Tanzania, Nyerere reacted by called the OAU a trade-union of tyrants, adding that "when African nations find themselves incapable of collectively punishing a single country, then each country must look after itself."

7) Inter-African functional integration remains unrealized. But economic integration is not an option, it is the only option in town.

8) The OAU has not preserved Africa as a non-aligned continent. More and more of its members have become entangled with the super powers contrary to

the policy of non-alignment. For example, the Soviets were in Ethiopia after having been expelled from Somalia. In the latter they were replaced by the USA which also gained "access to military facilities" in Kenya, Egypt, Sudan and Morocco. Egypt, Somalia and Sudan had even held joint military exercises with theUnited States on African soil.

9) For the OAU to be able to perform its functions fully and effectively it will have to be transformed from a functional organization to a political authority enjoying the sort of power which other supra-national authorities enjoy.

10) For the OAU to be effective, there is a need for international democratization. Today our people work harder, produce more, but get less for what they produce. The world economic system is disadvantageous to Africa.

11) Integration and unification are not to be seen as means of sharing what one does not have, but rather a framework for collective effort to resolve the same problems, in the face of the same difficulties and in the same environment.

12) Development in Africa can only be ensured, if it is first and foremost a process hinged on needs and interests of the continent. Development must not be limited to solving the problems of hunger, ignorance, and disease, or confining science to a secondary, if not a marginal role. Development must enable the Africans to reflect their differences, with the possibility of fulfilling and expressing themselves in all human dimensions.

13) Africa must find its own solutions to its own problems.

NOTES

1. L. Oppenheim, "International Law," London, 1948, Vol. 1, p. 47.

2. Charles Chey Hyde, "International Law Chiefly as Interpreted and Applied by the United States," Boston, 1951, Vol. 1, p. 84.

3. F. List, "International Law," Yuriev, 1917, p. 72.

4. Mazrui, A. A., "Pan-Africanism in the Cold War," East African Institute of Social Research Conference Paper, 1965, pl. 1; same: "The Legacy of Kwame Nkrumah in Africa: from Kenyatta and Mboya to Nyerere and

Amin," Historical Association of Kenya Annual Conference Papers, 1977, p 27; see also Shepperson, G., "Notes on Negro American influence on the emergence of African nationalism, Journal of African History, I (1960), p. 2.

5. See Padmore, George, "Pan-Africanism or Communism: the coming struggle for Africa," Dobson, London, 1956; Shepperson, G.,"Notes on Negro-American influence on the emergence of African nationalism,"Journal of an History, 1 (2); Kwame Nkrumah, "Africa must unite," London, 1963; Woronoff, J.,"Organization of African Unity," Meruchen, NJ, 1970.

6. See Odede, S. O., "Nigeria in the context of Pan-Americanism," 1945-1966. Mimeograph, Nairobi, 1969; Machyo, B. S., "Pan-Africanism," Makerere Adult Studies Centre, pamphlet, NO. 3, 1968.

7. Makonnen, R., "Pan-Africanism from within," Oxford University Press, Nairobi, 1973, p. 168.

8. Thompson, V. B., "Africa and Unity. The Evolution of Pan-Africanism," Longman, London, 1969, pp. 89-90, p. 133; Legum, C., "Pan-Africanism: A short political guide," Frederick A. Praeger, N.Y. 1965, p. 153-4.

9. Thompson, V. B., "Africa and Unity. The evolution of Pan-Africanism, Longman, London, 1969, p. 133.

10. Padmore, G., "Pan-Africanism or Communism: the Coming Struggle for Africa," London, 1956, p. 376

11. Haas, Ernest B., "The Uniting of Europe and the Uniting of Latin America," Journal of Common Market Studies, 5.

12. Lieber, Robert, "Theory of World Politics," George Allen and Unwin, London, 1972, p. 42.

13. Haas, Ernest and Schmitter, Philip, "Economies and differential patterns of political integration; projections about unity in Latin America," in A. Etzioni (ed.), International Political Communities, Garden City, New York, 1966, p. 259-99.

14. Legum, C., "Pan-Africanism: A Short Political Guide," Frederick A. Praeger, New York, 1965, p. 42.

15. Italiaander, Rolf, "The new leaders of Africa," (trans. J. McGovern), Prentice-Hall, 1961, p. 196; West Africa Pilot, 6 May, 1961; Nyandira, N., "Regional organizations and integration: the case of the OAU." Seminar paper given in the History Department of the University of Nairobi, 1980, p. 4; Legum, C., Pan Africanism: A Short Political Guide, Frederick A. Praeger, New York, 1965, p. 50-53.

16. Legum, C., Pan Africanism: A Short Political Guide, Frederick A. Praeger, New York, 1965, p. 51.

17. Wade, E. C. G. and Philips, G. G., Constitutional and Administrative Law, 7th ed., London: Longman, 1977, p. 5.

18. A. V. Dicey, "Introduction to the study of the law of the Constitution," Library Classics, Indianapolis, 1982, p. 278.

19. Cervenka, Zdenek, The Organization of African Unity and Its Charter, Frederick A. Praeger, New York, 1969, p. 140, p. 144-45.

20. Ibid, p. 140-141.

21. Divine, A. Robert, Second Chance: The Triumph of Internationalism in America during World War II, Aithineum, New York, 1967, p. 41, Cervenka, Zdenek, The Organization of African Unity and Its Charter, Frederick A. Praeger, New York, 1969, p. 2.

22. Ibid, 1969, p. 9.

23. The documents referred to above were written during the Kennedy administration and are available on microfiche published under the title "The Declassified Documents by the Carrollton Press, Inc., Washington, D. C., 1976-77.

24. Time, 20 May 1963; Newsweek, 20 May 1963.

25. Nkrumah, Kwame, Africa Must Unite, Long, 1963, p. 189.

26. Wolfer, Michael, Politics in the Organization of African Unity, New York, 1976, p. 16, p. 19.

27. Cervenka, Zdenek, "Major Policy Shifts in the Organization of African Unity", in K. Ingham (ed.), Foreign Relation of African States, Butterworth, London, 1974, p. 326; Thiam Doubon, The Foreign Policy of African States, New York, 1965.

28. Elias, T. O., "The Charter of the OAU," American Journal of International, Law, 1965, LIX(2), p. 246.

29. See U.N. Charter; Declaration on Principles of International Law concerning Friendly Relations and Co-operation among States in accordance with the Charter of the United Nations, (Resolution 2625) XXV.

30. See Res. 219 (XV). OAU Resolutions, Recommendations Adopted by the Ordinary and Extraordinary Sessions of the Council of Ministers, vol. two (1968-1973), Addis Ababa, May, 1973, p. 103-108.

31. AHG(XX) President Nyerere's address to the OAU Summit Meeting at Addis Ababa. November 1984, when accepting the Chairmanship of the Organization, p. 3.

32. AHG/117(XX), Part I, p. 11.

33. AHG/131(XX).

34. Edmond Jouve, "Africa and the Test of Its Borders", paper presented at UNESCO-sponsored Meeting of Experts of Contemporary Africa History, Ouagadougou, 17-22, May, 1979.

35. See "Decision on a Mechanism for Conflict Prevention, Management, "adopted at the OAU Summit in Dakar in 1992 (appendix no. 1).

SECTION II

MEDIA, LANGUAGE, AND LIBERATION

CHAPTER 4

LANGUAGE, OPPRESSION, AND LIBERATION

Marie-Josée Cérol

Most of the current debate on the necessity of making what African people are exposed to not only more relevant to their experience, but centered around that very experience, has pointed to the importance of language as discourse, as speech, in the Afrocentric quest. This view is best expressed by Molefi Asante, for example, when he states that "Language is essentially the control of thought. It becomes impossible for us to direct our future until we control our language. The sense of language is in precision of vocabulary and structure for a particular social context. Black language must possess instrumentality, that is, it must be able to do something for our liberation"(1988 [1991]:31). It would seem difficult to disagree with such a statement, since it is obvious that language provides one with a powerful tool of self-definition and/or of definition of others. Put otherwise, unless we are able to define ourselves, we cannot be in control of our lives. And in order to define ourselves in a meaningful way, we need to be at the center of ourselves, which makes Afrocentricity so relevant and so important for us.

However, this is only one dimension of the language question. Language also refers to a set of verbal forms, structures and rules. It is commonly assumed that the major if not only function of language, so defined, is simply to transmit information. Although the referential function of language is undeniable, language has other functions that will be highlighted here in order to uncover the privileged relationship between language and oppression, and by the same token, between language and liberation.

There are, in particular, two points that I would like to emphasize - the link between language and culture and the link between language and society in a colonial or neo-colonial setting.

LANGUAGE AND CULTURE

It is a commonplace assertion that language and culture are intertwined. This point was made quite forcefully in particular by two scholars, Sapir and Whorf, who argued that the language one speaks determines one's perception of reality. Whether one would agree or not with such a strong statement, it remains unarguable that language not only serves as a vehicle, as a carrier for a particular culture, but that it is also a fundamental part of that culture. It is, as Ngugi puts it, "the collective memory bank of a people's experience in history. Culture is almost indistinguishable from the language that makes possible its genesis, growth, banking, articulation and indeed its transmission from one generation to the next" (p.15). To speak a particular language is to be initiated into a particular world, a particular mode of thinking, of seeing, of feeling, of being. There exists, therefore, an obvious and strong link between language and ethnic identity; language is a visible marker of ethnic identity. Although for linguists all languages are equal, value judgments are often made about languages. Such value judgments may be mere reflections about those who speak these languages, a defining of a people by defining or qualifying their language.

The pride that one takes in one's language seems directly correlated to the pride that one takes in one's culture, which in turn, is an index of collective self-esteem. We know, for example, how much pride the French have in their language which they have tried to present as the most beautiful and most logical language. The idea is to convince themselves and the rest of the world that they, the French, are the most beautiful and logical people on earth, whatever this means.

Conversely, many African people show some distrust in their language's validity or ability to meet all their needs. As a matter of fact, many of us refer to our language not as language but as dialect. In the Caribbean and in North America where African people speak Creole languages, it is quite common for these languages to be referred to as 'broken English' , 'broken French', 'dialect' , 'patois' , all expressions with negative connotations based on the assumption that Creole languages are nothing but aberrant pathological versions of European languages. However, expressions such as 'broken English' or 'broken French' have very little objective basis since language 'breaking' is not an easily definable process. Such expressions are, at best, metaphors.

But what is the theme of the metaphors? The theme of the metaphors is the inferiority of African people, and it extends far beyond language. It encompasses all aspects of African culture. Since language is so important to culture and serves as an explicit marker of cultural identity, it is quite understandable that it would be included in any attempt to denigrate and ridicule a people. From a linguistic and historical point of view, the terms 'dialect' and 'language' are interchangeable. Yet, from a sociopolitical perspective, a nation has a culture, a religion, and its members speak a language; a tribe does not have a real culture but folklore, does not have a religion but rather magic and superstitions, and its members speak a dialect. A hierarchy, linguistic and otherwise, is developed, which relegates certain groups of people, and African people in particular, to the lower strata of human life and civilization.

It is well-known that African people have been afflicted by Europeans with that 'syndrome of savagery' so insightfully dealt with by Mudimbe (1988). Among the signs of that savagery are *nakedness* (associated with childishness) and *cannibalism* (clearly related to beastliness) (Mudimbe 1988:50). These two attributes are of particular relevance to the status of African languages in colonial discourse. Indeed, it is well-known that children do not have a fully developed linguistic system at their disposal yet, nor do animals speak. The assumption that language is unique to humankind (and should provide us with an invaluable and incomparable insight into humanity) is certainly central to modern American linguistics.

When such discourse is internalized by us, the result can be quite pathetic. It usually manifests itself through the praising of European languages and downgrading of African languages, as illustrated by Ngugi, who reports how the Senegalese writer and former president, Senghor, once stated that "French words send out thousands of rays like diamonds in the African darkness" (1986:19). Another such example is provided by the Haitian author, Archer, for whom "le francais est la forme évoluée et cultivée du créole" (1988:257), since Creole is "une langue simple parlé(e) par les esprits simples qui le conçurent (...)" (1988:369). More generally, many of us associate speaking 'properly', speaking 'right', with speaking 'white'.

Beside the devaluation of African languages, there is also the important question of the imposition of European languages as carriers of European cultures, and the alienation that it generates within ourselves. This issue has been dealt with very insightfully by many. Let us simply note here that colonial powers have always, at some point or another, tried to impose their language on African people as an attempt to establish and secure their 'superiority'. (This is particularly, but not only, true of the French who, again, thought so highly of their language [i.e., of themselves] that they saw it as a gift to the world and especially to the supposedly very needy African people.)

Whether, European languages were introduced in the first years of school or only later on is simply a matter of detail. The point that transcends is that European languages were indeed imposed on Africans, as part of the colonizing process and the civilizing mission. However, this dissemination of European languages has been and still is selective by necessity. And this is another aspect of the imposition of European languages and of the rejection of African languages in African speech communities to be investigated, the relationship between language and society.

LANGUAGE AND SOCIETY

Every nation has an official language, whether it is explicit or not. The appointment or use of a particular language as the official language does not, of course, happen by chance, but is the result of a particular language policy. Every state has a language policy, whether it is implicit or not, that is carried out through language planning. Language planning can be thought of as deliberate efforts to influence the behavior of others with respect to the acquisition, structure, or functional allocation of their language (Cooper 1989:45).

The prescription of a language as an official language means that all public transactions must be conducted in that particular language, and it will be the language required from anyone aspiring to social upward mobility. One of the major agencies of implementation of any particular language policy is the school. The official language is taught as a subject and is used as a medium to teach other subjects. The exclusive selection of a particular language to fulfill official functions automatically signifies the rejection of other language varieties. When questioned, this rejection (language planning by default) is justified in the name of the superiority of the language variety chosen and of the inferiority of those excluded. However, as has been stressed earlier, no language is intrinsically superior or inferior to any other.

In reality, the decision about which form to select and reject is made by those in power whose interest it is to promote their own language variety. It is in their interest simply because their language will be used in order to store and disseminate information and technology vital to the functioning and ruling of society (Devonish 1986). Therefore, only those who will have access to their language, beginning with themselves and continuing with their children, will be able to acquire a certain knowledge, and enjoy the power that it confers. Their language will also be the language of state institutions. Without an appropriate command of that language, one cannot expect to participate in any debate, for example, and therefore is excluded from the decision-making process. We know that those who have power do not particularly care about sharing it with others, certainly not in capitalistic countries. To make the language and the knowledge of power accessible to all would certainly be a nonsense from that perspective.

The French educational policy in French African colonies provides a clear example of selective dissemination of the French language and culture. There were indeed two different tracks, the African ladder and the European ladder (Mumford & Orde-Brown 1970:28). The first one was for the African masses, adapted to their needs and their aptitudes, as defined by the colonists: "Africa is not capable, as are India, China, or the countries of Islam, of evolving a fully formed intellectual culture of her own. The degree of European education to be given to educated natives must therefore be measured solely by their aptitudes and special needs" (Charton 1970:110). The second one was for French children and 'assimilated Africans': "The European educational system was restricted to European children who resided in Africa and to African children who came from French-speaking homes, i.e., those who were already half French in their outlook" (Mumford & Orde-Brown 1970:29). In other words, the French educational system aimed at the creation of an elite, European and African, while the African schools mainly, in the words of an Inspector-General of Education in French West Africa, were an "agency for toning down the wildness of native tribes" (Charton 1970:101).

In most African or Caribbean countries, even after two or three decades of flag independence, the language of the former colonial power is still used as an official language. Competence in the European official language remains limited to a few, the elite created by the colonial power in order to pursue a policy favorable to imperialism and economic exploitation of the land and of the people. For example, in Cameroon, the 1961 Constitution made French and English the official languages of the country. According to Fonlon (1976:199), the elimination of the colonial languages would have "set the country back forty years" because French and English are "the languages of science and technology". In addition, in his view, French and English also have a major role to play in the unification of Africa. In other words, English and French are a blessing for Cameroon and Africa! Cameroonian people, Fonlon claims, should be grateful and strive to "master these languages as well as their owners" (1976:204), and produce in them "works of art and science of the highest merit." (1976:202). It would be senseless to deny that, indeed, the lexicon of most African languages needs to be elaborated and modernized in order to meet the challenges facing official languages. However, African languages are not disqualified per se from becoming the languages of science and technology.

To argue the contrary, is simply to argue for the maintenance of the status quo. The real question, rarely raised, is: *who* benefits from the use of French/English in Africa (or the Caribbean)? Put otherwise *who* suffers from the use of French/English in Africa (or the Caribbean)? As for the "African mission" of English and French, one cannot help thinking that this is, indeed, a quite ambiguous way of proceeding towards unity. Again, the question is: *what* unity, (political? economic?) and for *what* aim?

The reluctance of Caribbean elites to address the language issue, and make Caribbean Creoles official languages, reveals the conflict of interests between Creole monolingual speakers, usually belonging to the working class, and bilingual speakers, usually members of the bourgeoisie. In many cases, the very existence of Creole as an autonomous language is simply denied. In other cases, the status of Creole is posed only in cultural terms, but never in terms of socioeconomic empowerment through its use.

CONCLUSION

Too often, essays on education focus solely on the discourse aspect and leave the language issue aside, or treat it simply as a peripheral question when it is, in fact, central. Whatever message one wants to convey, it seems clear that one will be successful only insofar as one uses the right medium, the right linguistic code for that message to be heard and understood. In addition, language is not simply a medium but is also content in itself because it is culture. In other words, language is part of that very experience, the African experience, that we need to valorize in our attempt to define ourselves positively.

However, the 'cultural' struggle is certainly not the only one to which African people should commit themselves. Language was used to keep most African people away from being in control of their labor and of the production process. As we move in the direction of true emancipation, we should think quite seriously about the role of languages spoken by African people in the process of political and economic empowerment.

REFERENCES

Archer, Marie-Thérése, *1988., Latinité du créole d'Haiti.* Port-au-Prince:Imprimerie Le Natal.

Asante, Molefi Kete, 1988 [1991], *Afrocentricity.* Trenton: African World Press, Inc.

Charton, Albert, 1970, The social function of education in French West Africa. *Africans learn to be French.* Mumford, W. Bryant & Major G. St. Orde Brown. New York: Negro University Press. 97-112.

Cooper, Robert, 1989, *Language planning and social change.* Cambridge: Cambridge university Press.

Devonish, Hubert, 1986, *Language and liberation: Creole language politics in the Caribbean.* London: Karia Press.

Fonlon, Bernard, 1976, The language problem in Cameroon: a historical perspective. *The search for national integration in Africa.* D. R. Smock & K. Bentsi-Enchi 11 (eds) . New York: The Free Press. 189-205.

Mudimbe, Valentin, 1988, *The invention of Africa.* Bloomington: Indiana University Press.

Ngugi wa Thiong'o , 1986, *Decolonizing the mind: The politics of language in African literature.* London: James Currey.

CHAPTER 5

LANGUAGE AND LITERATURE IN AFRICA

Augustin Ainamon

At the second biennial conference in 1986 of the Benin Association for Anglophone Studies held in Cotonou, scholars and eminent guests from America and the United Kingdom reviewed problems generated by the use and expansion of a 'world language' in Africa, e.g. English. There are problems concerning the learning process, literary or scientific creation, and translation as well as competition with the African languages (in most cases mother tongues or source languages). The central topic was *The English Language and African Renaissance.*

There are complex relationships between language and literature in the learning process as well as in literary production. Should one use literature (a specific creation and a vision of an artist) to learn a dynamic and complex language like English, French or Portuguese? Or, should one wait to be competent and fluent in the given language before attempting the study of a literary work? Should Africans carry on writing exclusively in European languages or should they reject the use of what some might term 'vehicles of disguised imperialism'? These are some of the many issues confronting Africans. These disturbing questions and misgivings were given a new expression at a session organized April 22, 1987, in homage to Wole Soyinka, the Nigerian playwright and 1986 Nobel Prize winner. That session was one more occasion to clarify some of the questions raised by African literature or more accurately literature in Africa.

Paulin Joachim, editor of *Bingo*, a Paris-based monthly magazine, has had this to say about the Nobel Prize:

> The most prestigious literary award (to Soyinka) means world recognition at last for the black man, the colonial subject who has managed to invent an original expression from within his own genius and under the linguistic domination of a foreign culture and who says, 'I exist, I am born again from under my ruins, I can transcend the colonial accident, I have

> colonized the master's language and have now regained my immemorial space (Joachin: 1986).

And yet, when Soyinka came back from Paris to break the news to his people in Lagos, his first words sounded something like: "This Prize is not ours. We want an African Prize and to wait 85 years to award it to a European (the Nobel Prize was instituted in 1901 and was first awarded that year to Sully Prudhomme, a French writer, for literature)." That hardy quip seemed to have rejected, in advance, worries about the long time taken by the Euro-Americans to discover Africa.

THE NOTION OF LANGUAGE

Before entering the core of the debate, a few generalizing statements about language are perhaps required at the outset. Any system as complex as a human language is bound to lend itself to a variety of independent approaches. This complexity is, of course, linked to its capacity of serving as a means of communication, a cultural vehicle, and as clues and vehicles to personality. Language can be variable and have a disruptive effect on social habits or, rather, it can be a factor of cohesion within a community. In the making of a nation, the progress of language is extremely relevant to the process of search for a cultural identity. Different cultural situations determine various communication media among which is the written language. Language and society are a dual concept in that the system of rules, conventions and relationships regulates behavior and corresponds to an overall cultural system. Modern linguistics is a code based on a finite set of rules which the user activates in order to produce an infinite variety of discourse. It is no mystery, then, that it is infinitely varied and that the speaker is continuously creating new utterances which he has never heard previously.

All humans are born with an innate capacity to learn and use any language. This does not happen in a haphazard way or by a simple memorization; the potentialities of a language are practically unlimited. Despite great differences between surface structures (morphology, syntax, and sound patterns, that is, actually oral or written produced sentences), all languages have the same deep structure (the abstract structure of the sentences which can be diagrammed) which amounts to the same deep logic, a logic inherent to all humans. To show that we cannot put words together in just any order we want, Noam Chomsky has pointed out that the sentence, "Colorless green ideas sleep furiously," is a nonsense in English and, indeed, in any language.

The main question now, after a necessary clarification, is when to start learning a language. Experience has shown that the earlier in life the better, whether it is a first language (mother tongue) or a second language. The four basic skills are listening/comprehending, speaking, reading and writing, but the stress is being more and more laid on an oral rather than written process. A child can learn as many languages as possible right at birth provided he is kept immersed in corresponding socio-linguistic environments. But the process should not be discontinued before the period of fixation and maturity if we want to get any efficient result from it. Ideally, however, the first language to be taught at school should be the mother tongue or the language of early experiences in life, the language corresponding to the socio-linguistic environment of the child as it is currently being experimented in many African countries.

But, unfortunately, this process of learning a language, started when the child is just one to two years old, is suddenly stopped for most African children when they begin nursery school or kindergarten where French or English is introduced. At that age, no child can be expected to have mastered a language, be it his mother tongue. The problem of African school children is that they are asked to tackle a second language without having the opportunity to master a first language (mother tongue). Experience has shown that in those conditions the acquisition of both languages is often insufficient or inadequate. This necessary bilingual education program requires, of course, additional educational tools including buildings and personnel. This task is made more and more difficult and many investments deployed at the grassroots level are ruined by a lack of continuity.

AFRICAN LANGUAGES UNDER HARD PRESSURE

The real problem confronting African languages is that they are submitted to a severe competition with imported languages, usually European. In a situation of mostly oral vernaculars confronted with languages refined by generations of writers and artists, the decay of African languages seems unavoidable. As Joseph Ki-Zerbo stated some time ago, "the Africans live in the present in which they feed (ineffectually) on the fruit of other people's work; they are latecomers on a train which does not belong to them and they live on other people's effort" (Ki-Zerbo: 1972). The reality today in African countries is that native tongues do not yet serve to mediate any aspect of modern life. The language of power and administration, of education, of the legal system, of economic activities and exchanges is a European language: English, French, Portuguese and so on.

The African who wants to communicate with the outside world finds himself compelled to learn a language which in many ways is alien to his environment. The aim of a foreign language learner is to communicate with the native speaker who represents for him the reference of excellence. A student of mathematics has no such problem. But not all native speakers are capable of generating the same variety of speech. All languages have regional, dialectal, socio-economic or intellectual varieties. In a normal class situation, the foreign language student is expected to aim at the most important variety, generally that of the most important metropolitan area. The B.B.C. has allegedly adopted the Hertfordshire variety of English. The target in a class situation is the language of the educated people, even though the models of exposure and learning are many and varied. This holds for first languages as well as for second and foreign languages. But the target of second language acquisition being simply to communicate with native speakers, a student of English (ESL/EFL), for instance, has no need culturally or socially to be identified with an Englishperson or an American unless he (or she) is intolerably alienated (even though in America one tends to behave like an American). The differentiation we are making here, however, holds only for oral and spoken language, because there is only one pattern of written English or French, etc., except for a few spelling modifications or simplifications (as for American English, for instance). The English language, a great borrower, is no longer automatically identified with one given national group.

WHAT IS AFRICAN LITERATURE?

The rather complex relationship between language and literature makes many critics wonder what could be the meaning and validity of a literary work mediated through a 'borrowed' language as is widely the case in Africa. "To create in a language," they argue, "the writer must master sufficiently well rules and conventions to be able to innovate competently and not out of sheer ignorance."

The Palm Wine Drunkard by Nigerian writer Amos Tutuola has often been alluded to as an accidental masterpiece. The writer proved rather talented, but with so little schooling and formal mastery of the English language, his achievement could have been disastrous. Literary creation, as everyone knows, makes use of an autonomous language that seemingly 'violates' structural and lexical conventions. And yet it appears to use conventional linguistic codes while at the same time diverging significantly from those codes. This duality is an essential feature to the way literature builds its messages and this is what creates the style that is peculiar to each writer. A methodology that systematically takes into account the quality of literary writing is necessary to guide both learners and writers in foreign or second languages toward their own discovery of the multifaceted meanings of a literary text as a creative use of language.

To create in a foreign or second language is to solve the problem of transposing moral, psychological and spiritual qualities of a people into another language, that is, to use a second language to illustrate and express a world view selected from a first language (a mother tongue?). The adopted language whose structure and articulation the writer is using has no semantic, syntactic or even 'ecological' parentage with the general conditions at the source of the work. The writer's personal capacity of perception and selection, and a good competence in both languages is necessary to convey a world view that is both lasting and plausible. Maybe nothing (short of a real feat) should be disregarded if the African writer wants to produce a work that is more than a curiosity for the outside world. To those who ask why we need literature in European languages in Africa, people like Achebe or Soyinka might give a flippant retort: "Isn't literature in African languages literature for minority groups? Don't we need for the time being to open up to an international audience? If some of our grievances are directed to the Western world, maybe we need to use their languages to express them."

This brings to my mind some of the questions or false alternatives raised in 1966 in Kampala-Makerere by some eminent writers among whom, however, there were no writers in Zulu, Swahili, Yoruba or Arabic. Arabic is, indeed, an African language. Neither Chief Fagunwa, who had already published several titles in Yoruba, nor Shabaan Roberts, then the most important poet writing in Kiswahili, was invited to that symposium whose title was: *A Conference of African Writers of English Expression* (it automatically excluded those who wrote in African languages, an absurd anomaly from today's perspective). The main issue, however, was to define *What is African literature* ? The debate which followed was very animated and Ngugi, who was also a participant, has summed up some of the questions:

> Was it literature about Africa or about the African experience? Was it literature written by Africans ? What about a non-African who wrote about Africa; did the work qualify as African literature? What if an African set his work in Greenland; did that qualify as African literature? Or were African languages the criteria? What about Arabic? What about French and English which had become African languages? What if a European wrote about Europe in an African language? (Nguji: 1986).

If..if..if...this or that, except the issue is the domination of our languages and cultures by those of imperialist Europe. In any case, there was no Fagunwa or Shabaan Robert or any writer in African language to bring the conference down from the realms of evasive abstraction. The question was never seriously asked: did what we wrote qualify as African literature? The whole area of literature and audience and hence of language as a determinant of both the national and class audience did not really figure; the debate was more about the subject matter and the racial origins and geographical habitation of the writer.

The participants at the Makerere 1962 Conference were at pains to find limitative criteria for defining African literature, turning around in a circle and overlooking the main issue: can we master a second language prior to gaining a sufficient grasp of a first one? The sad truth about African languages today is that they are massively invaded by alien cultures; imperialism is a global phenomenon pervading all aspects of life, including linguistic. Under the severe pressure of (and considering the unfair advantage given to) foreign languages and cultures, it is sad to note that Africans are no longer practicing their own languages, not even orally.

This massive invasion by alien cultures has led African writers, at least at a first stage, to want to prove at all costs to others their Africanness, to present to Europeans and Americans their Africa in a recognizable way, to present the life of Africans as Africans(?) as if concepts like *African* and *European* were defined and frozen in unalterable postures once and for all. European and American readers and critics had at one time incited the black African to present to them a really African life (whatever that means) and not men and women in an interdependent world with joys and sorrows which, though specific and contingent, are accessible to anybody who dares to look into our common human destiny.

By wanting to answer necessarily the question, is this writing authentically or sufficiently African or is it a copy of Europe, we inevitably turn African literature into 'News from Africa' ... for Europe or the Western world and we miss the only question worth answering: 'Is it good literature?' This extrovert desire to prove at all costs one's Africanness to others may inhibit and preclude creativity, spontaneity and originality.

It is no mystery that African history is linked to world history, the history of other peoples as men and women organized in society with close relationships to other societies for thousands of years. It is, therefore, scientifically inaccurate, or at least naive, to isolate Africans from other peoples, as some theories and practices in Africa and elsewhere are advocating. Christopher Wondji, a historian from Côte d'Ivoire has had this to say in a critique on 'African Authenticity':

> In black Africa as well as on other continents, history has been a succession of plural changes expressing conflicts between man and his environment, between different peoples and between various social groups within each society. It records during its development in Africa and elsewhere the discarding of the values that have gone stale and obsolete and the creation of new values, an expression of the innovating vitality of peoples the world over (Wondji:1977).

It is futile to always wait for outside (Western?) recognition before being convinced about the validity and specificity (and therefore universality) of African creations. Should one be surprised at the Western world having waited 85 years to grant the Nobel Prize in literature to an African? Such questions could also be applied to Third World-oriented rhetoric and lamentations against the alleged domination of the United Nations by the founding members (permanent membership to the Security Council and the right to veto resolutions). One is tempted to retort to those rabid nationalists: "Who prevented you from creating academy awards of your own and organizations in which you could be vested with permanent membership?" Tiny Switzerland is not a member of the United Nations or any specialized institutions linked to it. And yet it is at the center of that world organization and the venue of so many international gatherings. The Swiss and their country are courted by the whole world for their reliability.

Is there any secret or recipe to achieve universality? In 1966, at the first festival of Negro Arts in Dakar, the late Nigerian poet, Okigbo, created sensation by his scornful rejection of the first prize for poetry. Ali Mazrui was to write in his strange novel, *The Trial of Christopher Okigbo* in 1973:

> Who was Africa's greatest poet for the festival? Christopher Okigbo was offered the first prize for poetry. A sense of admiration pervaded the climate of judgment. Some other poets swallowed hard, proudly accepting the extra margin of greatness in Okigbo's lines. A poets were more skeptical, less convinced of the esthetic accuracy of the verdict. Some of the latter might have been envious. Buta startling pronouncement was made. Chris Okigbo had rejected the first prize for poetry awarded by the Festival of Negro Arts. Why? He had proclaimed: 'There is no such thing as Negro Art!' (Mazrui: 1981).

That proclamation of an aggressive and paramount universalist refused to dilute art with the milk of nationalism. The same Okigbo was to die later for Biafra, leaving the issue of universalism more obscured than ever.

In 1986, Soyinka did not reject the Nobel Prize, but his declaration when he came back to Lagos was no less significant as a warning to those who thought they were honoring an African artist and not simply a good artist. His warning to the African audience and citizens was not to substitute a new African chauvinism, even if extended to a whole continent, for the English, French or Portuguese colonial chauvisms and arrogance of the last few decades. The most urgent task for African intellectuals, according to Soyinka, at this end of the second millennium, according to Soyinka, is to place African experience into a world context and not to pretend to ignore the many influences the continent has undergone for centuries and the problems resulting from those contacts. African intellectuals are certainly not asked to do away with problems. Rather, let us know that an answer to a problem may hide even greater problems. Alien influences on Africa, though indelible, need no longer be preponderant in every aspect of life. By always turning their eyes away from home, Africans may deny their society the capacity to influence other people in a significant way. They must understand that underdevelopment is not an exclusively economic phenomenon, that it has also been and still is a hideous intellectual distortion and a mutilation.

Africans therefore have to reinvent new means of expression and creation. The carving of the African continent between the various colonial powers at the Berlin Conference of 1884 was certainly not a cultural enterprise, each metropolis having rather endeavored to project into her 'possessions' collective and individual habits from home. The new African must re-create his own history - evolve and harness the concept of African literature. African writers have already compelled cynical and skeptical minds to cast a new vision on Africa and to accept a necessarily different and original world view. Today's Africa is a quickly changing society. Its problems are complex, and, in literature as in many other fields, no one solution or answer is to be considered adequate.

AFRICAN LITERATURE IN AFRICAN LANGUAGES?

To try to define African literature in present conditions is obviously like wanting to square the circle. Chris Okigbo used to deny that he was an African poet. "I am a poet," was his simple insistence, and becoming more explicit later he asserted: "There is no African literature. There is good writing and bad writing. That's all" (Mazrui: 1981). Literature springs from so many different sources to be assimilated into an integral whole that it is difficult, if not futile, to want to sort them out completely. The factors of continuity in art, of civilized values and of eternity as a creative process all come into combination to produce a good work of art. Let us consider the problems arising from the use of African languages in literature.

The notion of literature is not defined once and for all. African creative minds have already shown that they can innovate in a field which was allegedly a 'Western' field; of course, one need not be necessarily a descendant of Henry Ford to know how to drive a car. Comparing car driving and creative writing, Achebe had this amusing comparison to make at a conference in Canada:

> Every visitor to Nigeria will tell you that we are among the most creative drivers (see *Morning Yet on Creation Day*, p. 54)! We are, indeed, getting tired of prescriptions (and proscriptions), babbles about universality and eternal varieties, proselytizing for European literary fashions and the hankering after hasty definitions. I am not willing to create futile and unnecessary anxieties about the existence or non-existence of an African literature. Creative minds have already grown mature, beyond self-doubt and self debasement. They have proved that in Africa, as anywhere else, they can use any kind of fiction according to their differing abilities, sensibilities and visions without asking anyone's permission (Achebe: 1975).

But the problem still remains that in producing exclusively in non-African languages, African creative writers may be looked upon (wrongly so) as unfinished Europeans and pale imitators of English, French or Portuguese literary traditions. The most honest Europeans recognize that the world needs the fresh vision of Africans writing in ex-colonial languages. But here they are on the begging side because there is no fatality in continuing to use exclusively non-African languages. At this point we must confess that nobody can tell for sure what an African language is and what it is not, and once again I am not in favor of any prescription or proscription. Achebe has looked into the language problem and has had this to say:

> There has been an impassioned controversy about an African literature in non-African languages. But what is a <u>non-African</u> language? English and French certainly. But what about Arabic? What about Swahili then? Is it then a question of how long the language has been present on African soil? If so,how any years should constitute <u>effective occupation</u>? For me it is again a pragmatic matter. A language spoken by Africans on African soil, a language in which Africans write justifies itself (Achebe: 1975).

Use European languages, certainly yes, but there is no reason why Europeans should continue being the eternal mediator between former colonial subjects through their languages. It would appear, then, as if African intellectuals can meet only on the mine-laden field set for them by the white man. About this peculiar predicament of ex-colonial subjects Jean-Paul Sartre, the French espouser of Negritude, has had a penetrating remark:

> The colonist rises between the colonials to be the eternal mediator; he is there, even though absent in the most secret councils. And since words derive from ideas, when the Negro declares in French that he rejects French culture, he takes in one hand that which he has pushed aside with the other. He brands himself with the thinking apparatus of the enemy as with an embossment (Okonkwo: 1979).

Some African writers of achievement have proved quite brilliant and complex using European languages, "but because of their very brilliance, ingenuity, and complexity," wrote Juliet Okonkwo in a very informative article, "these writers can at best appeal to a select audience, yet few ... can choose (like Okigbo who did not want to read his poems to non-poets) to limit his audience to a literary, sophisticated elite; but that, of course, cannot serve the national objective of revolutionizing the consciousness of the people, nor can such 'precious' writing prepare anybody except the already educated to try their own hands at writing" (Okonkwo: 1979).

The adoption of African languages for literary creation would, on the contrary, open new ways and accelerate the expansion of African literature (or literatures). It will also put a greater number of Africans in contact with various literary techniques old and new. Translation is an important area for exercising one's talents, but, unfortunately, it has been neglected after the first attempts by missionaries to translate the Bible and prayer books into African languages. Yet, under good guidance, this enterprise could bring to our people the best products of world literature. One feels freer (less inhibited) when transporting from one language to another. Until very recently we have insisted on what makes traditional Africa different from other cultures. But today in a world with fluid and uncertain values, even the most rabid nationalist will admit that Africa needs a synthesis of true values from her ancestry and those from ancient Europe in order to sustain stable and disciplined societies (see the article by Juliet Okonkwo).

In a quickly changing society like today's Africa, we must always seek to maintain a careful, if fragile, balance. But as far as the complex problem of language is concerned, three questions remain adamant:

> -What will happen to European languages? Shall we have to file them off as museum pieces? Surely not. The use of one's language does not prevent the study of foreign languages since the objective is to communicate with speakers of those languages. The world has come together more than ever before as one and it is futile to want to go back to the 'glorious' days of the ancestors.
>
> -The second problem is what about the limited audience literature in African languages can touch, hence the limited scope it can have? Until recently people haven't been buying works created in African vernaculars, first because they haven't been taught to read them, and even if they can read them, they don't expect to discover much or take much advantage from them. Why should they learn to read and write a language that cannot secure a job for them in the near future (ethnic chauvinism)?
>
> -The third question is which language should be chosen among the many African languages as a national means of communication? Languages cannot be regimented; they reflect the dynamism of the people who speak them. English has imposed itself as the national language in the USA, for instance, because the English settlers have been the most dynamic, not necessarily the most important numerically (the last census in 1980 has revealed that the people from German descent are as many as those who claim English ancestry). A language is first developed from the scientific, then from the practical point of view, then comes the political determination to polish it up as the French, Italians and English polished their own vernaculars a few centuries ago. Through conscious programs designed by the leaders of their literary movements and out of sheer determination to borrow, to adapt and to convert, those nationalists willing to fashion a specific identity have wonderfully developed their various languages while maintaining a proper balance. We have in those successful experiences the necessary guidelines; the process will be slow and long as far as African languages are concerned. It may take centuries to mature. But the longer we postpone this necessary assignment, the more difficult and even impossible it will continue to seem. Meanwhile, those for whom it is too late to start writing effectively in African languages will certainly continue using English, French or Portuguese.

The modern African is bound to be multilingual and multicultural if he or she wants to face the challenge and complexities of the technological age. Much is being done currently to teach at least 90% of black Africans to write and read their own languages. This effort must not be discontinued. A systematic and intensive use of African vernaculars in literary and scientific production and in journalism must allow those 'new literates' to be as creative as efficient. The sad truth is that Africans are practicing less and less their own languages, even orally. Why? Because of the hard pressure put on them by 'world languages'? We must be permitted to doubt the validity of such an argument.

REFERENCES

Achebe, Chinua, 1975. 'Thoughts on the African Novel,' in *Morning Yet on Creation Day*, London, Heinemann, p. 50.

Chomsky, Noam, 1968. *Syntactic Structures*. Gravenhage, 1957, p. 15 quoted in *English Transformational Grammar*, by R.. Jacobs and P. Rosenbaum, London, Ginn & Co. Ltd., p. 4.

Joachin, Paulin, 1986. Extract from editorial, *Bingo*, December. Translation mine. The text in French was: Le plus prestigieux des Prix littéraires du Monde, c'est le sacre de l'homme noir. Le colonisé qui est parvenu à s'inventer une expression originale surgie de son génie propre à l'intérieur même et sous la domination langagière étrangère, et qui dit: 'J'EXISTE, je survis à mes décombe. Je transcende l'accident colonial. Je colonise la langue du maître et je reconquiers mon espace immémorial.

Ki-Zerbo, Joseph, 1972. *Histoire de l'Afrique Noire, D'hier A Demain,* Paris, Hatier.

Mazrui, Ali , 1981. *The Trial of Christopher Okigbo*, London, HEB-AWS 47, p. 70.

Ngugi-Wa-Thong'o, 1986. *Decolonizing the Mind* (The Politics of Language in African Literature), London, James Curry (& Heinemann, Kenya), p. 6.

Okonkwo, Juliet, 1979. 'The Missing Link in African Literature' in *African Literature Today* 10, London, Heinemann, p. 101.

Wondji, Christopher, 1977. *Authenticité Africaine, Mythe et Realité' in Revue de Littérature et d'Esthetique Négro-Africaine*, NEA, Abidjan, p. 134.En Afrique Noire comme dans les autres continents, l'histoire se déroule en une sucession de luttes exprimant les conflits entre l'homme et la nature, entre les peuples et entre les groupes sociaux au sein de ces peuples. Elle enregistre au cours de son développement en Afrique et Ailleurs la chute des valeurs en déclin et la création de nouvelles valeurs, expression de la vitalité des peuples.

Williams, Raymond, 1983. Writing in Society. London, Verso, p. 72

CHAPTER 6

ADULT LITERACY AND THE IDEOLOGY OF PAN-AFRICANISM

H.S. Bhola

Social scientists tell us that there is, indeed, such a thing as the African culture, the African personality, and the African mind. But these concepts are not yet in the minds of ordinary African peoples. To become a reality, Pan -Africanism will have to be internalized by the ordinary peoples of Africa, both as an ideal and an emotion. In other words, Pan-Africanism as an ideology is not conceivable unless the ideal of an all-African identity is shared by all Africans. Therein lies a challenge for communicators and Pan-Africanists.

Indeed, cultures exist in communication. Naturally, the African peoples seeking Pan-Africanism must communicate with each other to articulate old and new commonalities. Given the present infrastructures and patterns of low mobility among peoples in Africa, there is a limit to how much such communication can occur through face-to-face social interactions. Therefore, much of this communication will have to be through media. Again, while mass media like radio may play an important role in the dissemination of the ideology of Pan-Africanism and in the internalization of the accompanying emotion, mass media alone will be insufficient. The most important role is likely to be played by print media. Adult literacy, in fact literacies in the mother tongue, in an African lingua franca and in an historically relevant European language, will be of crucial significance.

We posit a dialectical but not a deterministic relationship between the process of literacy promotion and the phenomenon of Pan-Africanism. Literacy by itself is not a sufficient condition for bringing about Pan-Africanism. It may not ever be a necessary condition. If, somehow, we could use mass media without the constraints of politics and limited availability of technology or resources, we could develop Pan-Africanism by radio or television. In terms of a more realistic scenario, we suggest that adult literacy will have to play an important facilitative role in actualizing Pan-Africanism. Yet, we are not suggesting that literacy will be an unmixed blessing. The "potential added" by literacy to individual adults as active participants in their societies could be manipulated by the corrupt or the tyrannical. This possibility for abuse is, however, not unique to literacy.

WHAT IS PAN-AFRICANISM?

The following are major component ideas of Pan-Africanism:

> Africa as the homeland of Africans and persons of African origin, solidarity among people of African descent, belief in a distinct African personality, rehabilitation of Africa's past, pride in African culture, Africa for Africans in church and state, and the hope for a united and glorious future Africa (Esendebe: 1992).

One can see, in the above components of Pan-Africanism, two general dimensions: ideational and emotional. Pan-Africanism is a historical statement, a political agenda, and an economic necessity for African nations trying to fight "neo-colonial Balkanization." It is also an emotion that must have psychocultural roots (Singer: 1968). For both the idea and the emotion of Pan-Africanism, African peoples everywhere must learn to use categories of self-definition that are as large as Africa itself.

IS THERE AN AFRICAN CULTURE?

Is there an African culture within which larger self-definitions can be made? Abraham (1962) has heard "responsive throbbings in the collective consciousness of Africa." In identifying a 'Paradigm of African Society,' he has found a certain world-view to which the central concepts of all African cultures can be related. These central concepts cover: philosophic aspects; theory of humankind and society; theory of government; the legal system; the military organization; literature, ethics and metaphysics; and institutions.

That is the good news for Pan-Africanism. The bad news is that this shared 'Paradigm of African Society' is dormant and needs articulation through communication among the African peoples.

CULTURE, COMMUNICATION AND LANGUAGE

Culture, community and communication have the same common etymological root. The great 'Paradigm of African Society' (or culture) needs communication for awakening. The throbbings of the collective consciousness of Africa must be translated into speech. Africans must speak to each other and must listen to each other. Without speech, neither the ideas nor the emotions of Pan-Africanism will become actualized.

THE LANGUAGE OF PAN-AFRICANISM

What will be the language of Pan-Africanism? The great 'Paradigm of African Society' is waiting to be articulated, but what will be the language of its articulation?

Through the contradictions of history, the first battles on behalf of Pan-Africanism were fought in European tongues. The African elite developed the ideal of Pan-Africanism and experienced the accompanying emotion in English, French or Portuguese. There were two important consequences from the use of metropolitan languages as vehicles of Pan-Africanism. First, Pan-Africanism was confined to the new African elite. The common peoples of Africa were not touched. Second, the movement was fragmented into the three streams of English-speaking, French-speaking and Portuguese-speaking Africans.

To match the throbbings of a collective consciousness of an African culture, one has to find an African language that is on the African side of the racial divide and in which Africans can hear echoes of their own collective memories. The solution is not easy. In Africa there are at least 1000 different and mutually unintelligible languages, divided into four language families: Congo-Rordofanian, Nilo-Saharan, Khoisan and Afro-Asiatic. These language families are as different from each other as Indo-European languages are from Chinese. At the same time Swahili, Bemba, Lingala, Kongo, Hausa, and Mandinco have become the lingua francas of their regions. Clearly, all or some of these languages will have to be the languages of Pan-Africanism. This is not merely an intellectual possibility, but a cultural possibility as well. Ngugi wa

Thiong'o (1986) writing about Africa during the colonial period says:

> The peasantry saw no contradiction between speaking their own mother-tongues and belonging to a larger national or continental geography. They saw no necessary antagonistic contradiction between belonging to their immediate nationality, to their multinational state along the Berlin-drawn boundaries, and to Africa as a whole. These people happily spoke Wolof, Hausa, Yoruba, Ibo, Arabic, Amharic, Kiswahili, Gikuyu, Luo, Luhya, Shona, Ndebele, Kimbundu, Zulu or Lingala without this fact tearing the multinational states apart (Ngugi: 1986).

Will the use of more than one lingua franca fragment Pan-Africanism? It will not if there will be enough people learning more than one regional lingua franca and if there is considerable contact between intellectuals and artists writing in these languages. Finally, intelligent use will have to be made of the metropolitan languages in concert with languages of Africa.

There will be another price to pay. Over the centuries, many of the African languages will perhaps disappear, not as does a river in the desert sand, but as smaller streams into a larger river.

SETTINGS FOR SPEECH ENCOUNTERS

Settling the language question does not dispose of the question of having a medium for communication or of the settings for people speaking to each other. We can communicate in face-to-face situations to build commonalities within the framework of an African culture. But such interaction, while essential, is insufficient. Articulation of the great 'Paradigm of African Society' through face-to-face interactions may take centuries.

The other solution is in the use of mass media, particularly the use of radio, to develop an African culture by cultivating an African audience. Several UNESCO documents have talked enthusiastically about the possibilities of radio teaching foreign languages and contributing to international understandings. This solution is technically possible but not as feasible as it might look at first sight. First, there are some practical problems. Radio is not as easily available in rural Africa as we sometimes like to believe. Also, it has become a tool of entertainment rather than of instruction. There are also several constraints inherent in radio as a means of communication. Radio in its instructional role (and even in its entertainment role) uses the grammar of print. Non-literate people do not understand radio as well as the literate do. Detailed historical records and philosophic systems are not possible in totally illiterate communities. Radio is not a good vehicle either for ideology or for the technology that genuine Pan-Africanism would demand. Indeed, radio can teach people to be dependent.

NOT WITHOUT LITERACY

The question of oral communication versus communication by reading and writing (literacy) must be settled. We may begin by posing the question in this form: Is Pan-Africanism possible among non-literate people? Theoretically speaking, some sort of Pan-Africanism is possible. But it will be, as we have mentioned earlier, Pan-Africanism of the elite. Or, it will be Pan-Africanism imposed by armies of one nation over the others. Imagine Christianity in Africa without literacy and without the Bible to read.

From historical experience, we know that literacy is able to carry both ideas and emotions. It is a medium that is highly versatile. It gives freedoms to the user that no other medium does. Once the book is in the hands of a reader, the reader has the choice of time and place of study and has repeated and random access to the material in the book. The ability to be with the book alone encourages reflection. The reader can be a writer as well without the need for anything more elaborate than pencil and paper. Thus, codification of reality is as much possible as decodification of reality as seen by others. By its very nature, literacy enables a person to rise above the physical-definitional reality and to have ideas and emotions about symbolically constructed reference groups and systems. Literacy is the antidote to isolation. Ngugi gave literacy an important role in his battle for the decolonization of the African mind. Its role in Pan-Africanism may be similarly irreplaceable.

We are suggesting that multiple literacies be taught to African adults: literacy in the mother tongue; literacy in the regional lingua franca and literacy in a metropolitan language. Literacy should be taught first in the mother tongue, except where it could be taught as easily in the regional lingua franca. Literacy, it is said, is learned only once. The literacy skills learned through literacy acquisition in the mother tongue can then be transferred to literacy in the regional lingua franca and then the metropolitan language.

Ngugi wa Thiong'o, even while analyzing the role of colonial languages in the process of colonization, accepted the role the metropolitan languages could play at this moment in the history of Africa and the Third World in general. Metropolitan languages will have to play a crucial role if Pan-Africanism is seen as a movement of the African people rather than African states. This larger conception brings the diaspora of black Africans into the movement - all of the 100 million blacks who live outside Africa in the U.S., the Caribbean and Brazil and who are equivalent to about one-fourth of the total population of Africa.

This three-language formula is, in fact, already emerging within the national education system of many countries including Kenya and India.

REFERENCES

Abraham, Willie E. 1962. *The Mind of Africa*. London: Weidenfeld and Nicolson.

Encyclopedia Americana. 1985. Vol. 1. Danbury: Grolier.

Esendebe., P. Olisanwuche. 1982. *Pan-Africanism: The Idea and Movement, 1776-1963*. Washington, D.C.: Howard University Press, p. 3.

Ngugi wa O'Thiong'o. 1986. *Decolonizinq the Mind: The Politics of Language in African Literature.* London: James Currey; Nairobi: Heinemann, Kenya; Portsmouth, N.H.: Heinemann, Harare: Zimbabwe Publishing House.

Singer, J. D. 1968. "Man and World Politics: The Psycho-Cultural Interface," *Journal of Social Issues* 24: pp. 127-56.

CHAPTER 7

ROLE OF THE PRESS IN KENYAN NATIONAL IDENTITY: HISTORICAL PROBLEMS AND POSSIBLE PROSPECTS

Diana F. Ryan

A generation ago, just when many African countries were becoming independent, communication researchers thought the mass media were going to play the key role in shaping how emerging countries developed. Their approaches grew out of a Western point of view that proved not to be translatable into the value systems of other parts of the world. In spite of the fact that communication media are no longer considered magic bullets that can inject developing countries with Western "modernization," most media experts and governments of new African states in the 1980's believe communication technology and the mass media do have an instrumental role in social change. They see the press, radio, television and other forms of modern mass media as an important part of the infrastructure that can link the often quite disparate groups of new nations. One of the ways the media form this link is by defining and validating the values these groups do share. In other words, it is believed the media can contribute to the effort to mobilize the national consciousness of a pluralistic country.

Kenya is one of the new African countries where strong ethnic traditions, as well as the more recent influence of Western, particularly British ideas, have created a complicated relationship. The Kikuyu, at 21 percent of the population, are dominant in number, most centrally located, and have tended to control Kenyan politics. Traditionally, the powerful alternative bases among the Luhya (14 percent), Luo (13 percent), Kamba (11 percent), Kelenjin (11 percent) as well the smaller groups such as the Maasai, Giriama, Nandi and others, have tended to work together to counteract Kikuyu political domination. In addition, there are 280,000 Asians, Arabs and Europeans. Kiswahili was made the national language in the early 1970's and is a required subject in school.

English is widely spoken, especially by the elites and is used in teaching secondary and university level classes. The major institutions, such as law and politics, and including the mass media, are largely modeled on the British system. The press typically is geared to the urban minority who are more educated and speak either English or Kiswahili.

At 224,960 square miles, Kenya is a relatively small country compared to some of the others in Africa - slightly smaller than Texas. Approximately 75 percent of the country's 20 million people live in 10 percent of Kenya (Ogunade, 1986, p. 103). The one-third of the land that is arable is in short demand for the mainly rural population. National political leadership, according to one University of Nairobi lecturer in 1979, envisioned a Kenya where each ethnic group, under its own elite, would slowly pull itself up to participate in ever-increasing national resources (Arnold, 1981, p. 2), but, in fact, phenomenal population growth has led to growing competition for limited resources and fears of ethnic favoritism.

Clearly, it is critical for the national leadership to find ways to respect minority cultures and yet supercede the multitude of intrinsic differences to promote national goals and self determination. It is believed the media can be instrumental. As one well-known Kenyan editor, Hilary Ng'weno, told an International Press Institute Assembly in Nairobi:

> The first duty of the press in such countries, as indeed of any other institution or individual, is to encourage greater national unity; for without a minimum amount of national unity all other human values in society become impossible. Freedom and justice become meaningless. Life becomes insecure. Where there isn't enough national unity, it is my view that the press should confine itself to the difficult tasks of helping to unify the nation and remove mistrust between communities or tribes.

APPROACHING THE PROBLEM

An examination of Kenya's press history and current status is a place to begin in the task of defining the media's role in promoting national identity. Is there any reason to believe the Kenyan press can help validate and define qualities that might be shared by Kenyans -- whether they are urban or rural, educated or uneducated, young or old, rich or poor, male or female, Kikuyu or

Luo? In 1980, Peter Mwaura, Kenyan communication expert, was doubtful. He said the Kenya press "lacks a well-defined concept of what is African about it. It is elitist and urban oriented. It is Western in orientation" (Mwaura, 1980, p. 62).

Some of the past and present circumstances have had a direct bearing on the press's role in helping Kenya evolve a national identity. A search of the history of the major newspapers in Kenya should illustrate some of the forces that have shaped and constrained the press's contribution to a national identity; There are prospects for the press to contribute to a Kenyan national identity in the future.

HISTORY OF THE PRESS IN KENYA

The newspapers in Kenya, and in East Africa generally, have had quite a different history from the newspapers on the West Coast. From early on, the major newspapers of Nigeria and the Gold Coast were organs of protest and political agitation. Kenyan writer Ali Mazrui has described many West Africa nationalistic leaders as journalists. James Brew of the Gold Coast in the 1870's, John Payne Jackson of the Lagos Weekly Record and other leaders established a tradition of nationalistic journalism followed by Nnamdi Azikiwe, Obafemi Awolowo and Kwame Nkrumah (in Condon, 1975, p. 228). This spirit of nationalism and identity-seeking was exemplified when Nkrumah told the Second Conference of Pan-African Journalists in Accra that African journalists had a duty to express views that "move the revolution forward," the revolution being for independence from the colonial influence.

In contrast, on the East coast of Africa, according to Communication Professor John Condon, Jomo Kenyatta's editorship from 1928 to 1930 of Muigwithania, a Kikuyu nationalist organ, made the only significant contribution in this direction. Rather, the roots of the Kenyan press were firmly based in the strong settler population and their interests (Condon, 1976, Gazette, p. 228-229). The major difference was that the press in Kenya was initiated by non-Africans who came to East Africa to pioneer an undeveloped area and exploit the possible economic opportunities. Both the large Indian population, many of whom initially came to build the East African Railway from Mombasa to Kisumu, and the English settlers had hopes of establishing farms and businesses. The roots of the press were set in these foreign interests rather than African interests and points of view.

THE EAST AFRICAN STANDARD

The earliest newspaper, the East African and Uganda Mail, was published in Mombasa in 1899, only four years after the British government declared the strip between Mombasa and the Rift Valley a protectorate. But the first major newspaper was founded in 1902. The weekly African Standard was founded in Mombasa, the largest and oldest city in the area. The paper was established by a prominent Indian businessman, A. M. Jivanjee, to serve British East African administrators and settlers (Condon, p. 229). In 1905, Kenya lost its protectorate status when it was transferred from the Foreign office to the authority of the Colonial Office. So, when the African Standard was bought out by an English partnership in 1910, the newspaper was moved to Nairobi, the new seat of government. The newspaper's name was changed to the East African Standard and it became a daily.

The E. A. Standard established itself as the leading newspaper of the colony. It became the first mouthpiece of European opinion (Carter, 1968, p. 86). Its policy was to support the government, and even in the 1950's, as the pressure built toward independence, the E. A. Standard was strident in its opposition to African nationalism (Mytton, 1983, p. 43-44). Today, a generation after independence, the Standard remains foreign owned by the Lonrho Corporation with its base in London. Ogunade of the University of Lagos reported in 1986 that the Standard's daily circulation figure was 32,000, (Ogunade, 1986, p. 108), the same number reported for 1973 by American researcher James Scotton - a decrease by 3,000 from 1968. Scotton says the Standard's survival as an independent newspaper is remarkable considering its settler roots and departing European readership (Scotton, p. 20). The Standard' s contribution to an African Kenyan identity has been minimal. It has been aimed at the most affluent Kenyans, particularly Europeans. It has attempted to compete with the other English-language dailies by concentrating on Kenyan news, but as it continues in the pattern set in colonial times with coverage of dog and horse shows (Scotton, p. 27), it is unlikely to present values that many Africans would associate with a national identity.

The Kenya Weekly News was an example of these slowly disappearing settler and colonial interests. This newspaper was founded in the late 1930's as a European farmer's paper published from Nakuru in the Kenya Highlands. It was known as "the Settler's Paper." In the early 1950's it was prosecuted for sedition when it published a letter that said "government programs to improve the African were a waste of time since he was inherently primitive and basically savage" (Scotton, Journalism Quarterly, p. 36). In those pre-independence days, Scotton points out, the Europeans in Kenya, unlike the Africans accused of sedition at the time, had a right to trial by jury and charges against the Kenya Weekly News were dropped. In 1968, it was taken over by the Standard Group. Carter says it did not survive the competition of other English-language newspapers (Carter, p. 86); without drastic policy changes, it seemed to have little place in the newly independent Kenya.

BARAZA

In 1939, the colonial government launched the broadsheet Kiswahili weekly, the Baraza. Although initially the Standard Company was opposed to a newspaper for Africans, the newspaper was so popular, the Standard management agreed to take it over (Scotton, p. 20). The colonial government encouraged the project by guaranteeing to meet any losses incurred by the paper. The government had ceased publishing its regular Swahili paper during the Depression and wanted to explain events, especially the outbreak of the war, to the African population of East Africa (Carter, p. 86).

According to Felice Carter, the Baraza followed a more independent line than its origins might suggest and never took money from the government. After 1945, the newspaper consistently advocated African political development. Its primarily rural circulation was not affected by Kiswahili and vernacular government newspapers before and after the war and, she says, "by maintaining a fairly moderate line it survived the Emergency in 1952" (p. 86). Graham Mytton, on the other hand, points out that although the Baraza became self-supporting in two years, its editorial policy was a British government responsibility until 1946 (Mytton, p. 43-44).

In 1973, the Baraza was East Africa's largest weekly with a circulation of 61,000 (Scotton, p. 19). Baraza was the first major attempt to reach the estimated 75 percent of Kenya's Kiswahili-speaking population. As a major African-language newspaper, Baraza played a role in drawing attention to the growing interest of these Kiswahili readers, in spite of the fact that it was a consistent supporter of continued settler rule.

DAILY NATION

A second major English-language daily, the Daily Nation, was founded in 1960 by Prince Karim Aga Khan IV, an international businessman and the spiritual head of the Ismalii Moslems. The Nation, a tabloid, successfully challenged the dominant position of the Standard. Both the Standard and the Nation are read by "all the Europeans, almost all the Asians, and by those upper and middle class Africans with enough education to belong to the English-speaking minority," according to Scotton's research in 1975 (Scotton, p. 32). The Daily Nation appeals to respondents who are 33 years old and younger, and is preferred by people with 13 years of education, according to researcher Frank Ogboajah of the University of Lagos in 1985. The Nation was preferred as the media with more information than any of the other major newspapers in Nairobi (Ugboajah, 1985, p. 155).

The Nation's circulation tripled between 1966 and 1973 to 75,000, and in 1986 was estimated to be at 100,572, putting it far ahead of the Standard at 32,000 (Ogunade, 1986, p. 108). Sunday Nation is published also by Nation Newspapers Limited. The Nation has had an African editor since 1964 and Africanized its staff early, although the Aga Khan's ownership may have been a factor in its reputation amongst many Kenyans as an "Asian newspaper," according to American researcher James Scotton. The editorial policy is liberal and historically has been supportive of African nationalism. The Nation has consistently supported African rule in Kenya with participation by all citizens, including Africans, Asians and Europeans (Miller, 1961, p. 48-51; Scotton, 1975, p. 21).

In 1960, the Nation Newspapers Limited began publishing what was for a long time the only Kiswahili daily, the Taifa Leo and its Saturday edition Taifa

Kenya (Baraza was a weekly) (Ogboajah, 1985, p. 155). An African editor and news staff produce the Taifa papers. The circulation of Taifa Leo has risen from 10,000 in 1970 to 49,000 in 1986 (Ogunade, p. 108). In a 1975 study of newspaper readership and ownership in Kenya, Scotton found that editors and vendors agreed the Taifa papers were read primarily by working class Africans although the editor of Taifa Leo believed there was a growing readership among educated, middle class Africans (Scotton, p. 22). Most researchers contend newspaper circulation figures do not reflect accurately the actual African readership of each copy. Due to the limited funds of many African workers, newspapers (especially the Kiswahili ones) often are bought jointly and passed around (Scotton, p. 22; Neher & Condon, p. 230).

Scotton found the content of the Taifa and Baraza stressed entertaining features and Taifa occasionally mixed news with moral admonishments concerning issues of national development (Scotton, p. 21-22). His content analysis indicated that in these Kiswahili newspapers, the most Kenyan aspect was the letters-to-the-editor. Often the form of poetry, a common traditional form of commentary, most letters addressed local social problems and a desire for more Africanization of businesses (Scotton, p. 27). In a 1985 study, Taifa Leo, unlike its parent organ, had an impact among respondents 46 years old and above (Ugboajah, p. 161).

From the outset, the policy the Nation series claimed to follow has been to appeal to a multi-racial readership, with an emphasis on African interests and a belief in press freedom. 2 Nonetheless, the fact that the Nation is foreign-owned makes it vulnerable to African criticism and government threats, Scotton says. Although both the Standard and the Nation are strong supporters of the government on most issues, they have been known to criticize government policies and officials. Some of their non-Kenyan reporters have been deported, but they have continued their criticism in moderate tones (Scotton, Gazette, 1975, p. 20). This principle of press freedom may be the major contribution the Nation and the Standard have to make to Kenyan national identity. African journalists are commonly subjected to government censorship and controls. Typically, government officials expregs concern over the fragile nature of national unity and stress that positive support should be the role of the press. This issue has been the subject of international debate for the last five or six years, and in many developing countries even moderate criticism of the government by the press is unusual. As widely respected newspapers, the Nation and the Standard play a role in keeping channels to alternative perspectives open until such time as the press creates a viable voice for the values of all Kenyans.

THE ASIAN PRESS

Long before the Daily Nation with its connection to the Aga Khan, the Indian community had English and Gujerati newspapers. By 1905, Indian interests in Kenya were the most serious challenge to the plan for British settlement. The large numbers of Indians in Kenya had a strong influence and, like the British, also were considering plans for a possible colony, according to East African historian Bethwell Ogat. A. M. Jivanjee in 1910 said "I would go so far as to advocate the annexation of this African territory (Kenya) to the Indian Empire, with Provincial Government under the Indian Viceroy" (Ogat, 1968, p. 256). In 1921, the Indian National Congress published an article in its official Kenyan newspaper, the East African Chronicle, detailing an Indian-administered Kenya, and even the Aga Khan suggested East Africa could be an Indian colony (Ogat, p. 256).

Although both Indian and European settlers had been encouraged by the British initially, the British pioneers and their interest in controlling the Kenya Highlands eventually took precedence in government policies. Although the 1923 White paper declared Kenya primarily an African country, Ogat says, Europeans got the best services, Indians the second best and Africans had to do with whatever was left over (p. 276). It was a policy of separate development. It was not until after World War II that the Indian press began to support African nationalism (Mytton, p. 44). In 1968, there was one remaining Indian paper, Africa Samachar in Gujerati. It had begun publication in the early 1950's and was owned locally by the United Africa Press Ltd. (Carter, 1968, p. 87).

THE PRE-INDEPENDENCE NATIONALIST PRESS

Only a few independent African newspapers existed prior to World War II

(Scotton, Journalism Quarterly, 1975). In 1921, Harry Thuku, the leader of the East African Association which was mainly a welfare organization concerned with the personal improvement of its members, published a few issues of Tanqazo, (Announcement), but it disappeared when he was arrested and deported in 1922 (Ogot, p. 282). In 1928, the Kikuyu Central Association (the East Africa Association's successor) began to publish Mwigwithania, (the Mediator or the Counselor), sometimes under the editorship of Jomo Kenyatta. The association put most emphasis on development and was mainly concerned with demands for fairer treatment from the British and to negotiate the return of alienated Kikuyu lands, according to Bildad Kaggia, a former KCA member. "It had no programme for changing the status quo or even for attaining independence" (Ogat, p. 282). As World War II threatened the colonial borders, a total ban was put on all political activity, including the newspaper of the KCA (Ogat, p. 282; Scotton, Journalism Quarterly, 1975, p. 31). 3

In Western Kenya some Luo papers had been published, but the only other publications for Africans before 1945 were religious periodicals or government gazettes (Scotton, p. 31).

Starting with Mumenyereri (He Who Looks After) in 1945, a series of post-war African newspapers appeared. The weekly Mumenyereri's circulation reached 10,000 by 1952 and was known as "the paper of Kikuyu patriotism" (Scotton, p. 31). The official paper of Kenyatta's Kenya African Union, Sauti ya Mwafrika (Voice of the African); The Luo weekly Ramogi (News); The Nyanza Times; Mwalimu (Teacher); Radio Posta (Radio Post); and Uhuru Wa Afrika (Freedom for Africa) were all among the most radical newspapers of the new group.

In 1950, the Kenya Legislature gave the government power to close seditious papers, "to protect Africans from Communism, but the editors turned to mimeographing news sheets. Under the Kenya Penal Code, says Scotton, sedition was defined as seditious intention, "which includes any attempt to 'excite disaffection' against the government or 'promote feelings of ill will and hostility between different classes of the population of the Colony.' The sedition law was only used five times against Asian newspapers and four times against African newspapers (Scotton, p. 36). These papers were a significant communication point for the common desires that formed the core of African nationalism and were used in battling the power of the settlers and the colonial government.

When the Kenya African Union was founded in 1952, its goal was to unite the African people toward an African nation and to foster social, economic and political interests of Africans (Ogat, p. 206), but the editor of the organization's newspaper, Sauti ya Mwafrika, resigned in protest against the rising domination of the Kikuyu in the organization. Jomo Kenyatta, president of the organization, insisted the XAU not be turned into a Kikuyu union. B. M. Kaggia, one of leaders of the rebellion which subsequently broke out, maintains the KAU was only used as an umbrella and KAU leaders knew nothing (p. 289). The uprising, known as the Mau Mau Rebellion, has been interpreted in many ways, but rather than a civil, religious or nationalistic movement aimed at political independence, historian Ogat suggests the movement was a multi -leveled revolution of many different interest groups, each with their own needs and wants presenting a united front against the colonial officials and settlers (Ogat, p. 288-289).

Scotton says that "Although many of the African newspapers had links with Kenya's nationalist leaders, Kenya's African press remained essentially a press of protest rather than nationalism" (Scotton, p. 32-33). He contends that the important African press continued to preach moderation in spite of the Kenyan colonial government's resistance to African demands for "common law for all citizens, equal opportunities in education, social and economic services, and equal representation" (p. 34).

On the other hand, British political scientist Graham Mytton says the anti-colonial, anti-settler Kikuyu language newspapers were a critical element in African nationalism similar to the nationalist press in British West Africa. He also says that these newspapers escaped scrutiny earlier because the British administrators knew Kiswahili, but not Kikuyu (Mytton, p. 44).

With the failure of separate development, the Colonial Office instituted a series of new constitutions promoting multiracialism. But African leaders wanted "non racial" policies with land redistribution and opportunities for African equality. The emergency continued with bitter constitutional battles in Nairobi and London. Finally, in 1960, with independence in sight, two political parties emerged, Kenya African National Union and Kenya African Democratic

Party. KADU claimed to represent the minority ethnic groups, but a year after independence in 1963, KADU dissolved, leaving ethnic suspicions and fears unresolved (Ogat, p. 292).

The press, like many of the other institutional forms inherited from the British in Kenya, was originally designed to serve a multiplicity of races, but not particularly to unite them. There was very little time to evolve appropriate structures for an independent Kenya between 1952 to 1963, and "when Kenya attained her independence, many of the old racialistic institutions still existed. The problem of creating a society based on authentic African values was therefore likely to be difficult" (Ogat, p. 292).

POLICY AND NATIONAL IDENTITY

When Kenya became independent of Great Britain in 1963, it was one of the last of the African countries to sever colonial ties. After 64 years, the British journalistic tradition ran deep and the press began its struggle to find its role in creating an African national identity. Although in many African countries the press was put under government control at independence, in Kenya the foreign-owned press was allowed to continue. Kenyatta, Kenya's first president, told the International Press Institute in 1968 that the "press should positively promote national development and growing self-respect. And the press should always seek to coalesce rather than isolate the different cultures, aspirations and standards of advancement which make up our new nation" (Wilcox, p. 575). As has been discussed, the foreign-owned press continues to dominate the newspaper scene. It often has been cited as one of the most free, lively and outspoken in Africa (Carter, p. 88), but the foreign-owned press treads a fine line. Kenyatta was never criticized in the press and the same rule applies to President Moi who succeeded him. On the other hand, the press has been influential in putting public pressure on corruption or incompetence in the lower echelons of government (Arnold, p. 9; Carter, p. 87).

Graham Mytton argues that because there is no established African pattern for the press, it often continues to draw on traditions from outside, and these traditions have often been at variance with local conditions and problems. Although national leaders and government officials recognize the significance of mass communication to national identity and unity, some critics claim the potential of the press in Africa has been sidetracked. The professed general policies of harnessing the mass media for the sake of the nation have, "in reality, been translated into using available communication facilities to project the image, policies, ideology and programmes of the government of the day" (Boafu, 1986, p. 40).

Very few national communication policies in sub-Saharan Africa have evolved or been implemented that are based on "preserving nationally recognized fundamental values which underline the socio-cultural life of the people" (Boafu, 1986, p. 40-44). In a mixed culture like Kenya's, the challenge of national unity and stimulating individual cultural systems is a delicate task.

In his study of Kenya's communication policies, Peter Mwaura noted the mass media were underdeveloped but were recognized as a "vital and integral part of Kenya's development strategy," that the media would grow if the interests and concerns of the Wananchi (citizens) were addressed more directly (Mwaura, 1980, p. 94).

RECENT EVENTS

In 1983, the Kenya African National Union (KANU), now the only legal political party, began putting out two new party newspapers. The Kenya Times was formerly the Nairobi Times, a private Kenyan African-owned newspaper in English which had been growing in popularity. Frank Ogboajah found the Nairobi Times to be more popular than the Standard and said there were indications it "would in the near future compete fiercely with the Daily Nation as the people's newspaper" (Ugboajah, p. 161). KANU also established Kenya Leo in Kiswahili in 1983.

But, in spite of the newspapers, it would appear that Wananchi concerns and interests are not being heard. Michael Maren, former assistant editor of Africa Report, who lived in Kenya from 1977 to 1981, says the lively commentary of the newspapers in the early Moi days is being discouraged and a dissident press is gaining momentum. Pambana, the organ of the December Twelfth Movement (DTM) was expressing ideas and goals in the interest of the poor and challenging the edicts of President Moi and his ministers from 1982-1984, he says, but they experienced little governmental repercussion or public support. Then, in March of 1986, the government announced the arrests of several University of Nairobi lecturers and dissidents, charging them with "membership in an underground organization (Mwakenya or the Patriotic Front for the Liberation of Kenya) and of possessing or distributing Mpatanishi (Kiswahili for "The Arbitern"). This organization has the same goals as the DMT, according to Maren. Although Maren notes that the Mwakenya are organized into cells along the lines of Kenya's anti-colonial (so-called) Mau Mau movement, these are all Kenya's middle class and no central ethnic group seems to exist (Maren, 1986, p. 67-71). In the past year, sedition trials have put 64 alleged members of Mwakenya in prison according to the Economist. Five of them have been journalists (February 21, 1987, p. 39).

As an article in Africa Events pointed out last year, the African journalist is required to exercise "delicate" judgement and exercise extraordinary awareness of political nuances. They quoted a speech titled "The Role of the Mass Media in African Development," by Hilary Ng'weno. He said "Some day, this state of affairs will change. In the meantime, communicators in Africa have no option but to do whatever they can to continue their involvement in the formulation and transmission of the message of development and in keeping the channels open through which the message must be transmitted" (Africa Events, January, 1986, p. 43).

PROSPECTS

The task of defining national character may have reached a critical point in the Kenyan press. Colonial heritage used to be considered Kenya's biggest problem and was the rallying point for national unity. But, rejecting the British is no substitute for knowing what it means to be a Kenyan. For one thing, Kenya's population is one of the fastest-growing in the world. In 1985, the population was estimated to be 20,194,000, having expanded by more than 50 percent since independence from Great Britain in 1963. More than half of the population is under fourteen years old. The memories of the struggle for independence are fading and, as one Kenyan put it, these young people "do not have an emotional firsthand knowledge of the pre-independence nationalism and the sacrifices which were made (during the struggle for independence)" (Africa Events, January 1986, p. 42- 43). Too, the pressure for successful national development plans increases as the ranks of poor and landless swell. Under the pressure for national development, the mass media have diverged into two paths; one serves the nation within the traditional Western form of the press, and the other path has gone into the field with the mass media serving as a tool in national development projects. The latter is commonly termed development communication (Boafo, 1985, p. 83).

SUMMARY

This paper has focused on the historical path of the press, but some of the concepts of development communication could be useful to the future press, and this would mean more than just critiquing development projects and issues. Often, mass media researchers interested in Africa suggest integrating traditional media such as dance and folkways with modern media to reach the rural masses for development projects. Turning this argument around, rather than focusing on the individual different cultural traditions, the press could focus on the core values that link urban, educated Kenyans with rural, less educated people. Rather than maintaining the separation of the urban elite from the rural poor, educated from uneducated, one ethnic group from the other, these values would seek a common core of sameness that both groups would identify with, whether in development projects or the press.

In 1968, Ali Mazrui believed three of the most important values influencing policy and political behavior in independent East Africa were equality, development and unity (Mazrui, 1968, p. 346), but these are vague ideas in the struggle for suitable balance between love for one's tribe and loyalty to one's nation. Other, perhaps more specific core values have been suggested by Isaac Obeng-Quaidoo. They are: 1) the role of the supreme God/Allah and lesser gods in the daily life of the African; 2) the African concept of time and its influence on him/her; 3) the African's concept of work and its relationship to how he/she perceives his/her own relationship to nature; 4) the nonindividuality of the African and how this affects his/her world view. Obeng-Quaidoo, a University of Ghana professor, stresses that, in the first value, the Supreme God is not manifest very frequently, while "the lesser gods exercise a profound influence on the thought, imagination and day-to-day activities of the African" (Obeng-Ouaidoo, 1986, p. 92). The African concept of time, he suggests, is not linear as in Western thought, but rather, "a composition of events which have occurred, those which are taking place now and those which are immediately to occur" (p. 93). The value of work relates to the ideal of cooperating with nature, rather than trying to subdue or conquer it, he says, and, finally, the value of non -individuality relates to the sense of attachment and responsibility the African feels for everyone in his immediate clan (p. 93). These are ideas that need testing and experiment. If the emerging generation is going to participate in the development of Kenya with the help of the press, it will need to be given some common links and bonds with the previous generations. New combinations from older traditions may be modified to create a new role for the press or used to define common values for communication through the press. The watchdog form of the press is not functioning as it does in the West. If it is to continue as a channel of communication and agent for national identity, the press must redefine its methods to include African points of view and African values.

REFERENCES

Arnold, Guy. 1981. *Modern Kenya*, Longman Group Limited, London.

Ainslie, Rosalynde. 1966. *The Press in Africa: Communications Past and Present,* London: Victor Gollancz.

Boafu, S. T. Kwame. 1985. "Utilizing Development Communication Strategies in African Societies: A Critical Perspective," *Gazette*, Vol. 35, p. 83-92.

Boafu, S. T. Kwame. 1986. "Formulating Comprehensive National Communication Policies for Development in African Countries, in *Africa Media Review*, Vol. 1, p. 35-47.

Carter, Felice. 1968. "The Press in Kenya," *Gazette*, Vol. 14, No. 2, June, p. 85-88.

Hachten, William A. 1974. *Muffled Drums : The News Media in Africa,* Ames, Iowa: The Iowa State University Press.

Hamelink, Cees. 1983. *Cultural Autonomy in Global Communication*, New York: Longman Inc.

"Kenya: A Sudden Chill," *Africa Confidential*, Vol. 27, No. 8. April 9, 1986, p. 1-3.

"L'Etat, C'est Moi." *The Economist*, February 21, 1987, p. 39-40.

Legum, Colin. 1982-83. *African Contemporary Record: Annual Survey and Documents,* New York: Africana Publishing Company.

Maren, Michael. 1986. "Hear No Evil," *Africa Report*, Vol. 31, No. 6, November-December, p. 67-71.

Mazrui, Ali A. 1966. "Political Censorship, Intellectual Creativity and Nation Building, "*East African Journal,* Vol. 3, No. 9, p. 34.

Miller, Norman. 1961.*Kenya's Nationalism and the Press 1951-1961*, an unpublished master's thesis, Indiana University.

Mwaura, Peter. 1980. *Communication Policies in Kenya,* Paris: UNESCO.

Mytton, Graham L. 1983. *Mass Communications in Africa*, London: Edward Arnold Publishers Ltd.

Neher, William W. and John C. Condon. 1976. "The Mass Media and Nation-Building in Kenya and Tanzania" in David Smock and Kwamena Bentsi-Enchill, eds., *The Search for National Integration in Africa*, New York: The Free Press, p. 220-239.

Obeng-Quaidoo, Isaac. 1986. "A Proposal for New Communication Research Methodologies in Africa, "*Africa Media Review*, Vol. 1, No. 1, p. 89-99.

Ogat, B. A. 1968. *Zamani*: A Survey of East African History, East African Publishing House and Longman Group Ltd., Nairobi.

Ogunade, Dele. 1986. "The Mass Media Systems of Kenya and Tanzania: A Comparative Analysis, "*Africa Media Review*, Vol. 1, p. 99-111.

Schramm, Wilbur. 1964. *Mass Media and National Development: The Role of Information in the Developing Countries,* Stanford: Stanford University Press.

Scotton, James F. 1975. "Kenya's Much Maligned Nationalist Press, *Journalism Quarterly,* Vol. 52, p. 30-36.

Scotton, James F. 1975. "The Press in Kenya a Decade After Independence: Patterns of Readership and Ownership," *Gazette*, Vol. 21, p. 19-33.

Ugboajah, Frank Okwu. 1985. "Media Habits of Rural and Semi-Rural (Slum) Kenya," *Gazette*, Vol. 36, p. 155-174.

Wilcox, Dennis. 1975. *Mass Media in Black Africa: Philosophy and Control,* New York: Praeger Publishing.

NOTES

1. The last year Baraza was cited in the Indiana University Acquisitions list was in 1978, suggesting it may not be published anymore, or may be under some other name.

2. The Nation Newspapers Limited became a public stock company in 1973, but the extent of African ownership is not known (Scotton, p. 21).

3. Mytton says it stopped publication when Kenyatta went to England in 1934, Condon cites 1930.

CHAPTER 8

EFFECT OF WESTERN PHILOSOPHIES ON MEDIA ORGANIZATIONS IN THE DEVELOPING WORLD

Mbella Ngomba-Maija

News dissemination is an important factor in the media's role of "informing," and it is a point of most contention according to critics who believe developing countries are dependent on Western news sources. The media in developing countries have come to replicate the "news values" and mechanisms of the Western media (Meyer, 1989). An example would be the way in which the unstructured media follow the West's lead in the focus of their media coverage.

The four largest Western news agencies, AP (U.S.), UPI (U.S.), AFP (France), and Reuters (U.K.), have largely shaped the presentation of news in developing countries and defined news values for their mass media (Martin and Chaudhary, 1983). This is not necessarily a choice made in accordance with developing countries' media philosophies; rather, it is due to economic factors. Few countries in the world have the financial ability to gather international news, so they must rely heavily on news services from those countries that do. A study dealing with news coverage within 14 Asian newspapers found that more than 75 percent of nonlocal news content came from the four Western transnational news agencies (TNNAS) (Schramm et al, 1978). Another study of Nigerian broadcast media found that 85 percent of the total news content came from Reuters, AP, AFP, and Visnews (Golding and Elliott, 1979).

Perhaps the political unrest in many developing countries can be attributed in part to overreliance on Western news agencies and, thus, the inclusion of Western political thought inherent in the news slant. This imbalance portrays the West as neoimperialists (cultural imperialism) which creates regional spheres of informational hegemony (Becker et al, 1986; Schiller, 1976). It should not be implied, however, that developing countries' news media rely on Western agencies to the extent that "newsworthiness" criteria are nonexistent. The majority of developing nations' governments use various techniques for controlling the content of news media in their countries (Martin and Chaudhary, 1983).

CRITERIA USED FOR EVALUATING INTERNATIONAL NEWS

Alcino Louise da Costa, director of the weekly, *Afrigue Nouvelle*, identified several criteria used by African editors to evaluate international news for their national audiences. These criteria are also used in other developing countries (1983):

1. The "psycho-political security" criterion.

It places importance on encouraging news coming from countries with which close relations are maintained. Any news items considered politically detrimental are excluded. State-controlled media regimes will not allow any news content that may disturb public opinion.

2. The "community of interests" criterion.

It gives priority to encouraging news about countries with the same political, economic, or ideological interest.

3. The "imperatives of national policy" criterion.

It legitimizes or strengthens current governmental ideologies (1983).

STATUS-QUO

It is evident that many developing countries place importance on their "Status-Quo" forms of government and do not tolerate any deviation therefrom. The minister of information in most developing countries and the heads of departments under him or her usually decide the editorial criteria for news. During war and emergencies, many ministers screen radio and television news before it is aired. Sometimes they draw up the content and headlines for certain news stories. A "gatekeeper" in Saudi Arabia will consider strict Islamic laws and the dominant Arab culture as part of the news criteria. Pran Chopra (1980) noted one particular distinction of Asian journalists; many have been schooled in the Western tradition. Thus, news criteria in Asia are largely influenced by the interplay of foreign influences as well as Asian cultural and sociopolitical influences (Martin and Chaudhary, 1983).

METHODOLOGY

Once again addressing the prevalence of the "big four" Western news agencies in developing countries' news media coverage, Schramm (1980) conducted research to determine the extent of agency newswire use in these countries. In a later study, five issues of each African newspaper for 1984, five for 1985, and four issues of each Latin American paper were analyzed and coded. The basic unit of analysis was the international news story. The samples were stratified in two ways: by issue and by week (no two issues were taken from the same week). Papers were analyzed from a six-month time period. Each story was coded for paper and publication date, the wire service carrying the story, the nation and region covered in the story, the theme, the column-inches lines for spot news as opposed to developmental news. Raw facts about diplomacy, wars, etc. were considered spot news whereas developmental news projected relationships between raw news and economic/political change (Meyer, 1989). The data were used to support three research questions: media dependency and patterns of news coverage; differences in news reporting between Western TNNAS and local agencies; and the structure of international news flows (1989).

Data were tabulated regarding the media dependency question. From the samples it was apparent that the African press is more dependent upon the TNNAS than is Latin America. Twenty-nine to thirty-six percent, the largest single group of all international newswire stories reported in Kenyan, Zambian, and Zimbabwean newspapers, came from Britain's Reuters newswire (1989). The apparent reason for this is the fact that all three of these nations are former British colonies.

However, the mass media in Latin America have been established on American commercial models and are heavily influenced by Western styles of journalism (Martin and Chaudhary, 1983). Nonetheless, while Latin America does take more news from the regional wire services, especially from EEE, the Spanish Service and IPS, a specialist in developmental news (Meyer, 1989), forty-one percent of all international news reported in the Latin American press came from the two U.S. TNNAS (AP and UPI). Arguably, this is because Central America is within the "imperial sphere" of North America (1989).

Critics of the Western philosophy claim that global print media is becoming homogenized in its coverage of world events (MacBride Commission, 1981). Newspapers from different developing countries are said to resemble one another (Schramm, 1980), with developing countries' papers closely resembling Western prestige dailies regarding topics selected for coverage (Stevenson, 1981). Without delving into the statistical data involved, Meyer (1989) concluded that there is no significant difference in coverage of developmental news versus coverage of other news between Western and developing countries' dailies. Results suggest that Asian, African, Latin American and Western dailies are similar to each other in percentages of news devoted to interstate reporting and regions covered. Western TNNAS often focus on crises and crime when reporting from developed or developing countries (Weaver and Wilhoit, 1984).

Evidence from developing countries suggests a heavy reliance on the West for international news. This might lead one to believe that Western news values have come to govern media in the South. According to Stevenson and Cole (1980), "Western agencies set the agenda for developing countries' media at the level of influencing what topics get covered."

RESEARCH FINDINGS

Research data indicate that dailies in Africa and Latin America might reflect this mentality. A dependency on the West for news becomes a form of cultural imperialism when it reaches the point at which media producers in the South begin to think like those in the West (Meyer, 1989). A substantial number of international reports in Latin American and African papers came from a TNNA. This illustrates a continued reliance on the Western newswires.
Also, developing countries' dailies show close similarities to one another and to U.S. "prestige" dailies regarding geographic areas and topics covered.

The findings demonstrate media dependency as well as the replication of Western values in the South. So, the four major news agencies (AP, UPI, AFP, and Reuters) have largely shaped the presentation of news in developing countries and have defined the news values for their mass media (Martin and

Chaudhary, 1983). Nearly all broadcast media in developing, non-Communist countries really have no other alternative than to rely on these wires for their main sources of international news.

The agencies have also influenced the concept of news in developing countries by playing the role of agenda-setter, as well as promoting speed and impartiality (1983). The "inverted pyramid" method of journalism originated in the West is now considered standard practice throughout most of the world.

Notably, the Western newswires have shaped developing world news values via training programs. For example, Reuters helped establish news agencies for several developing countries in Africa by training many of their staff members as did the Agence France Press and the Francophone African countries. Developing nations' media have also been influenced by Western journalism in other ways. Several magazines have closely modeled the *New York Times* and *Newsweek*.

Two television news agencies dominate the developing world: the Reuters-owned Visnews, which sells the news resources of NBC overseas; and UPITN, which is owned and operated by UPI and the British ITN television network. Each day, Visnews distributes news to 98 countries. Each station receives about 15 minutes of video material, of which about five minutes is used on newscasts.

The Western concept of the journalist maintaining a neutral stance, and the "two-sided" style of Western journalism have been easy targets for developing countries' politicians. Editors have been known to edit a two-sided story into a one-sided story for political purposes. For media under governmental control, the Western formula has allowed them to promote good news about allied countries and bad news about adversaries (1983). For the privately owned media, publishers have given priority to their commercial interests and have selected controversial and "soft" news that attracts more readers and more advertising revenue (da Costa, 1980).

GROWTH OF ALTERNATIVE SOURCES

The reliance of developing countries on Western agencies has slightly decreased, however, due to the development of alternative sources of news. In recent years, there has been a growth of national and regional news services in the developing countries supply of news through exchange arrangements and cooperation between national agencies (Martin and Chaudhary, 1983). A primary example of cooperation among developing nations is the Non-Aligned News Agency (NANA) initiated in 1976. Members from 85 nations swap objective and reliable information from the national agencies including news regarding the relationships between nonaligned countries and the rest of the world. The purpose of this organization was to overcome "the situation of dependency and domination in which the majority of countries are reduced to being passive recipients of biased, inadequate, and distorted information" (1983).

The Yugoslav news agency, Tanjug, organized the aforementioned news pool. The agency receives a daily limit of 500 words of news items from each of the 41 participating agencies. It then translates the news into English, French, and Spanish. A majority of the material is not critical of the participants' political positions, but is influenced by ideological rhetoric (1983). Inter Press Service (IPS) is supplemental to NANA. This agency was developed in Latin America in 1964, and reports primarily on problems of developing countries - development, liberation movements, and so on. Interestingly enough, IPS has rejected Western journalistic styles to adopt this specific political cause. More emphasis is placed on interpretation of economic problems in order to better educate developing nations' residents.

Other examples of countries that have organized regional news pools include Africa (Organization of African Unity, PANA, "Africa number one") and Egypt (MENA). The former Soviet news agency (TASS) is distributed free in several developing countries (How's that for subtle propaganda?)

NEW WORLD INFORMATION ORDER

The United Nations Educational, Scientific, and Cultural Organization (UNESCO) concerns itself with agreeing upon a new world information order. This order calls for regulation of the right of access to information, more balance in news coverage, the licensing of journalists, and the right of reply to false news reports (1983). In essence, the West wants the free flow of information to other nations. Of course, the majority of news products would be Western-flavored. Developing countries ask for balance because they are very aware of this fact.

Since the 1950's, UNESCO has helped create programs that benefit residents of developing countries. Its resolution of December, 1962, states that "information media have an important part to play in education and in economic and social progress generally and that new techniques of communication offer special opportunities for acceleration of the education process" (Schramm, 1978). In 1964, UNESCO stressed as a priority the educational role of television in Africa. Since this time, educational television has been widely used in African schools, perhaps to partially offset the lack of trained teachers.

In 1970, UNESCO passed a resolution authorizing the Director-General to "assist member states in formulating their policies with respect to the mass communication media." Two years later, another resolution was passed that gave the Director-General authority to further develop communication research, especially in its application to the formulation of policies and the elaboration of national strategies in the service of development (Martin and Chaudhary, 1983). In 1976, the UNESCO Latin American Intergovernmental Conference took place in San Jose, Costa Rica. Venezuelan President Andre Perez harshly criticized Western media ethics for subjecting developing nations to alien values that could threaten their national identity. UNESCO has also been blamed by some who claim it a bad idea to have concentrated on Latin America as the first region in which to propose and develop national communication policies (1983). By the mid-1970's, communication policy studies were ongoing that included such countries as Asia, Africa, Latin America, and Europe, as sponsored by UNESCO.

NEWSWORTHY

How do different nations go about deciding what is newsworthy for their populations? Whereas the U.S. emphasizes "soft core" news stories that appeal more to audience interests rather than to what people need to know in many instances, former Soviet gate-keepers consider basically anything which can be used to illustrate current party policy or economic fitness to be worthy of coverage. Almost anything else is considered unimportant. The comparison is somewhat oversimplified, since nothing can be considered this "black-and-white." There are always "shades of gray". Reports on many major political events, especially those considered crises, are often delayed. This gives decision-makers time to organize the propaganda machine; in other words, from what angle do Soviet officials want their constituents to "hear" news.

Before the reunification of Germany, the Soviet style of "brainwash" journalism was quite evident in East Germany (GDR). For example, *Neues Deutschland* conveyed the same world view and stereotypes about a happy population, prospering citizens, and a powerful economy as *Pravda*. The lead story on the front page of one issue was a report with a picture about a visit by Enrico Berlinguer, the Italian communist leader, to an exhibition in Rome of the achievements of the GDR. Page two was dominated by a major story about the opening of a dairy and meat plant, and page three by a glowing three-column review of party leader Ench Honecker's book on the role of the trade unions (1983).

There basically exist two different types of communication systems in the world - open and closed. An open receiver system means that anyone can be a member of the audience system. A closed system has little interchange with the system environment. The more closed the system, the more predictable the system states are.

OPEN AND CLOSED SYSTEMS

Here then, are descriptions of various open and closed systems.

Type 1 A: Controlled (Mass) Communication. Controlled mass communication means a communication system in which the audience system is as open as possible but the message system is relatively closed. The constraints of the message system may be political (censorship) or any other kind that limits the selection of messages. This is a typical situation for Communist countries, but also for any other centralized political system.

Type 1 B: (Open) Mass Communication. An open mass communication system is a system in which both the audience and message constraints are as open as possible. This system comes closest to the traditional Western form of mass communication as typified by the BBC in broadcasting or the New York Times in print.

Type 1 C: Private Communication. The opposite of an open mass communication system is private communication, where both the audience and the message systems are relatively closed. Typical examples are private letters and phone calls. In poor societies - those with less adequate mass communication systems - this is the mode of communication.

Type 1 D: Directed (Mass) Communication. Directed communication means a communication system in which the audience system is closed but the message system is open. There are few constraints in the selection of the messages, but not everybody can join the communication system. Typical audience constraints are economic or ethnic restrictions; for example, a linguistic minority may not know the language used by the dominant medium. Or media use is too dominant for a large part of the social system, as would be the case in many developing countries. The types are, of course, idealized, and there are many middle values in different social systems.

Type 2 A: Decentralized Public Model. This model is perhaps best typified by the broadcast media in Western and European countries such as France and Denmark. The broadcasting companies are publicly owned, but the control system is decentralized. No single political or any other interest group can totally control the messages.

Type 2 B: Centralized Public Model. This is a typical socialist or communist model in which the media are owned by society and controlled centrally by the dominant political party. Russia, China, and many Eastern European countries are examples of this model.

Type 2 C: Decentralized Private Model. The Western European press and U.S. media in general belong to this category. The media are privately owned and there is no centralized control.

Type 3 A: The Authoritarian Model. In this model, the right to send may belong to the individual, but the right to receive belongs to the society. The society allows only certain kinds of messages to be sent by the media. This model is applicable to many authoritarian states and dictatorships, (such as occurred in Nazi Germany or Franco's Spain).

Type 3 B: The Communist Model. According to this model, society controls both the right to send and receive. Society can give these rights to individuals on certain occasions, and it has the absolute right to recall these rights when individual rights conflict with the interests of society. Events in Poland during 1981-82 are very good examples of this model in nation.

Type 3 C: The Libertarian Model. The individual owns both the right to send and the right to receive, and the society can limit these rights only to protect similar rights of other individuals. This is a pure form model, and the U.S. media system comes closest to it.

Type 3 D: The Model of Social Responsibility. The individual owns the right to receive, but society owns the right to send. Accordingly, society also has some control over what is received. This right is used mainly to protect the members of society against "harmful" communication, such as too much violence, explicit sex, abuse of children, or unwanted advertisements. This model is used in most Western-type democracies, although there are large variations in the degree of social control. The U.S. comes closest to this model.

REFERENCES

Becker, J., G. Hedebro, and L. Paldian (eds), 1986, *Communication and Domination: Essays to Honor Herbert I. Schiller.* Norwood, NJ: Ablex-Norwood.

Chopra, P., 1989, "Asian News Values: A Barrier or a Bridge?" In UNESCO, *News Values and Principles of Cross Cultural Communication.* No. 85 Paris.

da Costa, A. L., 1980, "New Criteria for the Selection of News in African Countries." In UNESCO, *News Values and Principles of Cross Cultural Communication.* No. 85, Paris.

Golding, P., and P. Elliott, 1979, Making the News, London, England.

MacBride Communication, 1981, "Communication Problems Today," pp. 35-55 in J. Richstad and M.A. Anderson (eds.) *Crisis in International News: Policies and Prospects.* New York: Columbia University Press.

Martin, L. J., and G. Chaudhary, 1983, *Comparative Mass Media Systems.* New York: Longman.

Meyer, W., 1989, "Global News Flows: Dependency and Neoimperialism," *Comparative Political Studies*. 22(3). 243-264.

Schiller, H. I., 1976, *Communication and Cultural Domination*. White Plains, NY: M.E. Sharpe.

Schramm, W. et al, 1978, *International News Wires and Third World News In Asia*. Hong Kong: Center for Communication Studies, University of Hong Kong.

Schramm, W. L., 1980, "Circulation of News in the Third World: A Study of Asia," pp. 589-619 in G.C. Wilhoit and H. Debock (eds.) *Mass Communication Review Yearbook*. Beverly Hills: Sage.

Stevenson, R. L., 1981, "Beyond Belgrade: Prospects for a Balanced Flow of Information." Presented to the International Studies Association, Philadelphia.

Weaver, D. H. and G. C. Wilhoit, 1984, "Foreign News and the Western Agencies," pp. 153-185 in R.L Stevenson and D. L. Shaw (eds.) *Foreign News and the News World Information Order*. Ames: Iowa State University Press.

SECTION III

MILITARISM VERSUS COMPETING APPROACHES TO ECONOMIC AND SOCIAL DEVELOPMENT

CHAPTER 9

THE REALITY OF THE "SUCCESS" OF STRUCTURAL ADJUSTMENT IN GHANA IN THE 1980'S

Benjamin Asare and Clifford L. Staten

In the 1989 Per Jacobsson Lecture, Ghana's High Commissioner to the United Kingdom, Dr. J. L. S. Abbey, commented on the successful structural adjustment process in Ghana during the 1980's:

> Since...[1983]...real output has expanded by about 40 percent; real per capita income by more than 20 per cent; the inflation rate, while still bothersome, has been dramatically reduced; the balance of payments in surplus and the initial large stock of external arrears has been virtually eliminated. The net domestic public debt has been almost eliminated. In this and other ways we have begun to repay our debt to future generations (Abbey, 1989).

Ghana has been lauded by the International Monetary Fund (IMF) and World Bank as the model for structural adjustment among the developing states of the world. But, what is the reality of this structural adjustment? It is important to go beyond the reporting of macroeconomic indicators of growth in order to illustrate the continuing problems in the cocoa industry such as its inability to meet production targets, the ongoing market bottlenecks, the problems created by the semi-feudal land tenure system, and the impact of the lack of direct access to the world market by the cocoa farmer. Additional concerns are the declining terms of trade in food, the negative impact of structural adjustment on traders, and the impact of budget cuts in the areas of health and social needs.

GHANA AS THE MODEL OF STRUCTURAL DEVELOPMENT

The design of the economic adjustment and recovery program which was developed with the IMF and supported by adjustment loans from the World Bank focused upon both stabilization and economic growth. Stabilization was achieved through devaluations of the cedi, an increase in official producer price (the price of cocoa), liberalization of imports, a curtailing of domestic deficit financing, an incomes policy, and tax reform. Tax reform, an incomes policy for the entire economy, and restraints on imported "conspicuous consumption" items such as luxury cars were developed to create the perception that the burden of adjustment was being placed on all sectors of society.

The promotion of real economic growth focused primarily upon the production and marketing of the primary foreign exchange earner - cocoa. This was achieved through higher producer prices, providing farmers with hybrid seedlings to replace those trees lost through brush fires in 1983 (loans from World Bank were crucial here), a streamlining of the organization of the Ghana Cocoa Board that enabled it to reduce its share of the revenue from cocoa and thus allow the cocoa farmer a higher price, and the expansion of extension services to cocoa farmers (Okyere, 1990).

The IMF and World Bank cite macroeconomic growth indicators as evidence in support of the success of the adjustment program in Ghana. Such statistics may include the following: real gross domestic product (GDP) exceeded the IMF target figures and grew by 8.7 percent in 1984 and by 5.1 percent in 1985; domestic inflation was reduced by 39.7 percent in 1984 and by 10.3 percent in 1985; and the overall fiscal position improved significantly (Heller, et al, 1988). Statistics focusing upon the cocoa industry indicate that between 1984 and 1987-88, nominal cocoa prices increased by five times, although real cocoa producer prices did not increase until 1985-86 (Green, 1989), and cocoa production increased from a low of 159,000 tons in 1983 to 228,000 tons in 1987 (Green, 1989 and Okyere, 1990). These data (and others) are used to promote Ghana as the model for structural adjustment in the developing world.

Yet by 1982, the economy of Ghana had deteriorated to the point that structural adjustment was necessary. Real per capita income was lower than in 1970 by 30 percent, real export earnings by 52 percent, and import volumes by 30 percent (Heller, et al, 1988). Agricultural output declined at a rate of 0.3 percent per year through the 1970's (Green, 1989), per capita food production in 1979-81 was 74 percent of that of 1969-71 (World Development Report, 1983) and the average daily caloric intake was 86 percent below the minimum standard of 3,000 calories a day (Asare, 1989). Allocations to economic infrastructure declined from a level of 20 percent of fiscal expenditures in 1953-60 to 7 percent by the end of the 1970's (Akoto, 1987). Runaway inflation estimated at 80 percent between 1976 and 1981 (World Bank, 1984), low investment levels, a shift by producers away from tradables to non-tradables, and reduced access to foreign borrowing also characterized the economy of Ghana in the early 1980's.

Ghana's major export - cocoa - experienced a decline from 36 percent of the world market share between 1960 and 1965 to around 17 percent by the early 1980's. Cocoa production declined from a high of 403,000 tons in 1969-70 to 179,000 tons by 1982-83 (Asare, 1986). By 1982, cocoa growers were receiving less than 17 percent of the 1960-63 real price and the smuggling of cocoa to neighboring countries was common due to the rapid appreciation of the cedi during the 1970's (Green, 1989).

Factors which are said to have contributed to this economic decline include severe droughts, the influx of emigrant workers returning from Nigeria, declining terms of trade, an overvalued exchange rate, depressed real wages, and a misaligned domestic relative price structure (Heller, et al, 1988 and Green, 1989).

CASTING DOUBT UPON GHANA AS THE MODEL OF STRUCTURAL ADJUSTMENT

Macroeconomic indicators of economic growth, reduced inflation, and balance of payments indicators can not tell the entire story of structural adjustment and, in the case of Ghana, it should be noted that growth indicators overestimate increased outputs and income because producers have shifted from the black market to the official market. Cocoa production is a case in point. Prior to structural adjustment, a significant amount of cocoa was sold by producers on the black market to neighboring Togo and the Ivory Coast. This was largely due to the fact that the cocoa farmers could receive a higher price on the black market than from the official price paid to them by the Ghana Cocoa Board. The World Bank and IMF admit that the growth of income and output indicated by the official data significantly overestimates the actual increase because it may represent a shift away from the black market and a return to the official market (Heller, et al, 1988). In 1984-85, cocoa production was only at 80 percent of its targeted levels, and, according to Commander (1989), much of that increase was due to the return to official marketing channels. Cocoa production in some areas of Ghana declined under structural adjustment. For example, production in the Ashanti region (a prominent cocoa producing region in Ghana) declined from 36 percent of the nation's total in 1981-82 to 25 percent in 1985 (Commander, 1989). Finally, if one accepts the increase in cocoa production at face value, it is still below the peak levels of the late 1960's (Commander, 1989).

A more important criticism of the focus on macroeconomic indicators is that economic and social development factors are just as important, if not more. There are some unanswered questions. Which sectors of Ghanian society have benefitted (experiencing growth) and which have not? Has income been redistributed and in what direction? How has it impacted indigenous food production? What about social programs? Have they suffered under structural adjustment? Is there a gender bias in the consequences? Answers to these types of questions will give one a more complete picture of structural adjustment in Ghana.

Mining and extractive industries and service sectors have grown at a faster rate and at the expense of the other sectors of the economy (Manuh, 1992). Those farmers that produce food for local consumption have not fared well during the structural adjustment process due to a 50 percent decline in real prices. There is no incentive to produce food for local consumption at current prices. Even though food is plentiful now, at current consumption levels and price trends, it is estimated that Ghana will experience significant food deficits by the turn of the century (Commander, 1989). The lack of access to credit by local food producers also exacerbates the future situation. In a survey of food producers in 1991, 91 percent stated that they had no access to credit facilities (Asare, 1991).

A staff study by the United States House of Representatives Subcommittee on Africa issued in March of 1989 noted a worsening of social inequality and poverty among some sectors in Ghana despite impressive economic growth. Manuh (1992) points out that higher cocoa prices worsen the differences in rural incomes because 32 percent of cocoa farmers earn 94 percent of cocoa income. In fact, this skewing of income among cocoa farmers is made even more dramatic when one notes that cocoa farmers receive only 30 percent of the total income from cocoa; the Ghana Cocoa Board receives 35 percent and the government receives the remaining 35 percent (Commander, 1989). In addition, devaluation of the cedi has resulted in higher costs to the cocoa farmers because tools, insecticides, sprayers, and other necessary items are imported.

Traders (most of whom are women) play a vital role in the economy because they serve as a link between producers and consumers (Clark, 1988), and they have witnessed a declining quality of life as a result of the structural adjustment program. Falling demand for their products caused by the devaluation of the cedi has resulted in no significant increase in the volume of trade since before the structural adjustment program. A lack of capital (about 90 percent have no access to institutional credit and must rely on money lenders or relatives) and increased taxes have adversely impacted traders. Higher costs for water, electricity, transportation, and health care have also adversely effected the standard of living for many traders and Ghanians. Goods are more available and there is a greater choice, but higher prices bar access to goods and services. Traders are excluded from the Programme of Action to Mitigate the Social Costs of Adjustment (PAMSCAD). Manuh (1992) argues that this exclusion reflects the historical pattern of the group's lack of power in the Ghanian political structure.

Capital outlays by the government collapsed to less than 2 percent of the GDP by 1986. As a result there has been a deterioration in basic infrastructure. Health and education expenditures have remained virtually the same throughout the period of structural adjustment. Health expenditures fluctuated between 1.1 and 1.3 percent of the GDP between 1985 and 1988, and education expenditures only increased from 3 to 3.5 percent during the same period, notwithstanding an estimated population growth rate of almost 3 percent (Republic of Ghana Statistical Service, 1988 and 1989). Real allocations in health and education fell considerably in the first phase of the structural adjustment program. By 1987 spending on health by the government was half the 1979-80 level if measured on a per capita basis (Commander, 1989).

Per capita incomes for urban inhabitants and non-cocoa farmers have fallen. It is important to note that income benefits for cocoa farmers have been extremely skewed toward the large cocoa farms. Furthermore, unemployment has continued to rise, to some extent due to layoffs in the public sector (Heller, et al, 1988).

A CRITIQUE OF STRUCTURAL ADJUSTMENT IN GHANA

A look at the macroeconomic indicators of structural adjustment presents a very different picture of Ghana than if one looks at the economic and social development indicators. Short term growth masks the economic and social indicators which show that future economic development in Ghana is in question. There are three major problems identified with the structural adjustment program of the IMF in Ghana. They are as follows: (l) the failure to address adequately the institutional bottlenecks to the development of agriculture - in particular the continuing lack of supporting inputs for agriculture, such as insecticides and extension services, the land tenure system, and the operation of the Ghana Cocoa Marketing Board; (2) the failure to use existing information sources, such as the Institute of Statistical Social and Economic Research at the University of Ghana, which would prevent the IMF from repeating past mistakes; and (3) the continued focus upon short term growth rather than long term economic development in Ghana.

1. Institutional Bottlenecks

The structural adjustment program in Ghana has failed to address the bottlenecks in the production of food for local consumption. Adequate extension services are crucial for the future production of food, but a recent survey 50.5 percent of the farmers indicated that there had been 2 or less visits by extension officers to their farms in the last season and 28 percent indicated that there had been no visits by extension officers in the last season (Asare, 1991). (Coupled with a decline in real prices this will produce food shortages in the near future).

Institutional bottlenecks in the production of cocoa have also not been addressed. Between 1982-83 and 1986, the price of pesticides quadrupled in nominal terms and the cost of mistblowers tripled in nominal terms from 1984-85 to 1986-87. The high cost and the unavailability of insecticides have led to a decline in their use, thus reducing the yield from the cocoa trees (Asare, 1986 and Commander, 1989). (It should be mentioned that low use of insecticides is perhaps a blessing for the environment and wildlife in Ghana.)

Another major obstacle to increasing the output of cocoa is the semi-feudal nature of the land tenure system. All land in the forest belt is communally owned by the local people and administered by the local chief who is the sole authority in the allocation of that land. A local citizen can establish a permanent right to the land as long as he or she cultivates it on a more or less continuous basis. Land not being used reverts back to the chief.

Non-local citizens or migrants gain acquisition to the land through tenancy. In most parts of the country, tenancy is the predominate mode of land acquisition. A study of the Sankore and Sehwi Asawinso districts indicates that 65 to 70 percent of the cocoa farmers are migrants (Asare, 1988). They must pay rents, tributes, and/or land taxes to the local chief. Commercial timber, minerals (note that in recent years the central government now allocates mineral concessions), and other natural resources from the land always remain the local and exclusive properties of the chiefs. At any time, the chief may grant the same land as a concession to a timber contractor (as an example), who in turn can cut down cocoa trees and destroy crops without compensating farmers. In the Asafo and Benchemaa districts, tenant farmers can not pass the land down to their heirs.

Since these tenant farmers do not hold titles to the land, it can not be used as collateral for farm improvement loans. This makes access to credit even more difficult for cocoa farmers. Rent paid to the chief amounts to 10 percent of the proceeds of the farm (note there is an effort to increase this to 33.3 percent) (Asare, 1988). In a survey of cocoa farmers, 67.5 percent indicated that the rent was too high and was not conducive to growth in cocoa production (Asare, 1988). In addition to rent, the migrant farmers must pay all expenses in any litigation that may involve the chief and they have social obligations which include bearing the cost of funeral expenses of any royalty and contributing towards the annual festival of the chiefs.

As a result, the land tenure system discourages innovation and development in the cocoa industry. Rent based on a fix proportion of the produce deters hard work because the more a farmer works and harvests, the more he/she must turn over to the rent collectors or the land-owning group. Most farmers are unwilling to spend money on improving their crop and increasing their productivity. The uncertainty of cocoa production and prices is aggravated by the uncertainty of land holdings and titles. Long term plans and investments are discouraged under such a system. Neither the government nor the IMF have addressed the land tenure problem. Future development of the cocoa industry and agricultural development in general will require a change in the land tenure system in Ghana (Asare, 1988).

The Ghanaian government operating through the Cocoa Marketing Board, which originated during the colonial period, determines the price the cocoa farmer receives for his produce. This prevents the farmer from gaining access to the world market. The income the farmer receives from his produce is the result of a bureaucratic decision rather than a function of the world market price. Thus, currency devaluation under IMF structural adjustment has no effect on the producer price and incomes of cocoa farmers (Asare, 1986).

2. **Existing Information Sources**

The Institute of Statistical Social and Economic Research at the University of Ghana contains a wealth of information concerning past experiments and studies of the cocoa industry, privatization, and economics in general. The IMF should establish a working relationship with the institute and make use of the already existing pool of data. This would avoid duplication of effort and prevent the IMF from repeating mistakes made in the past. A case in point involves the current effort to privatize the distribution of insecticides and other inputs to cocoa production. Past efforts and evidence indicate that privatization has failed for the following reasons: (1) given the nature of price fixing concerning inputs to agriculture, there are no incentives for private individuals to enter this economic sector, and (2) the need to establish depots (not to mention other infrastructure problems) throughout the country is cost prohibitive (Asare, 1986). The IMF must address these problems before privatization will occur.

3. **Focus on Short Term Rather Than Long Term**

Perhaps the major criticism of the IMF structural adjustment program in Ghana is its short term stabilization and growth orientation rather than placing emphasis upon a long term economic development strategy. Typically, once the IMF becomes involved in the economic and political processes of a developing country, it is an on-again off-again relationship over several years. In other words, it is there for the long term because, in most cases, its successes have been few. Future development (access to loans from the World Bank and other multilateral banks and private banks, as well as future private investment capital) is also dependent upon the IMF issuing a "bill of good health". Since the IMF is, for all practical purposes, in the business of long term development it makes sense for the IMF to begin with the assumption that a long term plan focusing upon development is necessary.

In Ghana, the IMF has been preoccupied with cocoa and cocoa production (cash crops in general). The primary reason for this focus is that it earns foreign exchange and in theory corrects the balance of payments. The problem is that this reflects the short term growth orientation which will contribute very little to long term economic development. If Ghana remains dependent upon the export of one primary commodity - cocoa - with its inelastic demand structure and increased production elsewhere, it will remain poor. A brief survey of other developing countries that export one primary commodity with an inelastic demand structure will find that the countries have one thing in common; they are all poor. What is needed is a strategy for economic diversification which will allow Ghana to begin to move away from dependence upon cocoa. Without this, Ghana is forever doomed to repetitive or continuous structural adjustment programs administered by the IMF.

Another problem created by the structural adjustment program is the growing external debt of Ghana. Total debt service as a percentage of exports of goods and services increased from 24 percent in 1985 to 61.4 percent in 1988 (World Bank Debt Tables, 1988-89). This will have a debilitating impact on the future prospects for the economic development of Ghana.

CONCLUSION

This brief study indicates comparison of aggregate, macroeconomic growth data with social and economic development data documents a mixed picture concerning the "success" of structural adjustment in Ghana. There are three shortcomings of the IMF structural adjustment program in Ghana: 1) the program does not adequately address the structural bottlenecks in the cocoa industry; 2) it does not take advantage of existing data concerning the cocoa industry; and 3) it focuses upon short term growth rather than long term development. Long term development of the cocoa industry will not improve until the semi-feudal nature of the land tenure system is addressed and until the cocoa farmer has direct access to the world market.

It is especially important that the IMF take advantage of the expertise and data which already exist in Ghana. This will save time, duplication of effort, and, perhaps more importantly, it will allow local experts to participate in the design of the program, not just in its implementation.

> ... an adjustment program must be... designed to fit local conditions. Indigenous research institutions... have a major role to play. Local design is the most important factor for reform programs to be perceived by the population as their own. In addition, the credibility of the government and the population's confidence that the economic policymakers know what they are doing will be enhanced (Mills, 1989).

The major criticism of the structural adjustment program in Ghana (and in most of the developing countries for that matter) is that it is preoccupied with short and medium term stabilization and growth rather than long term economic development.

> The time horizon for adjustment has been biased toward the short and medium terms, with a tendency for such longer-term variables as education, skills development ... thrust aside (Mills, 1989).

Future development in Ghana is dependent upon diversification of the economy, the ability to meet its own food demands, a favorable international environment, and a population that has confidence in the government's ability to meet its needs. Even if the bottlenecks in the cocoa industry are solved, this will not benefit Ghana in the long run. The IMF has been working with Ghana for many years now. It is time to develop a long range plan in cooperation with local officials rather than a continuing series of short and medium term stabilization and growth plans.

BIBLIOGRAPHY

Abbey, J. L. S. 1989. On Promoting Successful Adjustment: Some Lessons from Ghana. In *The 1989 Per Jacobsson Lecture.* Washington, D.C. International Monetary Fund.

Akoto, O.A. 1987. Agricultural Development Policy in Ghana. *Food Policy.* August.

Asare, Benjamin. 1986. *Urbanization and Agricultural Development: The Cocoa Economy in Ghana.* Unpublished dissertation. Temple University.

Asare, Benjamin. 1988. Land Tenure Norms Among Cocoa Farming Communities in Ghana An Approach to Land Reform. Paper delivered to the Association for the Advancement of Policy and Research in the 3rd World, Myrtle Beach, S.C.

Asare, Benjamin. 1989. The African Food Crisis, Cross-Cultural Factors in the Problem: A Study of Ghana and Uganda. Unpublished manuscript.

Asare, Benjamin. 1990. Sociology of Urban Population Growth in Ghana. Paper delivered to the Association for the Advancement of Policy and Research in the 3rd World, Mexico City, Mexico.

Asare, Benjamin, 1991. Survey, Tono Irrigation Project in Ghana. (Grant from Indiana University President's Council on International Programs, Bloomington, IN.)

Clark, Gracia. 1988. *Traders Versus the State.* Boulder: Westview Press.

Commander, Simon, John Howell, and Wayo Seini. 1989. Ghana 1983-87. In Simon Commander, ed. *Structural Adjustment and Agriculture.* London Overseas Development Institute.

Green, Reginald Herbold. 1989. Articulating Stabilization Programmes and Structural Adjustment Sub-Saharan Africa. In Simon Commander, ed. *Structural Adjustment and Agriculture.* London Overseas Development Institute.

Heller, Peter, A. Lans Bovenberg, Thanos Catsambas, Ke-Young Chu, and

Parthasarath Shome. 1988. *The Implications of Fund Supported Adjustment Programs for Poverty Experiences in Selected Countries.* Washington, DC: International Monetary Fund.

Manuh, Takyiwaa. 1992. Structural Adjustment and Women in Ghana. Paper delivered to the International Consortium for International Programs Conference on Economic Liberalization and Political Transformation: Perspectives from Africa, Asia, and Latin America. Brown County State Park, Indiana.

Mills, Cadman Atta 1989. *Structural Adjustment in Sub-Saharan Africa.* Washington, DC World Bank.

Okyere, W. Asenso. 1990. The Response of Farmers to Ghana's Adjustment Policies. In Zafar Ahmed, et al, ed. *The Long Term Perspective Study of Sub-Saharan Africa: Economic and Sectoral Policy Issues.* Washington, DC World Bank.

Republic of Ghana Statistical Service. 1988. *Ghana Living Standards Survey.* Accra: Government of Ghana.

Republic of Ghana Statistical Service. 1989. *Quarterly Digest of Statistics.* Accra: Government of Ghana.

Staten, Clifford L. 1991. Comparative IMF Conditionality, Income Inequality, and Political Instability: A Research Note. Unpublished manuscript.

U.S. Congress, House Committee on Foreign Relations, Subcommittee on Africa. March 1989. Report on Senegal and Ghana. 101st Congress, Washington, DC: Government Printing Office.

World Bank. 1984. *Ghana: Managing the Transition.* Washington, DC: World Bank.

World Bank Debt Tables. 1988-89. Washington, DC: World Bank.

World Development Report. 1983. Washington, DC: World Bank.

CHAPTER 10

DIALECTICS OF INSTITUTIONAL VIOLENCE: THE CASE OF ZAIRE

Ezabele Wa Yasak

Zaire produced enough food to be self-sufficient in 1960 but has subsequently had to depend on food aid continuing into 1992. Is this decline in food self-sufficiency due to lack of resources, climatic and geographic reasons, or to political factors resulting in the exploitation of farmers?

There are many interesting and outstanding facts about Zaire. With an area of 2,344,885 square kilometers (905,365 square miles), Zaire is Africa's third largest country in land area, and Zaire is richer in minerals than other countries in Africa. In addition, the soil is rich and soft for agriculture and its tropical climate has an average temperature of 27 Celsius degrees (80 Farenheit degrees) and an annual rainfall of 150 to 200 centimeters. In spite of these favorable factors, Zaire has performed poorly in food production.

This study is meant to provide a better understanding of the structural and political issues in the agricultural system and to establish internal and external responsibilities. It will address such questions as: 1) Are farmers consulted by government and international organizations about social and economic policies that affect them? 2) With their income, can farmers afford fertilizer or seed at the government ordained prices? 3) Do farmers have access to credit for machinery, fertilizer and seed, efficient methods or modern tools, and other facilities used to avoid losing crops? 4) Do farmers get technical, financial, marketing or any other assistance from State/Central Government agencies ?

THEORETICAL APPROACHES

The general rule of social theory states that when seeking to explain a part of something such as oppression and exploitation of farmers in Zaire, it is of the metropolis-satellites structure of capitalism.

In 1960, agricultural production was sufficient to meet the usual needs of urban and rural populations. In 1992, there were nutrition problems primarily affecting poor people who are about 80% of the population in rural areas according to U.N.D.P., (1990:58). Zaire is potentially one of the richest countries, yet it has performed poorly in food production. The decline in food production is due not to a lack of resources or climatic and geographic reasons but mainly to political factors leading to the exploitation and oppression of farmers (institutional violence). A proof that Zaire has performed poorly can be seen in an excerpt from the World Bank Annual Report (1990:105) as pointed out by the table below.

Table Nº1. Africa: 1988 Population and Per Capita GNP of Countries That Borrowed during Fiscal Years 1988 - 1990.

Country	Population[a] (thousands)	Per Capita GNP[b] (US$)
Benin	4,449	390
Burkina Faso	8,539	210
Burundi	5,140	240
Cameroon	11,184	1.010
Cape Verde	360	680
Central Africa Republic	2,869	380
Chad	5,398	160
Congo, People's Republic of the	2,139	910
Cote d'ivoire11,225770		
Djibouti	n.a.	n.a.[c]
Ethiopia	47,356	120

Gabon	1,077	2,970
Gambia, The	822	200
Ghana	13,977	400
Guinea	5,401	430
Guinea-Bissau	940	190
Kenya	22,446	370
Lesotho	1,676	420
Madagascar	10,859	190
Malawi	7,960	170
Mali	7,983	230
Mauritania	1,909	480
Mauritius	1,051	1,800
Mozambique	14,943	100
Niger	7,256	300
Nigeria	110,068	290
Rwanda	6,656	320
Sao Tome and Principe	119	490
Senegal	6,996	650
Somalia	5,902	170
Sudan	23,777	480
Tanzania	24,728	160[d]
Togo	3,381	370
Uganda	16,211	280
Zaire	33,366	170
Zimbabwe	9,303	650

Source: The World Bank Annual Report 1990.

Note: The 1988 estimates of GNP per capita presented above are from the "World Development Indicators" section of World Development Report 1990.

n.a. : not available.

b : World Banks Atlas methodology, 1986-88 base period.

c : GNP per capita estimated to be in the lower-middle-income range.

d : GNP per capita refers to mainland Tanzania only.

Violence is presented as the exclusive property of the poor in the slums, the minorities, street gangs, and so on. However, if we analyze the concept of violence, we can easily understand that there are two kinds of violence: 1) individual violence and 2) institutional violence. Within Zaire, the political and economic systems violate farmers in their daily lives by denying opportunities for adequate incomes and decent living conditions. Farmers may even be removed from their land, with or without compensation.

Alexander Liazos notes that institutional violence is much more destructive than individual violence (1976:91). In Zaire, violence is committed daily by the government through imprisonment, expropriation, fires, and other neo-colonial administrative pressures.

POLITICAL PRESSURES

In Zaire, the constitutional crisis during 1960-1965 led to many deaths including the assassination of Prime Minister Lumumba; even more people have been killed since then (from 1965 to 1992) than before. In addition, people have been living under a military dictatorship regime. The symbolic division of power between the Government, the Legislative Branch, and the Judiciary have become the institutions of the M.P.R, the sole political party known as mono-party-state (Movement Populaire de la Revolution). All citizens became automatically life members from birth! The President was the only person not considered an organ of the M.P.R as described in the Constitution until its revision in 1978. The President incarnates the M.P.R and is the embodiment of Zaire in its political organization; he stands above the organs of the M.P.R such as the Congress, the Legislative, the Executive, and the Judiciary Councils; he presides over all. The President has been free to change, at will, any membership of the organs described above.

The so-called presidential election has led very often to a result of 99.99% voting for the victor! People have been obliged to vote or they will be in trouble (paying fees, imprisonment when they fail to show the proof requested everywhere at any time in Zaire of participation in the election process). In fact, in rural areas, the farmers who do not carry their proofs of participation in the election process into the fields may have to pay fees (cash orders or goods such as pigs, goats, bananas) or work as a punishment in the field of the local President of the M.P.R. People may be jailed or forced to work for several months as a punishment for not having come to the M.P.R meeting or for having refused to sing and dance for the M.P.R or for having criticized the M.P.R

In addition, the rural areas have been neglected, and, therefore, being sent back to the home village is considered to be a punishment. Any seller in the city who increases the prices of his articles may be sent back to the home village. Many professors and students have been sent to their villages for criticism against the M. P. R. It is not permissible to establish another political party or to congregate at home without written permission signed by the head of local government; thirteen members of the National Legislative Council were imprisoned and sent to their villages for establishing another political party known as the Union Pour la Democratie et le Progress Social (U. D. P. S.).

According to Campbell (1991:303), "land conflict and intensification of land use are characteristic of contemporary conditions in a number of African countries. The most common explanation for this is the population growth and high rural population densities." However, the greater reason is political oppression. The political violations that have been described have had economic and social implications.

ECONOMIC AND SOCIAL IMPLICATIONS

Farmers are not consulted by those in their own government or by international organizations about economic and social policies that affect them. As a result, many projects in Zaire and even throughout Africa have failed as pointed out by David Simon (1989:42). "Many supposedly sustainable projects that have been implemented in recent years turned out to be totally unsustainable for various reasons, including lack of appropriate objectives or scales or inadequate provision for participation and control by the supposed beneficiaries". Furthermore, the transport system for export built since colonization has not been sufficiently modified. Zaire did extend the transport system by building, for instance, Kisangani International Aeroport, Marechal bridge, and so on. However, local roads needed to transport goods have not been improved. To illustrate current transportation problems, you may fly by plane from Kisangani to Belgium in six hours, but it may easily take two to seven days by car from Kisangani to Opala (125 Km). Farmers lose crops because roads are inadequate for transportation of perishable goods to areas where they are needed and could be sold.

The economic and social policies have resulted in farmers having insufficient income to afford fertilizer or seed at the government ordained prices. They do not have access to credit for machinery, fertilizer, or seeds. They do not have the opportunity to learn efficient methods or to use modern tools to avoid losing crops. Because the price of cotton or coffee is low, many farmers have abandoned agriculture for gold, diamonds and ivory (1985:7-16). Hence, Zaire has to rely on food aid and in 1992 cannot even afford to import food! Food costs are high, and in many cities such as Kinshasa, Kisangani, Lubumbashi, Kananga, Mbuji-Mayi, people live from day to day (1990:3), eating whatever they can get. People seldom eat fish and meat in 1992 because they are too expensive; people are vegetarians despite Zaire's rivers with abundant fish.

The economic and social situations were better in 1960 than they are in 1992. According to F.A.O. Food Aid Figures (1991:152), Zaire is one of the low-income food deficit and less developed countries. The national budget is not used for agriculture development, social welfare or education but for maintaining an army which includes a paramilitary force, the Gendarmerie and a civil guard responsible for securing the regime and anti-terrorist operations. According to the *Europa World Year Book*, (1991:152) and U.N.D.P. (1990: 77) defense expenditures for 1989 were estimated at 27,119 m Zaires (7.5%) of the total expenditure by the central government while social welfare was estimated at 5,427 m Zaires (1.5%) of the total expenditure. According to estimates by UNESCO, the average rate of adult illiteracy in 1990 was 28.2% (males 16.4% and females 39.3%). Yet, in the budget for 1989, only 24,291.5 m Zaires (6.7%) of the total expenditure by the central government was allocated to education.

Zaire has served as a convenient battle ground for cold war rivalries between the superpowers. Aid received has led to re-colonization of Zaire (Mende, 1973; Jaler, 1968). As highlighted by Ted Trainer (1989:99), "in giving aid the primary purpose of most capitalist governments... is to preserve their own economic and political interests in the recipient countries." Aid has been wasted in the form of luxury consumption and unproductive investments and expenditures, often resulting in expensive projects without direct benefit for the majority of people.

CONCLUSION

In 1960, agricultural production of foods in Zaire was sufficient to meet the usual needs of rural and urban populations, and commercial crops, largely for exports, were also produced in large quantities, earning about two-fifths of Zaire's annual foreign exchange receipts (1979:206). This situation changed drastically, however, between 1960 and 1966 as civil disturbance and physical insecurity affected rural populations in rural and urban areas. The transport system -agricultural feeder roads and the like were damaged or deteriorated from lack of maintenance (1979:206). While wages and salaries have remained very low, there has been a continuous increase in the price of food, especially in urban areas, and hence a spread of malnutrition. Furthermore, Zaire's capacity to import food has been hampered by both low prices for exported raw materials and a heavy debt burden. Finally, the share of foreign exchange earned by the agricultural sector is declining.

So, Zaire's capacity to feed itself has declined as a result of colonial and neo-colonial development as well as internal and external factors. As pointed out by Campbell (1990:236): "Africa's capacity to feed itself has declined as a consequence of colonial and post colonial development. One aspect of this decline is a reduction in availability and efficacy of traditional strategies for coping with food shortage related to the change in local production patterns and their incorporation into national and international systems".

The logic of the world market makes it "sensible" for a country to let its people hunger while it fattens up foreigners. Institutional violence is exemplified at the international level by allocation of the best land in Zaire for producing export crops rather than for production of food for Zaire's people. Danman (1979:95) estimated that 110 million acres of Third World land was allocated to produce crops for export to rich countries. "For the cultivation of coffee, tea and cocoa alone, the rich countries use about 40 million acres in the third world". Harrington (1977:157) noted that: "The poor countries make a major contribution to the diet of the rich. And the rich want to keep it that way".

In Senegal, American Transnational Bud Antle... has established huge irrigated "garden plantations" on land from which peasants have been removed. These plantations produce vegetables in the Winter and feed for livestock for export in Summer. None of these products are eaten in Senegal... This process is occurring in all of North Africa. In Ethiopia, thousands of people were evicted to make way for agribusiness and then starved to death. International firms are producing alfalfa to feed livestock in Japan... During the Sahelian famine, the acreage planted to groundnuts in Senegal was increasing, while that planted to sorghum and millet for local consumption was actually decreasing" (1989:110).

Structural and political issues at national and international levels have led to low income of farmers and perpetuation of poor living conditions. For instance, the transportation system in Zaire as well as in other countries in the Third World is designed for exportation and not for the development of the people. The hospitals and schools are in poor condition and are very often closed in the rural areas of Zaire. Farmers have low income, few resources and cannot afford fertilizer or seed at the government ordained prices. According to F.A.O., (1984), Zaire has an abundance of available land, but available land use for permanent crop production per farm operation is less than 1 hectare (the average size in the U.S.A. is 85.52 hectares per farmer). Mbongolo Ndundu Mputela (1992) pointed out that "Zairian fertilizer consumption per hectare of available land is only 1.3 Kg of plant nutrition while in a developed country such as Belgium, fertilizer consumption has reached the high level of 499 Kg". Agriculture for what and for whom is the question.

Zaire needs a political and moral renewal with new established institutions, not old wine in new bottles. The government in Zaire has been used to check Soviet expansionism. Aid has been provided without attention to massive violations of human rights including institutional violence against farmers. In 1992, the geopolitical equation has changed and we hope the end of the military dictatorship and its institutional violence is at hand. The people of Zaire hope to get back their rights of political, economical, cultural and social choices that have been denied since 1960. Successful economic development in Zaire must begin with modernization in the agricultural sectors. The national budget must be used for scientific, technological and agricultural developments. Farmers must be consulted about economic and social policies that affect them rather than having communications that are only uni-directional from rather than having communications that are only uni-directional from government and international experts to the people. All should work together to help people in countries like Zaire determine their economic and political priorities.

REFERENCES

American University, Foreign areas studies: Zaire, A Country Study, 1979.

Bongeli Yeikelo Ya Ato.Pour un autre development des entitités rurales au Zaire Le cas de zone rurale de Gungu, *Analyses Sociales.* Volume II, Numero 4, Juillet - Aout 1985. pp. 25 - 42.

Campbell David J. Community Based Strategies for Coping With Food Scarcity: A Role in African Famine Early Warning Systems, *GeoJournal.* 20, 3 March 1990:231 - 241.

Campbell David J. and Olson Jennifer M. Environment and Development in Kenya; Flying the Kite in Kajialbo District. *The Centennial Review* 35, 2 (Spring 1991): 245 - 314.

Danman, E. *Future in Our Hands.* London, Pergamon, 1979 pp. 79.

Europa World Year Book. Volume II, 1991.

Ezabele Wa Yasak. Exploitation antisanale d'or et son impact sur la societé environnante. *Analyses Sociales.* Volume II, Numero I Janvier - Fevrier, 1985.

Ezabele wa Yasak. "Gong Unique" Problems of Nutrition in Zaire. In Zaire - American Language Institute Newsletter. Kinshasa, Zaire, Volume I, N°2, 1990.

FAO 1990. Food Aid Figures Volume 8/1, cited by *The EUROPA WORLD*, Year

Gunder Andre Frank. Dependance and Underdevelopment, Latin America's Political Economy, *Anchor Books Edition*, U.S.A., 1972.

Harrington. *The Vast Majority*, London, MacMillan, pp 157.

Jaler, Pierre. *The Pillage of the Third World*, Monthly Review Press, New York, 1968.

Kennedy John F. Some Important Issues in Foreign Aids. Committee on Foreign relations, U.S. Senate, Washington, D.C. Report prepared by the Legislative Reference Service of the Library of Congress, 1966, pp. 15.

Liazos, Alexander. Deviance and Social Control. The Poverty of the Sociology of Deviance; Sluts and Prevers, in Readings in Social Problems. 76/77 Annual Edition 1976 Dushkin Publishing Inc.

Mende Tibor. *From Aid to Re-colonization, Lessons of failure* . Pantheon Books New York, 1973.

Mbongolo Ndundu Mputela. The Role of Women Farmers in Managing Cassava Production in Bandundu (Zaire). Paper presented at the 11th Annual Symposium Farming Systems Research and Extension in the 1990s, Critical Issues and Future Directions. Michigan State University. October 5 - 10, 1991.

Murdoch, W. *The Poverty of Nations: The Political Economy of Hunger and Population,* Baltimore, Johns Hopkins. 1980.

Sengi Bangama Likondo. De l'articulation des mode de production dans la zone rurale de Wamba. Memoire de Licence en Sociologie Rurale, Université de Lubumbashi, Juillet, 1982.

Simon, David. Sustainable Development: Theoretical Construct or Attainable Goal? *Environmental Conservation.* 16,1 (Spring 1989): 41 48.

Trainer Ted. *Developed to Death: Rethinking Third World Development.* The Merlin Press Ltd., 1989.

UNDP. Human Development Report 1990, New York, Oxford, 1990.

World Bank. Annual Report, 1990.

World Bank. Agricultural Research Sector Policy Paper, June 1991.

CHAPTER 11

SOMALIAN CRISIS AND PAN-AFRICANISM

Safro Kwame

In the wake of the 21 year old dictatorship of ousted President Mohammed Siad Barre, Somalia has attracted global attention. Nowhere do so many millions of people continue to be poised so precariously on the brink of death, the United Nations Secretary-General reports. Nowhere are the margins of survival so slim, the resources so scant and the future so bleak. Somalia is a country where (a) there are "incredible scenes of hunger, disease and dying children," (b) hospitals are without water, electricity, drugs or even basic medical equipment, and (c) political and military leaders with their armed teenage escorts rob their own people of the food that has been donated to the starving.

> It was like the apocalypse, the end of the world, reported French photojournalist Maya Vidon after a three-week tour of tragedy-stricken Somalia. There she witnessed sights - looting, shooting, starvation, death - which she said, "made me forbid myself to think, to feel" (UN Chronicle: 1992).

LESSONS FROM SOMALIA ON PAN-AFRICANISM

If Kwame Appiah is right, conflicts such as the Somali one - like the Liberian, Ethiopian, Angolan, and Nigerian (Biafran) ones - point out the problem with Pan-Africanism as a movement for the unity of people of the black race or, as Appiah puts it, Africa as a racial mythology. Pan-Africanism cannot account for the disunity among Africans that establishments such as the Organization of African Unity (OAU) have been struggling unsuccessfully against:

> Race disables us because it proposes as a basis for common action the illusion that black (and white and yellow) people are fundamentally allied by nature and, thus, without effort; it leaves us unprepared, therefore, to handle the "intraracial" conflicts that arise from the very different situations of black (and white and yellow) people in different parts of the economy and of the world (Appiah: 1992).

A biologically rooted conception of race is both dangerous in practice and misleading in theory.

African unity and African identity need securer foundations than race. This was evidenced by Kwame Nkrumah's abortive efforts to establish an executive arm of the OAU's Assembly of Heads of States and Government about which he lamented in the last years of his life (Nkrumah: 1973). Africa is a geographic entity - the second largest continent in the world - with a population of over 500 million people speaking more than 1,000 languages

Not all of its inhabitants (e.g. some in North Africa and the Comoro Islands) consider themselves part of the same race. Hence, a Pan-Africanist movement such as Nkrumah's which is rooted in DuBois' and others' attempts to unify the black race is bound to fail if, in addition, there are all those political differences (e.g. in ideology) and superpower alliances with which to contend.

Any attempt to unify blacks or Africans is unlikely to be successful without an understanding of black-on-black violence and some resolution of disunifying factors. When both the victims and aggressors are black and often the perpetrators are (otherwise) relatively free and responsible adults, racial explanations - especially of a Pan-Africanist type are neither interesting nor enlightening.

It is important to note, as Appiah does, that the attempt to ground Pan-Africanism in racialism is not, exclusively, an American project. Nkrumah's conception of Pan-Africanism, like DuBois', was more deeply rooted in socialism than some of his American and, also, African counterparts. DuBois told the Sixth Pan-African Congress held in Accra, Ghana, in 1958: "your bond is not mere color of skin but the deeper experience of wage slavery and contempt" (Paschal: 1976, 465). According to Nkrumah, "the Pan-Africanism which found expression at the Congress (1945) and the All-African People's Conference (1958) was based on the age-old aspiration towards unity of all peoples of African origin exploited as workers and as a race" (Paschal: 1976, 465). This, for Nkrumah, implies (i) the eradication of imperialism, neocolonialism, and foreign oppression in all forms, (ii) a socialistic and continental form of government in Africa, and (iii) a military high command for Africa:

> At the core of the concept of African unity lies socialism and the socialist definition of the new African society ...the unity of the African people expressed in a Union Government is necessary... Members of AAPRA (The All-African People's Revolutionary Army) will be the armed representatives of the African people's socialist parties struggling against colonialism and neo-colonialism (Paschal: 1976, 466-467, 487).

An effective Organization of African Unity with a Union Government and an All-African People's Revolutionary Army should be able to do both what the American-led military relief mission to Somalia did - i.e. provide immediate food aid - and what the American-led military relief mission under Operation Restore Hope could not do - i.e. end the war. Unfortunately, Pan-Africanism, as conceived by DuBois and modified by Nkrumah, was not meant to deal with the exploitation of Africans by Africans (Black-on-Black exploitation) or to deal with African dictators of whom Nkrumah was one. It mainly aimed at ending White-on-Black exploitation as if that was not only necessary but sufficient. From all indications, the Somalis as well as the Liberians would rather see American forces and personnel than an all African force or secretariat. Unfortunately it seems that Africans have been less successful than foreigners in trying to solve such problems in the post cold war era.

Even though Nkrumah recognized at Ghana's 1957 independence that "our independence is meaningless unless it is linked up with the total liberation of the African continent, Appiah noted how puzzling such Nkrumalist claims sound when elaborated upon:

> To a person unencumbered with the baggage of the history of the idea of race, it would surely seem strange that the independence of one nation of black men and women should resonate more with black people than with other oppressed people; strange too that it should be the whiteness of the oppressors--"the white man"--as opposed, say, to their *imperialism*, that should stand out. (Nkrumah: 1973, 45).

A NEW WORLD ORDER

Nkrumah's remarks - like DuBois' - concerning the connection between socialism and socialism and Pan-Africanism are particularly interesting in the light of the new world order marked by the collapse of the socialist world of the Soviet bloc and the lack of competition for the support, sympathy and solidarity for/with African and other Third World countries. Without the cold war and without the need for the support or allegiance of Third World countries in a fight among superpowers, Africans must devote more time, effort and resources to our own political, social, and economic problems. Dictatorships practiced in the name of socialism or capitalism are not adequate to the tasks of African governance, and the Somali case appears to be a confirmation of this thesis. Siad Barre's flirtation first with Soviet socialism and then with American capitalism while practicing dictatorship helped neither himself nor his country avoid poverty, violence or disaster.

There is no reason to think we Africans can succeed where the Soviets have failed. Socialism did not succeed in freeing the masses from the dictatorships and the scarcities in the East. There is hardly enough evidence to think that it will do so in Africa. A dictatorship, even of the proletariat, is a negation of freedom and is subject to the abuses that were evident in the administrations of the Nkrumahs of Ghana, the Mengistus of Ethiopia, the Siad Barres of Somalia, the Idi Amins of Uganda, and the Bokassas of the Central African Republic. Such dictatorships have no checks on abuses, no balances to unlimited power, no reason to honor the wishes of the masses, and no fear of losing power to the opposition. One of the lessons from Somalia and elsewhere in Africa is that, unless we move away from the brutal and insensitive dictatorships that have persisted for many years over an impoverished majority, Somali-type disasters are likely to occur in a world in which the superpowers no longer compete for allies in the Third World. Herein lies the problem with Karl Marx's and Fredrich Engles' dictatorship of the proletariat as the means to a free and egalitarian society and also the problem with Nkrumah's requirement that socialism be the means to a free, united and egalitarian African continent.

Both capitalism and socialism can be practiced in the worst forms of dictatorships. An alternative for Africa could be a system in which there would be room for both a type of socialism and a type of Pan-Africanism which recognized African solidarity while building an efficient and sensitive welfare system of some sort for the bulk of Africa's hungry, poor, and sick masses. African governance should not be a dictatorship of black people exploiting black people while maintaining opposition to the exploitation of black people by white people who are capitalists! A foundation is needed for development of a system of accountability and efficiency that takes account of human fallibility and imperfection as well as the African experience.

Ultimately, the lesson from Somalia on Pan-Africanism in the new world order would be one about responsive internal government and continental cooperation such as would put the interests of the poor, sick, and hungry masses above those of military and civilian dictators. That is a way to make a serious attempt at avoiding tragedies such as the Somali one or to attempt to solve them when they occur. That is a way to try to ensure total internal and external liberation of the African continent and meaningful independence. To depend on the whims of a dictator and the generosity of charitable foreign organizations - which, in my opinion, is an accurate description of the Somali experience - is to be independent of nothing but reality. In this sense Nkrumah was right, that African independence was meaningless unless it was linked up with the total liberation of the African continent. However, Nkrumah also thought African independence was meaningless unless it led to a union government of Africa under socialism. This interpretation amounted to a Soviet experiment in Africa. If we are right, that kind of experiment would fail, not because it is socialism, but because it is dictatorship.

To ensure the kind of meaningful independence we envision, no one should be allowed to rule for more than 10 years. Preferably, governments should rule for 7 years or less in short terms of approximately three and a half years each. Such changes in government generate hope and are necessary, though not sufficient, for progress in solving our economic and political problems and getting rid of useless governments. If this were guaranteed on a continental basis (a) by recognizing a moral, human or natural right to overthrow any government which overstays and (b) by not recognizing such governments which overstay in power, then other African countries and societies may, thereby, be able to apply some form of social sanctions and pressure for accountability in Africa. Additionally, Africa needs its counterparts to the International Red Cross and Peace Corps that will provide a network of voluntary and humanitarian services on a regular basis without having to rely on the generosity of American or foreign governments and charitable organizations as in the Somali relief effort.

Coming in the wake of famine in Ethiopia, the Sudan, and elsewhere in Africa, and the economic and political disintegration of the Soviet bloc, the famine in Somalia suggests that there will be more hunger, suffering, and death in Africa if the following conditions prevail: (a) there is no serious superpower rivalry, (b) Africa does not have a peaceful way of getting rid of dictators - benevolent or otherwise, and (c) Africa does not pull its human and natural resources together in an effective way. The argument for Pan-Africanism in the wake of the cold war needs more grounding in African internal affairs rather than African external affairs. The old African order of tribalism and dictatorship needs to give way in the new world order, and the arguments for and against Pan-Africanism need to be revisited.

REFERENCES

Appiah, Kwame, E. 1992. In My Father's House: Africa in the Philosophy of Culture. New York: Oxford University Press.

Encyclopedia Britannica. 15th ed. Vol. 13. Chicago: Encyclopedia Britannica Inc. p. 60, 62.

Nkrumah, Kwame. 1973. Revolutionary Path. London: Panaf Books Ltd.

Paschal, Andrew. ed. 1976. A W.E.B. DuBois Reader. New York, Collier Books: MacMillian Publishing Co.

U.N. Chronicle. 1992. XXIX, No. 4, p. 5.

SECTION IV

CULTURAL AND SPIRITUAL CONNECTIONS

CHAPTER 12

THE ROLE OF ISLAM AND CHRISTIANITY IN DEVELOPMENT IN WEST AFRICA

Donald Bobb

Neither Islam nor Christianity is inherent in West African culture. Though brought to some parts of the Sahel perhaps a millennium ago, Islam has, by its absolute revelation and foreign nature, periodically struggled to make its communities more orthodox, hence, more Arabized, while at the same time permitting a syncretism with African culture. Christianity, strong in the southern coastal regions, is also absolute and foreign, but has historically rejected syncretism; within the past two decades, Christianity has consciously sought to permit the faith to become rooted in African culture, hence Africanize.

With the exception of the Sudan, the confrontation between the two world faiths is unique and more acute in West Africa than in other parts of the continent.

This paper draws its material from articles that have appeared in periodicals during the years 1984-1986, from books and writings of Christian and Muslim scholars over the past two decades, and from personal experiences in Christian-Muslim relations in francophone West Africa, 1978-81.

Based on 1972 statistics in The Gospel and Islam: A 1978 *Compendium*,[1] which lists the total population of fourteen West African countries committing Mauritania and Cape Verde as 105,565,000 (now probably doubled), 44.6% of the population was Muslim, 19.1% Christian. It is a safe estimate that easily another 10-20% has identified with one or the other religions, with a larger number adhering to Islam. In Nigeria today, with probably 100,000,000 people, the percentages are much closer, with Islam having a slight majority.

The purpose of this paper is to look at the role that these two faith communities have played in the overall development of the peoples of West

Africa. By "development" is meant those programs and projects that include education, agriculture, community organization, social services and vocational training. Also included are the emotional stabilization and spiritual enrichment provided by affiliation with one of the two world religions. They will be studied in their: 1) functions as religious groups, 2) involvement in development, and 3) relationships and community life. An attempt at a prognosis for the future will serve as conclusion.

FUNCTION AND RELIGIOUS GROUPS

Robin Horton has referred to traditional African religion as a two-tiered cosmos, with lesser beings in close touch with humans, and a Supreme Being overarching all the universe. It is his claim that Islam and Christianity came on the African scene as catalysts for changes that were "already in the air." [2]

In a debate with him spanning more than a decade, Humphrey Fisher has maintained that Africans have incorporated the religions as their own and have not merely mused them as catalysts. Unlike Horton, who feels all Africans share the same cosmic view, regardless of their religious persuasion, and seriously doubts their real "conversion," Fisher maintains that "conversion" is a positive element in African development. His alternative theory suggests three stages of religious growth: 1) quarantine (the coming of the trader, of missionary as stranger), 2) mixing (conversions create a new religious community), and 3) reform (the new community must analyze its position and relevance to the larger indigenous community).

In the reform stage, Islam and Christianity followed different patterns. Islam followed external models from the Muslim world in developing *tariqas* or mystical brotherhoods, now being critically reformed today by Saudi-inspired Wahhabi orthodoxy. Christianity has demonstrated greater identification of the faith with the African context, in an "incarnation within" Africa, as opposed to an "adaptation to" Africa. Because Christianity omitted the mixing stage, it must now recover the values overlooked. [3] Both faiths move under their own momentum, always acting and reacting to the external world to which they are related.

Both Islamic and Christian communities reveal divisions, making it difficult to generalize and make authoritative statements. For example, in Nigeria during the constitutional crisis and proposed inclusion of the *sharia*, it was found that Muslims might be related to a Sufi-type brotherhood, orthodox *ulamas*, millennial Mahdi movements or militant fundamentalists, not necessarily sharing the same viewpoints. Christians may be Roman Catholic, Protestant/Anglican, or Evangelical/Fundamentalist. Therefore, development may take on different hues with each community.

Islam is structurally a holistic religion, historically attempting to avoid separation of church and state, thereby incarnated in a culture as a political theocracy. But there are two ruptures that occur in Islam.

The first is that of the theological system as opposed to the political system. Though the spiritual ruler is obligated to give deference to the political ruler, the latter is nevertheless appointed by God and obligated to live under the Word of god as revealed in the Quran. Thus, one type of tension is created.

The second rupture is that of government as opposed to the opposition. The political opposition always has the tendency to explore or erupt into the religious realm because the political power does not permit its presence, seeking rather to guarantee total control over the political and religious spheres in an official Islamic state. Hence, the opposition uses non-political approaches, often in the form of the *jihad*, to accomplish its ends. 4

The modern Muslim philosopher, Mohammed Arkoun, traces the historical and philosophical relationships between Arab and European civilization to explain present-day Arab political thinking. He notes the mutual impact of each civilization on the other and the "modification of relations" between the Arab and Mediterranean worlds beginning in the 11th century. The colonial period reinforced the psycho-socio-economic imbalance in Arab culture and exacerbated the tensions between traditional and modern thought. Only after a struggle did the Arab states undertake the difficult task of obtaining their intellectual and cultural freedom, inseparably linked to the whole task of economic development. New political crises confronted them as they faced political consolidation of the state, protection of the national unit, illiteracy, demographic growth, the welfare of the disinherited, and the control of the acculturation process, so as not to lose their Arab-Islamic identity. 5

This historic-cultural background has affected the political and economic concepts of Islam in West Africa. A passion for recognizable unity of the Muslim *umma* community has motivated all states with a sizable Muslim population and a Muslim president to affiliate with world Islamic bodies. Since the religion includes the political realm within its ideological structure, it is only natural for "Islamic states" to seek to reinforce their power with international political alliances, hence uniting spiritual and political institutions in an orthodox state. A common historical experience as colonized peoples, as well as the racial inclusiveness and pragmatic methods of missionary expansion, has made the Arabization efforts easier to swallow.

Christianity, on the other hand, is not doctrinally political, its kingdom being on the spiritual level. Identified with the colonial movement, it comes from a civilization characterized by a dichotomy between the spiritual and the secular. This has produced several types of socio-political conflicts in Africa, not the least of which is preserving the rights and privileges of the Christian community in an aggressively Muslim society. Nigerian government money spent on pilgrimages to Mecca brought outcries of discrimination on the part of Christians who proposed pilgrimages to Jerusalem, not a tenet of the Christian faith. Muslim power became a more vocal Christian concern when, in the early 1980's, all of the governors of the Nigerian states were Muslim. The problem stems more from the divergence in concept between a political theocracy and a secular state than apathy on the part of Christians.

Lamin Sanneh of Harvard University's Center for the Study of World Religions, as a West African, feels that Christian missions should be congratulated for having adopted the local language and culture as the irreplaceable vehicle for the transmission of their message. Unlike the Islamic penetration, Christian missions can be seen as a "translation movement with consequences for vernacular revitalization, religious change and social transformation [more] than as a vehicle for Western cultural domination. . . [and he concludes]. . . Such an assurance should help alleviate some of the Western guilt complex about missions." [6]

In an intensive study conference on Islam, held by the Roman Catholic Church in Koumi, Burkina Faso in 1980, it was stated that Christian communities in West Africa are more often than not living as a minority with a ghetto complex. In the cities, they are often an amalgamation of different ethnic groups and lack the homogeneity ideal for expansion. They often carry a defensive attitude towards Islam and because of a highly developed hierarchy may discourage initiative on the part of their members. The Western cultural "garments" are also an obstacle. 7

The differences between the historical backgrounds, theological and political concepts, and cultural identities cause tensions that go far deeper than doctrinal differences. At the same study conference, it was observed that as long as the Muslin community does not realistically accept the existence of the Christian community and manifest an interest in sharing a community life together, no real dialogue is possible. 8 This broad statement must be tempered by the recognition of great African Muslims such as Tierno Bokar and Amadou Hampate Ba, who have not hesitated to fraternize with Christians. The traditional tolerance of the authentically African community permits this, but the external pressure of the world Islamic community to "Arabize" thus far militates against it. The church, on the other hand, by its very nature and mission, is compelled to dialogue with the world, though it too may often have sought to impose rather than relate, to proselytize rather than witness.

By the same token, it must be recognized that the Islamic sense of community attracts Africans in search of stability in the midst of their uprootedness. It serves people in the areas of family life, education, business and trading, politics, recreation and religious devotion. It is a clearly defined but closed community that gives security, reveals an almost oppressive strength, celebrates and prays; and it is a community that is egalitarian, without hierarchy or clergy. 9 Newcomers to a town or city will find immediate room and board at the mosque, with devotees or with Quranic school teachers.

The opposing doctrines "Christian Trinity" vs. "Islamic Monotheism" do cause tension, as do the views of Christ. Yet both claim a common faith in God as children of Abraham. Both are in the prophetic tradition of divine revelation, providence and supremacy.

Since the West is more familiar with the Church's stand on human rights and dignity, and social and economic justice, statements should be made on behalf of the Muslim community. The Quran calls for justice, distribution of wealth, assistance to orphans and an elimination of economic disparities. The

Senegalese, Mamadou Dia, even consider Islam an authentic socialism, realistic and spiritual. [10]

In a socio-juridical context, three types of Muslims can be identified: 1) those who scrupulously obey the Law of God, the only legitimate Legislator, 2) those who consider the legal prescriptions as examples of great principles of justice for their period, and 3) those who follow the spirituality of the faith and, by imitation of the various attributes of God, hope to become personally more just, peaceful and merciful.

If Muslim scholars were to write about Christians, they would no doubt come up with similar classifications. Relationships will always be somewhat one-sided and tense, until the day that Muslim scholars grant to Christianity the same recognizable attention and study that has come in their direction. Each has much to learn from a close association with the other religion.

Certainly, a Muslim-Christian seminar in Tripoli, Libya, in 1976, recognized that as creatures of God, all persons are "free and equal, subject to certain rights and duties, destined to find happiness through the practice of justice according to the will of God." [11] Each religion seeks to establish a society based on a solid and stable judicial system, made possible by the realization that each person is a servant of God, responsible to submit himself to the order established by God.

The foregoing has seemed necessary, in order to trace the interaction between the two communities and the roles they have played in development in West Africa.

INVOLVEMENT IN DEVELOPMENT

Muslim communities are often accused of being backward, slow to enter the modern world in comparison with Christian communities. For example, the emirs of Northern Nigeria have been blamed for resisting sending their sons to European-style schools out of fear of undermining their authority and losing their sons to conversion to Christianity. Yet, it has been shown that the emirs were not *de facto* rulers of their emirates. British governors were more concerned about their political control than the development of education. Once the schools were established in their regions, the emirs supported them wholeheartedly.[12] Similar explanations could be made for other areas.

They did have their Quranic schools that prepared their children for life in an Islamic context and certain areas of national life. As educational pressures have grown, an increasingly European-style curriculum has been added to the Islamic educational system to supplement the preparation for a western-type job market.

Still, the prevalent pattern of Islamic education is the Quranic school. While the instruction in learning to read, write and memorize verses in the Quran is standard, the patterns of school life will differ. In the rural areas, the students may live in the household of the teacher and assume their assigned duties. Their masters send them out to beg for their food, to teach them humility and subservience.

The Quranic school farm is considered an alternative to European-style education. The students share responsibilities for farm labor and are fed in return. Some teachers can develop large plantations in this manner. This is frequently a means of supplying grain to the marketplace. It is considered advisable for boys to leave home, for they will work harder for a teacher than they will for their own fathers. Some students may continue their studies in theology and Quranic texts elsewhere. Attending the Quranic school gives students a certain material role in society. A family may hope that their son will become a religious professional, able to write medicinal charms and serve as marabout or holy man. This system of education is considered by some to be advantageous over the European system in that: 1) there is no tuition, 2) the student works while going to school, and 3) it avoids the hopes held up to the student in a European-type school with its veneer of foreign culture and threat of unfulfilled expectations for the future.

The Mourides in Senegal are well-known for their organized farm communities, though not possessing the instruction considered essential for advancement. The women of Dakar, upon discovering that the enormity of child-beggars on the streets was stemming from abusive marabouts, hired other marabouts of integrity to teach and absorb the *talibes* in the community in order to get them off the streets and prepare them for a mature role in society.

The inclusiveness of the Muslim community permits anyone able and willing to profess the *shahada* (There is no God but Allah and Muhammad is his Prophet) to be set up in business or with a job, small though it may be. Muslims may be hired, promoted or advanced because of an exclusiveness that does not offer non-Muslims the same opportunities.

The prevalence of Muslim writers who, without questioning the Islamic faith, satirize Islamic practices and abuses, the charlatans and the use of fetishes for protection and personal power, reveals the naivete of the masses whom they are trying to instruct.

Popular Islam, usually associated with the Sufi brotherhoods, is often accused of hindering the progress of the masses. Holy men write Quranic texts on slates which are then washed into a potion to be drunk by the client. Orthodoxy and reform, though Arabizing, is considered essential by most scholars and leaders, to correct this distortion of the true religion of the Prophet.

The deficiencies in Islamic education can be seen in the Yan Tatsine movement in Kano, the result of a growing contradiction between the casual wage labor market provided by the Quranic school students and the economic, political and social order in Kano, suddenly changed by the oil boom of the 1970's. The uprising is more an indication of class antagonism and anti-materialist message than it is of a movement of popular millennial Islamic ideology. 13

An educational reform movement in Mali is establishing a new, dominant class of *neo-ulamas*, condemning the French atheistic system and its destruction of Islamic values. This movement portrays Sufi *ulamas* as perpetrators of popular Islam semiliterate and doctrinally aberrant. Literacy in Arabic separates establishment Islam from popular Islam. 14 However, popular Islam is too complex to define in this paper.

Petro-dollars from Saudi Arabia and the Arab world have been sent to West Africa. Complaints are heard, though, that the money is often primarily used to build mosques. Some ventures, working jointly with governments or development programs, have produced fish hatcheries in Togo and irrigation projects in Mali. Many a young man is sent to the Arab countries for further schooling. He returns to his own country as a professional, a laborer or teacher. He may also return a militant for orthodoxy, perhaps fundamentalism. Some development projects have been initiated in the name of Islam through the Ahmadiyya community from India, which has established schools and projects much along the lines of Western missions.

There is a lack of information and documentation included in this paper on Muslim developmental programs which more time and research might have permitted. UNESCO, FAO, United Nations and World Bank documents would be helpful, as well as a review of bulletins from technical assistance programs, both private and governmental.

Many books have appeared on Islamic values, jurisprudence, human rights and its future economic order. [15] They often seem to be an apologetic for Islamic doctrine rather than a statement of reality in action. While loyal to their faith, some Muslims will observe the generosity of Christian development projects that distribute assistance irregardless of religious adherence, unlike the Muslim distribution to Muslims alone. Yet there are cases where Muslims and Christians have helped each other build mosques and churches in the same community. In Ouagadougou, one Muslim builder, so grateful for the Christian aid to his region, built several churches free of charge as an expression of his appreciation.

But, on the Christian side, there are many weaknesses too. It has been stated in different ways that the lack of vision for social responsibility and economic development illustrates how the church is out of touch with economic realities. The political economy of Africa is dependent on a neo-colonialist system, with it wealth and resources sucked away by international capital. There are needs for achievement of peace and stability, a minimum standard of living consistent with human dignity, and a more rational economic order with equal economic opportunities among nations. But agricultural production falls; underemployment and unemployment prevail; growing indebtedness, social discontent, corruption, human rights abuses, and violent change in government all occur.

Even Lome I and Lome II Conventions were merely recognized as the transfer of resources from the developed world to developing countries, into a beggar's neo-colonial framework. Such plans as the Lagos Plan of Action, encouraging self-sustaining development, self-sufficiency and conservation, or the OAU Plan of Action, urging every nation to accept full responsibility for its destiny, should be promoted by Christians and Muslims alike. [16]

Christian action plans have been proposed by Colin Winter,[17] whereby a transformed church serves as an instrument of the people, and by a Renewal Course for African Progress (RECAP), which looks towards a renewal and transformation of society (see Footnote 16). The ecumenical movement, through the World Council of Churches and many denominations, works toward alleviating poverty and suffering, promoting solidarity with the poor, and education through peace and justice. The All African Conference of Churches is often a coordinator of such programs and projects. Not to be forgotten is aid given by Church World Service and World Vision. Parts of the Sahel have been transformed into orchards and vegetable gardens through the development assistance of churches and governments in well-digging, solar pumps and irrigation projects.

Two comments can be made about the strategy of Christian missions by way of suggestions for the future. Though the present development in schools and health services is due to the impetus of Christian missions, converts were often given an inadequate faith. The church became a sanctuary, bringing people within its walls. An adequate faith would call the church to be a sign, witnessing to the involvement of God wherever people struggle for development, freedom, peace, improved health and working conditions, political self-determination and everything that makes for humanization.[18]

The other comment regards the educational system brought by Western missionaries and governments. Traditional education was informal, holistic and useful; it sought to instill traditional values and mores in children and build character. It dealt with personal relations and was practical and vocationally oriented. Learning was experience-oriented with extended family members serving as teachers. Proverbs and folk tales, music and dance, play and games, ridicule and laughter have all been important traditional methods of education and socialization. Intellectual training has been combined with physical activity and group projects capitalizing on the communal bent of the African people. Could these ideas assist in development?[19]

Mention should be made of Christian communities living as a tiny minority in West African cities, often composed of strangers to the region, who are not comfortable with only a worship service on Sundays. These small communities, such as those in Dakar, Nouakchott and Niamey, break out of their Christian "ghetto" and engage in development projects with results far beyond their numbers. In such communities as well as elsewhere throughout West Africa, Caritas and Catholic Relief Services often study and respond to the social needs of the nation in these delicate situations, offering a discreet collaboration and a witness of compassion and service. Christian communities in both urban and rural areas carry on a "ministry of presence" in Muslim milieu, establishing schools (often with a curriculum that teaches Islam along with Christianity), women's training centers, youth activities, vocational training and crisis and emergency assistance and friendship.

RELATIONSHIPS AND COMMUNITY LIFE

In a number of communities, particularly among Yoruba in Western Nigeria and Berlin, Muslims will offer their lambs in commemoration of Abraham's sacrifice at Id-al-Adha and the breaking of the fast of Ramadhan at Id-al-Fitr in a communal celebration with Christians. Christians will share their turkey or chicken with Muslims at Christmas and Easter. They will exchange greeting cards and visits. The social and blood relationships are thus shown to be much stronger than religious divisions.

In Christian minority communities, Christians will often share in the celebration of the Muslim festivities. It would be hoped that in Muslim minority communities, Muslims would share in the celebration of Christian festivities.

In some communities, Muslims and Christians together have joined hands in meeting some of the severe crises in their communities, such as theft, mendacity, youth vagabondage and poverty. At the present time, these efforts use an informal friendship model or work through existing community organizations or social service. In the future, they may demonstrate, in a more organized and overt manner, their obedience to God (Allah) through service and love for their neighbor.

Muslims have traditionally been concerned about their people worshipping many gods and losing faith in the one God. With Islam's recounting of legends and stories, it aims to give people universal moral and philosophical values that tend to result in strict observance of rules and practices. Christians share a similar concern, though expressed more aptly in terms of a divine-human relationship, which precedes rather than follows the adherence to moral and ethical standards. Christianity, being a historical religion, deals more with perceptual images than legal practices. It is also imbued with more ritual and mystical practices than is orthodox Islam, characterized by rational calculation.

Muslims and Christians are now discussing ways whereby they can work together. Muslims think in terms of a third system, an alternative to capitalism or communism, while Christians are not apt to think in terms of a particular socio-economic structure. The Muslim appeal to Christians to join forces to bring into reality this third system hence falls on deaf ears with Christians, who cannot identify with an Islamic political and theocratic world view.

Both communities must stretch to go beyond the "cement" which holds them together. Both claim to be the best of communities and to have the final truth of God. Muslim faith in the verbal inerrancy of the Quran as the final Word of God is met by Christian faith in Christ as the ultimate Word of God. Each community will be required to make special efforts in order to develop bonds of friendship between them. "to do this, it is essential that the community life be open and viable. Certainly, together they can share the joys and sorrows of everyday life, respond constructively to the problems confronting youth, combat underdevelopment, work for a more just society, learn tolerance and how to live in a pluralistic society." 20

Conflicts often go beyond divergent world views and faith expressions. Conversions may present problems in social cohesiveness. Sometimes this leads to alienation or disownership of the converted. At other times, a family will include both Christians and Muslims among its members and will enjoy religious harmony through the joint festival celebrations. Intermarriage is another threat, in particular, where a Muslim woman marries a Christian man. Children of interconfessional marriages have traditionally adopted the religion of their father but that too is changing.

CONCLUSION

Two remarks may be made to indicate a future direction of the two communities in West Africa. One is socio-political, the other is spiritual.

Amidst the social and political turmoil and violence taking place in Nigeria, political and religious leaders are speaking out in favor of an "ethical revolution" based upon the model of redeeming sacrifice that is presented in each religion i.e., Christ as Redeeming Sacrifice, Abraham's sacrifice of obedience and ancestor sacrificial rites. This "redemption" (term issued by a revolutionary Peoples' Redemption Party) would permit a people's liberation from feudal structures and colonial systems. It would allow them to manage their own affairs, assume a political role and conquer different levels of power in the federation. Nigeria is facing a class struggle, bearing resemblances to the *jihads* of the 19th century. Religious and moral crusades are organizing to call for a periodic celebration of the Great Pardon. Though by pretext the movement proposes a secular regime, in reality the motto "Unity and Faith" reveals its goal as a new form of theocracy. Suicidal tendencies of fundamentalists toward martyrdom are hereby avoided. However, atheists have no place in this model. 21

A call is being issued to both Muslims and Christians to work and witness together in service to a world at large. The word "witness" in both Greek and Arabic comes from a root implying suffering. Both can convert "back to God" pray and worship together at times, while at the same time preserving their doctrinal integrity and faith convictions. As creatures and children of God, they are called to be "caretakers" and "servants" in West Africa today. Much of the future direction and influence of both faiths will depend on their relevance and approaches to socio-economic crises, the political context and personal/cultural identity of the African peoples. A centripetal movement towards Africanization of values and institutions is and will be challenged by a centrifugal movement towards an active role in the world community.

As one old Muslim saint in Abidjan once said, "The more we each know and follow our own Scriptures, the deeper the respect we will have for each other."

NOTES

1. Adegbola, Adeolu. "Christian Responsibility in the Politica Economy of Africa." *The Ecumenical Review*, 37, 1, 1985, p. 65-97.

2. Arkoun, Mohammed. *LaPensee Arabe*. Paris: Presses Universitaries, 1975, p. 122-4.

3. Brenner, Louis and Last, Murray. "The Role of Language in West African Islam." *Africa*, 55, 4, 1985, p. 432-46.

4. Elboudrari, Hassan. "Islams, Politiques et Ideologiques au Maghreb. Etudes Recentes." *Archives Sciences Sociales des Religions,* 1983, 56/2 (Octobre-Decembre), 177-189.

5. Fisher, Humphrey J. "The Juggernaut' s Apologia: Conversion to Islam in Black Africa. " *Africa*, 55, 2, 1985, 153~173.

6. Griffith, Henry. "We can teach better using African methods" *Evangelical Missions Quarterly,* 21, 3, 1985, p. 248-252.

7. Guy, Nicholas. "Dieu, Marx et les Modeles de la 'Guerre Sainte' et du sacrifice au Nigeria." *Archives Sciences Sociales des Religions,* 56/1, 1983 (Juillet-Septembre), 123-46.

8. Hoballah, Mahmoud F. "Islam and Modern Values." Washington: The Islamic Center, no date. "Islam and Humane l'enets." Washington: The Islamic Center, no date.

9. Horton, Robin. "African Conversion." *Africa*, 41, 2, 85-108 and "On the Rationality of Conversion." *Africa*, 45, 3, 219-235; 4, 373-399.

10. Imasogie, Osadolor. "The Church and Theological Ferent in African *Evangelical Review of Theology*, 9, 4, 1985, p. 359-71.

11. Islam,Mamadou, Dia. societes africaines et culture *industrielle*. Dakar: Les Nouvelles Editions Africaines, 1975, p. 111-2.

12. Khallaf, Abdel Monem. *Islamic Materialism and Its Dimensions*. Cairo: The Supreme Council for Islamic Affairs, 1971.

13. Koumi, op. cit., p. 325-7.

14. Mansur, Abdul Azim. *Islam: Allah's Eternal Jurisprudence*. Cairo: The Supreme Council for Islamic Affairs, 1973.

15. Sanneh, Lamin. "Christian Missions and the Western Guilt Complex." *Christian Century*, April 8, 1987, p. 334.

16. Stamer, P. J. "Perspectives pour un dialogue entre communautes en Afrique de l'Ouest." *Bulletin*, Secretariatu pro non Christianis, Citta del Vaticano, XV/3, 45, 1980, p. 324.

17. Stewart, C.C. "Introduction: Popular Islam in Twentieth Century Africa." *Africa*, 55, 4, 1985, p. 363-8.

18. Tibenderana, Peter, Kazengsa. "The Emirs and the Spread of Western Education in Northern Nigeria, 1910-1946." *Journal of African History* 24(1983), p. 517-534.

19. Winter, Colin. *The Breaking Process*. London: SCM Press, 1981.

20. Ibid., p. 319.

21. Ibid., p. 321-2.

REFERENCES

The Gospel of Islam: A 1978 Compendium, ed. Don McCurry, Monrovia, California, MARC, 1979.

"Convergences Spirituelles et Humanistes entre l'Islam et le Christianisme."

Troisieme anniversaire du Seminaire islamo-chretien de Tripoli. *Bulletin*, Scretariatu pro non Cheistianis, Citta del Vaticano, XIV/I, 40, 1979, p. 16.

Conferences on Moslem Doctrine and Human Rights in Islam. Beirut: Dar Al-Kitab Allubnani, 1972.

The Muslim World and the Future Economic Order. London: Islamic Council of Europe, 1979.

CHAPTER 13

ETHICS, PERSONHOOD AND DEVELOPMENT IN THE AFRICAN TRADITION

Kwasi Yirenkyi

African political elites (including the military) have erroneously believed that their pursuit of national development which often focuses narrowly on infrastructural, technological, socio-economic, and political development may be separated from issues involving human dignity. Consequently, in pursuing their development projects, these ruling elites often trample upon the rights of those who criticize their policies. This has created alienation, apathy, a culture of silence and has sometimes led to the flight of many people from their countries. As a result, these nations have been robbed of some of their most talented people who are supposed to be at the center of development.

Using Ghana as a case study, this Chapter argues that development has a moral dimension. Therefore, in order to achieve meaningful development, Africans have to pay particular attention to traditional moral values that celebrate the dignity of human beings. The analysis begins with the examination of the nature of African traditional ethics.

THE NATURE OF AFRICAN ETHICS

Africans view the universe as an interrelated whole with an inseparable relationship between the Supreme Being, lesser gods, human beings, and nature. The search for balance between them is the key to success and that is what defines the nature of African ethics. Social harmony and peace constitute the fundamental goal of society which all members of any given community should pursue collectively. The search for harmony is the essence of development. The emphasis on collective responsibility demands strict adherence to the principles of ethics which govern the whole universe.

Ethics or morality is universal, indeed, essential to all human communities. The term "ethics" (derived from Greek "ethikos" and Latin "ethicus" meaning custom) describes the principles of behavior governing individuals and collectivities, or the standards by which persons determine what constitutes right or wrong, virtue or vice in various societies. Codes of ethics also enable a society to determine the rules that govern the distribution of available wealth. [1] It needs to be noted that by using the term "African ethics," one risks conveying the erroneous impression that all Africans have the same customs or rules that govern their moral lives. The reality is that there are well over one thousand ethnic groups in Africa, [2] each of whose ethics is underpinned by social forces that govern it in that particular ethnic group. However, since there are some commonly held ethical values throughout the continent, one ventures to speak (albeit cautiously) of African ethics. [3] As will also be noted in the discussion below, African ethics shares some similarities as well as differences with its Western counterpart. [4]

In describing the nature of African ethics, I will focus on the Akan of Ghana. [5] Unlike Western societies where ideas have been recorded and systematized for a long period, African traditions, with the exception of a few areas, have generally remained at the oral level until recently. As Professor Ackah has said:

> Akan ethics like Akan religion is not systematically presented, or stated in a series of coherent and logically related propositions. It is a system of ethics worked out pragmatically in the day-to-day living of the people (1988:20).

African ethics are embedded in morals, beliefs, customs, rules, laws, maxims, idioms, proverbs, folk-tales, drum language, traditions, myths, rituals, folk-songs, and taboos (Gyekye 1984:200). These are believed to have been handed down by the gods and ancestors from earlier times to protect society - therefore, any disregard for them may have negative repercussions on the whole society. Africans claim that ethics originate from within the community and may change only with the consensus of the community. Its strict observance is a concern of the whole community. The pursuit of ethical behavior leads to wisdom and those who abide by the ethics of society are considered heroes. Since ethics is considered ethical concerns. In fact, the African "weltanschauung," with God at the apex of its hierarchy, is heavily influenced by morals.

African ethics is socially rooted and expressed on two levels, namely, personal and communal. The latter is of greater significance, since African societies believe that individual existence is possible only in the context of corporate existence. The Akan have a saying: "Onipa fi soro besi a, obesi nnipa krom" (when a human being descends from heaven s/he enters a community of other human beings). This means that in African ontology (human existence), a person's identity as a human being is recognized as inseparable from that of the community of which s/he is a part. From West Africa, Pobee expresses the Akan thought as follows: "Cognatus ergo sum - I am related by blood, therefore I exist, or I exist because I belong to a family" (Pobee 1979:49). From his experience in East Africa, Mbiti aptly sums up the African view: "I am, because we are; and since we are, therefore I am" (1970:108-9). These ideas make it clear that the life of the community takes precedence over that of the individual.

What our analysis indicates in African ethics is the interrelatedness of nature and the emphasis that all human activities including privileges and responsibilities have social dimension. The fundamental goal of society is social harmony and peace. Since the search for harmony is the essence of development, the emphasis on collective responsibility demands strict adherence to the principles of ethics which govern the whole universe.

THE CONCEPT OF PERSONHOOD AND ITS ETHICAL IMPLICATIONS

This section examines the African philosophy of human nature and its ethical implications for life, human dignity, individual and social identity, and development in the community. Our specific focus is the Akan whose concept of the creation of a human being, as already stated, has a corporate dimension. Among the Akan, a person is composed of four elements which are jointly provided by God and the child's parents. At conception, God gives the "okra" (soul) and "honhom" (the breath of life). The father supplies a "sunsum" (spirit) or personality as well as "ntoro" (the individual's hereditary traits). During the period of gestation, the mother provides "mogya" (blood) and the physical flesh. The "okra" (soul), the part of God which makes a person a living human being, constitutes the inner self and the immortal part of the individual. Among all creatures, only human beings uniquely possess an "okra," and its departure from the living person at death marks the completion of one's destiny. Without an "okra" (the life-giving force) the individual is merely blood and spirit (Appiah-Kubi 1981:10).

The "okra" is the "crucial factor in personal identity" (Abraham 1962:59). The "okra" and "honhom" (the breadth of life) constitute the divine speck in a human being, the essence of the image of God in a person. In Akan metaphysics God is held to be eternal and immortal; thus, the possession of the "okra" gives immortality to a person. A human being, therefore, is indestructible, and even at death continues to exist in the world of the spirits. One Akan maxim articulates this belief as follows: "Onipa wu a na onwui" (When a person dies s/he is not really dead), or "Onyame bewu na mawu" (I shall only die if God dies). The implication here is that since the "okra" is part of God, and God is immortal, so is the "okra" (see Opoku 1978).

The Akan theology, like Calvinists, have a strong predestinarian view. Akan people believe that when God gives the "okra," he also gives "nkrabea" (destiny) which is fixed and unalterable. Only God can change a person's destiny. This belief has often led people to accept things that happen to them with resignation: "Eye me nkrabea" (It is my God-given destiny/fate) or "Nyame na waye" (it is God who ordained this event to take place). Such a view, if interpreted narrowly, could impede development when a person resigns himself/herself to adversity.

The second component of a person, is the "sunsum" (spirit), given by the father, which is the spiritual substance responsible for one's "suban" (character). "Sunsum" is moral in its operation and is received from God, the creator. Character is of great importance because the Akan believe that human beings are innately good and can achieve moral excellence and avoid evil if they strive to do so. This belief is expressed in a number of proverbs such as: "Obi nkyere abofra Nyame" (nobody needs to teach a child who God is). This means that a human being, qua human being, has divine knowledge or a moral conscience that enables that person to distinguish between right and wrong. Individuals bear responsibility for their moral behavior (Ackah 1988:60). Since human beings are capable of achieving moral excellence, traditional moral education is generally inculcated in children at the very early stages of life, and it is this code of ethics which is essential in any community's development and which helps members of that community resist the pressures to engage in unethical acts such as dishonesty, callousness, extreme individualism, bribery and a horde of other problems which might impede development of the community.

The third component of a person is what Akan call "ntoro" which, unlike the "okra" and "sunsum", is hereditary. The "ntoro" is transmitted from a father to his children, and helps to account for their inherited characteristics. The "ntoro" does not depart at death with the "okra," but goes down to a person's children or by extension to his nephews and nieces through his brother. The father's "ntoro" may act on behalf of the child's "ntoro" until the latter attains puberty. It is the cooperation of the father's "ntoro" with the mother's blood which forms the fetus and moulds it into a human form. "Ntoro" helps to build a spiritual bond between the father and the child, and balances the relationship between the child and the mother. As Abraham puts it: "This bond establishes the `modus operandi' in family relations" (Abraham 1962:60-61;Opoku 1978:98). The clear establishment of a child's identity and the social bonding with both father and mother is regarded as crucial for development. It has to be noted here that the concept of a "father" may sometimes be emphasized in terms of responsibility. In some African communities, this responsibility may be performed by a woman who may by custom be considered to be married to another woman (with no sexual relationships between them).

The fourth component of a person is "mogya" (blood) which is given by a mother to her child, thus establishing a physiological bond between them. This relationship forms the basis of the "abusua" (clan), also referred to as "nton." The "mogya" received from the mother gives a child her/his status and membership within the family and clan. It also delineates the child's obligations as a member of the Akan matrilineal society. In contrast, patrilineal clans derive their membership from the male line (Abraham 1962:61; Opoku 1978:98-99).

Abraham has summed up the Akan theory of human personality in the following words:

> From the Akan theory of man it is evident that human personality and character were seen by them to rest on a number of factors and influences comprising the "okra," which above all was the ineducable and

unswervable element; the "sunsum," which was educable through precept and a system of punishment and reward, and was the foundation of personal and moral responsibility; the "ntoro" which was inherited and related mainly to the prescription of certain practices and avoidance of others, thereby moulding temperament through the operation of taboos; and finally the "mogya" which insured that one was amenable to reason, made one a human being. In the Akan theory of man, consequently, spiritual factors were primary (Abraham 1962:61).

The African concept of personhood delineated above points to the intrinsic worth of a human being who is made in the image of God, a view expressed in an Akan proverb: "Nnipa nyinaa ye Onyankopon mma, obi nnye asase ba." (All human beings are the children of God, none is a child of the earth). It further shows that in the analysis of personhood spiritual factors dominate. The analysis has also emphasized the fact that personal identity is defined mainly in terms of corporate identity. The very essence of the person is socially defined. This intricate relationships establishes a strong sense of identity and stability which is crucial in an increasingly impersonal modern society.

The analysis also stresses the unique character of the person whose dignity is to be affirmed by members of the community. Any attempt to dehumanize a person - beating elders (including parents), striking or kicking a spouse, or rampant military brutality - is regarded as an infraction against the creator and the ancestors. Ansah states such infractions:

> incur the defilement of the dignity and worth of the person....In the case of a male, there is the additional possibility of his becoming impotent, a chilling thought because sexual potency is believed to be the source of parental immortality (1989:246).

The African ontology which defines personhood in a social context is fundamentally different from the Sartrean existentialist view that a person is a "free unconditioned' being, a being not constrained by social or historical circumstances" (Menkiti 1984:178), or the Cartesian philosophy of "Cogito ergo sum" (I think therefore I exist/ I think therefore I am). The implication for Descartes' statement is that a person's being and dignity resides in her/his essence as a conscious (thinking) being, with emphasis on the individual. Descartes' rationalism, for instance, advocates following one's "inner light of reasoning," and not that of the community. The African view "moves from society to individuals, the Western view moves instead from individuals to society" (Menkiti 180). It is clear, therefore, that a crucial distinction exists between the African concept of personhood and that found in Western societies.

It is fair to point out that while Western individualism is stressed in contrast to the African sense of community, in practice no society can escape the reality of the social character of the human existence. Some cultures are better able to maintain a healthy balance between individual and society than others. The focus on traditional society, as described throughout this paper, is in Weberian language the "ideal type" situation. 7 It is an attempt to describe the social structure as if it had not been affected by any cultural diffusion such as colonization, Westernization, Christianity, Islam, or any ideologies for that matter (see Yirenkyi 1984:18). In practice African societies, like all other societies, have periodically exhibited conflict and contradictions.

THE CULTURE OF VIOLENCE AND THE PROBLEM OF DEVELOPMENT

Dehumanization of the populace by various African regimes is impeding development. During times of economic prosperity and/or social harmony, few people question the unequal distribution of society's resources, but in difficult times as most African societies face today, social forces rise to challenge the status quo. Such challenges in many African countries have often met with brutal repression.

Political repression in many African countries is well-known. Examples follow which gained notoriety because of repression during the 1970's and 1980's (for details see Chazan et. al.1988; Sandbrook 1985: passim). In the Central African Republic under Emperor Bokassa I (1965-79), the masses suffered while he lived in opulence and terrorized his critics (Sandbrook 1985:89). Although the Emperor fell from power in 1979, the repression in that country still exists. For instance, on August 1, 1992, when the 14-party United Democratic Party coalition marched to demand a national conference to bring democracy to the Central African Republic, soldiers beat the marchers and killed Dr. Claude Conjugo, the opposition leader. Another example occurred under Idi Amin (ruled 1971-79) of Uganda whose repression allegedly resulted in the murder of about three hundred thousand people (Sandbrook 143-44; 103-4). A notorious dictator who is still in power and continues to brutally repress his own citizens is Mobutu Sese Sekou of Zaire (Sandbrook 112-113). Mobutu's critics claim that he is one of the richest people in Africa today, with much of his wealth in foreign banks. Meanwhile Zaire, a nation with rich resources, is in economic shambles and is experiencing very serious social tensions.

In all these three cases the economy declined while the leaders amassed personal wealth, resorted to a strategy of repression, created a culture of violence, and silenced and drove many of their citizens into exile. While these are among the most severe examples of abuses, forms of dehumanization are rampant in Africa.

In Ghana, indications are that incidences of repression increased as the socioeconomic situation worsened. One of the reasons is that the decline and lack of realistic solutions always brought vocal opposition. In response, various regimes, including those cited below, engaged in suppression to silence their critics. The Nkrumah (1951-1966), Acheampong (1972-79) and Rawlings (1981-present) regimes are cited because their regimes lasted longer and their repressions were considered more severe than other governments in Ghana.

After independence (1957), Ghana's economy under Nkrumah's civilian regime was relatively healthy until about 1963 when the nation began to experience serious socioeconomic hardships. Unable to control the downward trend, the opposition intensified its criticism of Dr. Nkrumah's policies. In response, the regime ordered many of these critics to be locked up in prison without trial. A number of them died in prison including Nkrumah's leading opponent, Dr. Joseph Boakye Danquah. Systematic suppression and brutality increased when different groups attempted unsuccessful coups to unseat Nkrumah. Other repressive tactics included dismissal of critics who were employed by the government, house arrests, harassment, confiscation of private businesses of critics, or denial of import licenses leading to the demise of private companies. Nkrumah was finally overthrown in a coup by the military in early 1966.

Acheampong's and Rawlings' military regimes were not different in their repression of citizens during periods of socioeconomic crisis, and with a few exceptions, any conclusions drawn from one easily apply to the other. The former gained notoriety for corruption while the latter for human rights abuses and discipline in the military. In contrast to Acheampong, Rawlings has personally avoided corruption and an ostentatious lifestyle.

On January 13, 1972, Colonel Ignatius Kutu Acheampong's coup toppled Dr. Kofi A. Busia's democratically elected government (1969-72). The coup was condemned by many people, particularly the intellectuals and professionals whose sentiment had been well articulated by Professor Boahen, currently the leading opposition leader in Ghana's Fourth Republic. First, Boahen argued that the coup was "unnecessary and unjustifiable" because Ghana's socioeconomic problems could not be solved by that coup. Second, he pointed out that there was no evidence that the civilian administration had violated the terms of the nation's constitution (1989:8). He noted that a coup could be justified if a civilian government:

> refuses to hold fresh elections in accordance with the terms of the constitution... that the military may intervene - and even then only to enforce but not to overthrow the constitution (Boahen 8).

In analyzing Acheampong's regime, Boahen has said that by the end of 1974, the nation was united and agriculture was in full bloom with "Ghana's pride and confidence restored" (9). The second phase of Acheampong's administration from 1975 to 1978 was nothing but a disaster. According to Boahen, the period was

> characterized by falling agricultural and industrial productivity,... shortage of essential inputs and spare parts, a breakdown of the infrastructure... general moral degeneration... inflation rate rose from 3% in 1970 to 10.1% in 1972 and to the all-time record of 116.5% in 1977" (9).

By 1979 the country was unable to meet its loan repayments and the nation was bankrupt (Boahen,10-11).

Business people were made scapegoats for the economic ills of the country. Accused of hoarding and selling goods above government controlled prices, many were harassed and had their homes and goods confiscated and sold by the government. Some of them were flogged publicly. The lucky ones were freed after heavy fines, but many of them had prison sentences. Ghanaians looked on helplessly at such unparalled dehumanization (Yirenkyi 1992:147-148).

Unfortunately, the military would not allow civilian courts to prosecute or defend those who had been victimized. Military courts, dubbed "kangaroo courts" by Ghanaians, were established to deal with all such cases.

Rawlings' regime faced socioeconomic difficulties similar to those in Acheampong's regime. Rawlings' worst period was between 1981 and 1983 when the cost of living escalated, food was scarce, and imported goods and raw materials were non-existent. Boahen expresses the sentiment of many Ghanaians when he states that "never in the history of the country have such long queues been seen for every conceivable item" including such things as local foods and petroleum products. People have felt humiliated, hungry, impoverished, and subjected to traumatic experiences and disillusionment (49).

MORAL DIMENSIONS OF DEHUMANIZATION

Our focus is on the moral dimension of the problems, namely, the repression and dehumanization of persons in Acheampong's and Rawlings' regimes. Under both regimes, military acts of brutality often provoked students and professional associations into open rebellion. The universities were closed down on numerous occasions because of students' protests. In 1977, the Ghana Bar Association invoked a writ of *Habeas Corpus* to secure the release of 451 people detained by Acheampong's military government. Soon after the first coup, Rawlings summarily executed three former military officers who, like himself, served as heads of state in Ghana. In addition, he executed several other people who were accused of corruption.

Many Ghanaians (including lawyers) charged that these executions and additional brutal murders as well as the military government's overt human rights violations were against basic principles of the rule of law. Subsequently, the Ghana Bar Association boycotted the courts (Howard 1985:342-343).

This culture of repression and economic difficulties helped to undermine Ghana's social values. For example, it led to social apathy on the part of many responsible people who had previously made meaningful contributions to the nation. Some of the people who were invited to serve in the government declined. As a result of unprecedented economic hardships, decent people engaged in unethical means such as bribery and corruption in order to sustain themselves and their families. In the early 1980's, there was a mass exodus of men and women to neighboring countries such as Nigeria in search of jobs. Unfortunately, when the Nigerian economy declined, about one million Ghanaians were declared "persona non grata" and their return to Ghana compounded the unemployment situation. Armed robbery posed a serious problem until the government began to curb it by executing some of the robbers. Again, this summary execution of criminals (supported by many Ghanaians) raised ethical issues. Did the crimes justify the severe punishment? Were the trials considered fair?

SILENCING THE OPPOSITION

Various African governments including Ghana have used such strategies as dismissing editors who are critical, closing down independent newspapers, mistreating journalists, intimidation, imprisonment, kidnappings and killings of outspoken people to silence the media. The Ghanaian and other African experiences cited above indicate political leaders sought by any conceivable means to silence their critics. In response some of the victims of dehumanization adopted a culture of silence characterized by:

> apathy, indifference, refusal to accept appointments from the government, or take part in communal activities and official celebrations, premature retirements from the public service, and refusal to register and/or vote" (Boahen 56).

A small minority remained vocal, ignoring the risks to their lives. Some died for their beliefs in free speech. It is a paradox that a country like Ghana which was desperately in need of its most highly skilled people - doctors, professors, economists, engineers, artists and others - to help develop the country would drive those very people away through repressive tactics.

RETRIEVING THE CONCEPT OF DEVELOPMENT

The moral issue this analysis raises is that various regimes in Ghana have pursued development at the expense of the people. Their policies, to invoke

Boahen, "do not have a human face, and they must" (51). Unless Ghana (indeed Africa) learns the lesson that a nation cannot separate development from humane treatment of all its citizens (supporters of regimes and critics alike), it will continue to lose its most valuable asset for development - the people.

Some of the answers to our modern problems, with particular reference to development, may be found in the traditional value systems. Therefore, if Africans want to pursue any meaningful development, they need to retrieve some of their social values. This call for reevaluation and retrieving of African values is aptly described by an Akan expression: "Sankofa" (return to retrieve), to retrieve some of the relevant values in African culture. A number of African scholars have issued similar calls. For instance, Opoku has argued that in any meaningful discussion of development, "we cannot ignore our African sense of values, for it is within the context of values that development takes place" (1989:17). As Mazrui (1986:292) has also pointed out, no revolutionary government has defended Africa's indigenous values and customs. He states that the "journey of modernization must be restarted under indigenous impetus" (21).

In African traditional society, people come first for they are the object of development. However, it needs to be noted that their development is never separated from the inhabited universe as a whole. If people are the focus of development, then the concept of personhood analyzed above is relevant. Discovering one's identity in a rapidly changing world is crucial for personal and social development. For instance, when people feel alienated from the impersonal urban society and the modern political system, the traditional bonding and sense of belonging described above has tremendous advantages. Within the Akan traditional system, a child may learn that the greatest value is the realization of a new sense of communal belonging, obligation and collective moral responsibility that may form the foundation of development. The child may learn that shirking individual responsibility may lead to a diminution in a person's status within the community of which he/she is a part. Unfortunately, these traditional values are no longer stressed in the home and are practically ignored in the modern educational system. There is need to stress these values in the socialization process at home, in the formal educational system, and in other social institutions such as the church.

One of the fundamental principles of personhood in traditional society is the freedom to participate in every aspect of the community. Isolating a person from the community is a very powerful instrument in the hands of the members of African traditional society. Marasinghe states that the:

> principles of 'respect' and 'participation' (emphasis his) provide a general basis of the rights to family membership, to freedom of thought, speech, beliefs, and association, and the freedom to enjoy property (see Marasinghe, 1984:32-45).

The development of the society was based on these principles. Marasinghe further points out that the validity of these rights is not derived from Western constitution but enshrined in traditional social values as a set of basic principles which are supported by at least a substantial majority of any given society. These values stand the test of time because they symbolize some of the basic elements which hold society together. In contrast to this tradition, we have described the strategies which modern ruling elites have adopted to isolate their critics.

Political stability is a *sine-qua-non* for African social and economic development. In view of the numerous coups in Africa which have obviously created serious instability, there is need to examine values in African political systems. The argument can be made that some traditional socio-political structures are democratic. Some political scientists state that African pre-colonial political institutions were stable because they were widely accepted by the people, since they allowed for free expression and full participation of the citizenry in political affairs. The legitimacy of the leaders derived in part from a religious basis. Chiefs served as political heads of communities and had religious functions as well. The traditional system had checks and balances that enabled the people to deal severely with leaders whose rules were characterized by cruelty, arbitrary and capricious behavior, and other forms of dictatorship. For instance, Akan traditional leaders are installed with the consensus by the society at large through long established traditions. The institution made room for the people to remove chiefs who became dictatorial and therefore, unacceptable to the people. From the traditional standpoint, coups d'etat are undemocratic and morally unjustifiable because they are staged without the consent of the people and sharply depart from traditional customs.

Since modern states are ethnically diverse, it is impossible to maintain traditional political institutions based mainly on ethnicity. The challenge will be to find ways to adapt ethnic institutions to suit modern national interests, a difficult but not insurmountable challenge. Since we have been able to borrow from various Western nations, we can do the same with our own institutions. Opoku has argued that it is possible to evolve commonly agreed procedures for political office which will command the respect and adherence of the people (Opoku 1989:16).

Tolerance of criticism has been enshrined in African traditions. Development takes place in an atmosphere where all segments of the society can express their views. There is an Akan saying:" Nea otwa sa nnim se n'kyi akyea" (The person who is clearing a path does not realize that the section already cleared behind her/him is crooked). The person needs the help of another who stands at a distance. Used in this context, it means that our leaders who are actively planning development need others behind them to communicate whether they are on the right path. In other words, objective criticism brings progress and is a crucial part of development. This is a lesson the African ruling elite need to learn.

Meaningful development takes place in a society where the rule of law is respected by its citizens. The traditional moral and social basis of law and its relationship with the people have been ignored by African law makers. For example, when lawyers and other defenders of the principles of Ghanaian laws and human rights speak about dehumanization and other violations, they often invoke Ghana's constitution based mainly on British and American constitutions and the United Nations Universal Declaration of Human Rights (1948). What needs to be noted in the African context is that these violations were not only infringements upon the rights of the individual but also upon the society, the gods, the ancestors and, in some cases, against the environment as a whole, and thus their collective indignation.

The lack of reference to African moral traditions in nation building is noted by Dickson, and his admonition should be taken seriously. He writes:

> African countries would have done well to determine what they wanted to achieve. It is true that they might have believed that the goal of development had been defined for them by reference to a Western standard, but this would only serve to frustrate their development plans and

> achievements, for they would not have themselves defined their goal, taking into account the need for their peoples to develop integrity, in full knowledge of who they were. This largely explains why the path leading to development has become the path leading to stagnation and confusion. In other words, as long as the conception of development does not take into account the African cultural reality, it cannot but lead to much dislocation and uncertainty (Dickson 1985:49; cited in Opoku unpublished manuscript:17-18).

A major legacy of African ethics is its reverence for nature and the sense of harmony between the living environment and its inhabitants. Unfortunately, African acceptance of Western values and models is posing a serious threat to our development. Since the latter part of the nineteenth century and the beginning of the twentieth century, Africans have been increasingly adopting Western models of development. In addition, they have allowed the interest of the industrial nations to dominate African policies because Africans are desperate for foreign aid. The devastating effects of Western industrial exploitation have become a matter of serious concern in the world today. Environmentalists, ethicists, politicians and many others are discussing environmental issues, and we are increasingly hearing such terms as "environmental ethics," "eco-justice" or "environmental theology."

While Africans are not entirely blameless in the misuse of the earth, it is one area in which Africa does not need to borrow Western values or allow industrial interests to supersede African survival. Rather than discarding various African ideas about human beings and their relationship with nature as being out-of-step with modernization, it is necessary for Africanists to emphasize our interdependence and human responsibility toward the environment. The 1992 conference by world leaders on the environment in Brazil is a clear indication that concern for the ecology is rightly becoming a global issue, and true to the Akan world view and ethics, the world is like a spider's web - what affects one affects all.

Africans believe that God created human beings and placed them at the center of the cosmos, not as master but as caretaker. Human beings are expected to remain in harmony with the universe since they are part of it (see Opoku 1978). For the African traditionalist, this is a moral imperative that compels members of the society to take collective responsibility seriously. If there is room for borrowing in a global village, the West has some lessons to learn on environmental ethics from Africa and other traditional societies. While African nations may be awed by development in the West, they should never forget the exploitation (both land and people) and depersonalization that has accompanied Western industrialization. Africans need to heed Opoku's warning about development:

> development is not trying to frantically catch up with Western industrialized nations; if there is any catching up to do in development, it is with ourselves as a people by building on our own foundations (1989:4-5).

CONCLUSION

The Chapter has examined the nature of African ethics and has emphasized the unique character of the person whose development takes place in a social context. The African ruling elite, particularly the military, have ignored the traditional concept of society as one in which the members become the focus of development. They have consequently trampled upon human dignity in their attempts to develop Africa. From the African traditional perspective, dehumanizing persons by flogging, unlawful imprisonment, abductions, executions and/or any other unethical methods is a rebellion not only against society but also the Creator. This incalculable human cost and the erosion of confidence in institutions that protect the community are some of the factors hindering African development.

African societies should not ignore their indigenous ethical values. In pursuing development along Western models, we should be reminded that for the African, the search for harmony is the essence of development. If Africans can lead the way, they will contribute to the call for peace in the modern world which seems to elude all of us. One of the fundamental principles of personhood in traditional society is the freedom to participate in every aspect of the community. This is absolutely essential in political development.

As the judiciary and other lawmakers tackle many of our legal issues, they need to realize that the time has come for them to critically examine our traditional values and take an active role in incorporating the progressive aspects of these values into our constitutions. While Africans should promote human rights issues along with the international community, they need not look mainly to the West for values of human dignity but should begin to draw from their own traditional resources.

NOTES

1. The term is also used to describe the branch of philosophy that concerns itself with the reflection and analysis of the nature and validity of rules that constitute the moral dimension of human life. For the purpose of discussion the author makes no distinction between "ethics" and "morality.

2. I use the term "ethnic" rather than "tribe" because the term "tribe" sometimes carries a pejorative connotation. A dictionary definition of the word 'tribe' includes: "Any primitive or nomadic group of people of generally common ancestry, possessing common leadership" or "any group of people having the same occupation, habits, ideas, etc.: chiefly in a derogatory sense" *(Webster's New World Dictionary of the American Language,* College Edition, Cleveland and New York: The World Publishing Company, (1968: 1554). Quite frequently the term has been applied to Africa and other non-Western societies and never to contemporary Western societies. I substitute the term 'tribe' with the term 'ethnic.' The latter refers to "... any of the basic divisions or groups of humankind, as distinguished by customs, characteristics, language, etc." (ibid., p. 499). There is no sociological reason why the latter meaning can not apply to African groups.

3. Some of the common values include social order, the quest for peace and harmony with the gods, ancestors, the living, social integration and respect for nature, the primacy of society over the individual considered crucial to the life of the community, breaking of certain moral codes or taboos regarded as evil and punishable by the gods and ancestors. These are moral ideals shared by all Africans (see Opoku 1978: 153).

4. I believe that a study of ethics in one culture may share some light in

understanding another since human issues, irrespective of differences in cultures may have some similarities. With that in mind, I will occasionally compare and contrast African ethics with that of the West.

5. The Akan live predominantly in the Western, the Eastern, Central, Ashanti and Brong Ahafro regions of Ghana. They constitute about half or nearly two-thirds of the population of Ghana (1985 census was about 14 million). Some Akan people live in Côte d'Ivoire. This narrow focus on the Akan obviously poses a severe limitation and makes any generalization difficult to defend. Scholars studying the nature of African ethics have to be constantly aware of the danger in generalization even though this may be necessary to socio-ethical analysis. In addition to this problem, scholars (including Africans who are often trained in the West) should avoid the danger of superimposing a Western system on African ethics.

6. It answers the Aristotelian question: "What is the great goal or end (telos) of human striving?" In the words of Beach, it is the "ethics of the good, the ethics of aspiration" (Beach 10; see Beach and Niebuhr 6). Ethics becomes the discipline that delineates the means by which certain goals are realized. This long-established Western traditional distinction between deontological and teleological ethics does not exist in African ethics.

7. In Weberian analysis, an ideal type is a mental construct formulated by the researcher to heighten significant components of social structure under study enabling one to make some meaningful comparisons (Weber 1949).

8. In my brief analysis of Ghana, I have freely used material from Professor Adu Boahen's insightful annual J.B. Danquah Memorial Lecture, *The Ghanaian Sphinx: Reflections on the Contemporary History of Ghana 1972-1987,* Accra: Ghana Academy of Arts and Sciences, 1989. When I met Professor Boahen in Baltimore at the African Studies Association Conference in 1990, I briefly discussed with him my intention to use this material. I am indebted to him.

REFERENCES

Abraham, W.E. 1962. *The Mind of Africa..* Chicago: The University of Chicago Press.

Ackah, C.A. 1988. *Akan Ethics.* Accra: Ghana Universities Press.

Ansah, John K. 1989. "The Ethics of African Religious Tradition" in *World Religions and Global Ethics.* New York: Paragon House Publishers.

Appiah-Kubi, Kofi. 1981. *Man Cures, God Heals.* Totowa, New Jersey: Allanheld, Osmun and Company Publishers.

Beach, Waldo. 1988. *Christian Ethics in the Protestant Tradition.* Atlanta: John Knox Press.

Beach, Waldo and H. R. Niebuhr.1973. *Christian Ethics.* 2nd. Ed. New York: John Wiley & Sons.

Boahen, Albert Adu. 1989. *The Ghanaian Sphinx: Reflections on the Contemporary History of Ghana, 1972-1987.* Accra: Ghana Academy of Arts and Sciences.

__________________. 1985. "Education, Culture and Development" in E. Emeyoyonau et. al. eds. *Education, Culture and Development in Africa.* New York: P.W.PA.

Chazan, Naomi et. al. 1988. *Politics and Society in Contemporary Africa.* Boulder, Colorado: Lynne Rienner Publishers.

Dickson, Kwesi. A. 1975. "Research in the History of Religions in West Africa" in *Religion*. August.

Green, Ronald M. 1988. *Religion and Moral Reason*. New York: Oxford University Press.

Gyekye, Kwame. 1984. "The Akan Concept of a Person" in *African Philosophy*. Richard A. Wright ed. New York: University Press of America.

Hessel, Dieter T. ed. 1992. *After Nature's Revolt: Eco-Justice and Theology*. Minneapolis: Fortress Press.

Howard, Rhoda E. 1985. "Legitimacy and Class Rule in Commonwealth in Africa" in *Third World Quarterly*. 7: 323-47.

Marasinghe, Lakshman. 1984. "Traditional Conceptions of Human Rights in Africa" in *Human Rights and Development in Africa*. eds. Claude Welch, Jr. and Ronald Meltzer.

Mazrui, Ali. 1986. *The Africans*. Boston: Little Brown and Company.

Mbiti, John. 1970. *African Religions and Philosophy*. London: Heinemann Educational Books.

Menkiti, Ifeanyi A. 1984. "Person and Community in African Traditional Thought" in *African Philosophy*. RichardA. Wright ed. New York: University Press of America.

Opoku, Kofi Asare. 1989. "The Traditional Foundations of Development." Address to the 40th Annual New Year School, Institute of Adult Education, University of Ghana. Unpublished.

________________. 1978. *West African Traditional Religion.* Jurong, Singapore: FEB International Private Ltd.

Pobee, John S. 1979. *Toward an African Theology*. Nashville: Abingdon Press.

Sandbrook, Richard. 1985. *The Politics of Africa's Economic Stagnation*. London: Cambridge University Press.

Yirenkyi, Kwasi. 1992. "The Church and the Quest for African Modernization" in *Twentieth-Century World Religious Movements in Neo-Weberian Perspective*. ed. William Swatos, Jr. Lewiston: New York.

CHAPTER 14

WARFARE: SOWER OF THE SEEDS OF FAMINE

Father Carroll Houle

Proverb in Kihaya (Tanzania)
"Obworo Ntare Kotarashaine Yakulya"
"Poverty is like a lion, if you do
not fight you get eaten."

In 1984, Fr. Kenneth Thesing, a Maryknoller, did a survey in his area of the Diocese of Shinyanga, Tanzania, about the disaster facing the Sukuma people if the rains did not come. He concluded that 39,000 people risked starvation and death. The rains did not come, but thousands did not die of hunger. In early January, 1986, I was talking about this to the former president, Julius Nyerere, and his wife, Maria, indicating that we did not know how the people survived. Maria reflected that what probably saved the people is the custom of sharing in times of crisis. Julius said, "Thank God we still have those cultural values, but my fear is that, with the changes taking place, individualism will overtake our sense of sharing and lead to even more problems that we have now."

To my mind the two realities, of hunger and change are the biggest challenges for the African nations. Hunger stalks the continent. The recent drought caught almost every African nation on a downhill slide economically. When this will bottom out no one seems to know. The local, national, and international factors at play intensifying poverty are vast and interconnected.

I have travelled to countries still affected severely with starvation. Carrying a dying girl in a refugee camp in Sudan, being surrounded by legless young men and women in northern Ethiopia, seeing children digging roots of plants for food behind the house of the bishop of Huambo (Angola), and so many more personal experiences in the last year and a half could easily lead to discouragement and despair. From a worldly point of view, the reality seems hopeless. From a faith perspective, it is confusing, because while I believe in God's special love and care for the poor and voiceless, I also see this problem is ours as humans. There is so little progress being made to address the roots of and solutions to hunger.

I have attended many meetings and conferences in the United States of people - in relief and development, advocacy, peace, or academia - who have discussed Africa at great length. For many Americans it is a humanitarian undertaking. For some there are memories of times in Africa, but few have co-workers living and struggling with the poor and hungry in a life-long commitment as I do. Perhaps the greatest contribution that many Maryknollers like myself have made in Africa is simple presence with the people, walking with them in their search for a better life however material the expression of it is for the average person.

CHANGES

In countries like Tanzania or Kenya, which I know best, a better material life is wanted. Besides the basics like soap and sugar, people of the younger generation think they have a right to radios, bicycles and modern clothes. This seemingly new, modest materialism is only the visible tip of vast changes taking place in the mentality and awareness.

Obvious traumatic changes are taking place in countries like Mozambique, Angola, Ethiopia, and the Sudan. People want freedom and justice, an end to oppression, terror and starvation. These latter countries were far from my consciousness when I was in the missions of rural Tanzania. Both my travels to these countries and contacts in the United States have widened my understanding of the cultural and national problems, as well as the involvement of the superpowers in fermenting unrest and confusion. Warfare in these countries is the immediate reason hunger and starvation will continue for the foreseeable future. The United States and Russia are involved 'up to their ears'. Neither Ethiopia nor Sudan are making any significant peace initiatives, nor, up to this point, are the U.N. or OAU (Organization of African Unity). Certainly the U.S. and Russia are not. The Southern African countries will never achieve peace until the overthrow of apartheid in the Republic of South Africa.

DEVELOPMENT

Some of our people in Africa keep telling me that the wider systemic issues should not be my primary concern, that I should be concentrating on hunger. I probably would feel the same way if I did not have the opportunity the African Desk at Maryknoll offers me to see things in a new light. Most agree that drought leads to famine because of poverty. The answer to poverty is development. But development itself is a many-headed creature.

For countries like Tanzania and Kenya, development is the key challenge. But the possibility of development is limited, even if these countries had perfect governments and plans, given the debt problem; the plummeting prices of their exports on the world market; the rising prices of imports; and the present, persistent donor model of developing cash crops for foreign exchange despite the fact that it has not led to many results. Larger economic and political considerations play a major role in development beyond the transfer of material goods, machinery and technology. All of us, who have lived for years in rural areas of Africa, become experts on the peoples' disgruntlement with the policies and plans of the government, the corruption and inefficiency of the local bureaucracy, as well as the local cultural restraints that limit economic progress. Certainly this is part of walking with the people, but it could also be simply passively standing still on the path of hopelessness.

WARFARE AND FAMINE

Until 1978, Tanzania was lurching along making some economic progress. Soon after the war was launched against Uganda, this uneven economic progress came to a stand-still; $500,000,000 was borrowed to finance arms for the war. Tanzania was broke. The economic downhill slide of the country began, and it has not recovered. There were a host of other factors that came into play, but it seems that the war with Uganda was the straw that broke Tanzania's economic back. Most of the countries of Africa are going through a similar traumatic economic stage of stagnation, with the growing militarism playing a small or large role.

Definitely, for four of the five countries most severely affected by hunger and starvation in 1986 (Ethiopia, Sudan, Mozambique, Angola), warfare and the large amount spent on arms have made it impossible to get to the task of development. Drought was the immediate reason for famine in Ethiopia and the Sudan. Warfare is the deeper reason millions continue to face this tragedy. Both the U.S.'s and Russia's main concern in these countries is for the oil fields of the Middle East. The continued militarization of the economy and the savage wars prevent people throughout this region from peacefully pursuing the structural changes necessary for development.

The famine in Mozambique and Angola is directly connected with the extension of apartheid's violence into these countries. The South African government has attacked every country in the region in the past decade in order to intimidate, to prevent economic readjustment, and to assure that the independent states remain dependent upon apartheid's economic domination. South Africa has supported the rebel forces in both Mozambique and Angola, and has continually invaded Angola with its own military forces. U.S.'s support for Savimbi and UNITA of Angola has not only allied us with South Africa's apartheid regime but has left thousands maimed and caused millions to flee their homes to live in starvation and terror.

WILL IT PLAY IN PEORIA?

Maryknollers in Africa no longer have hundreds of hungry people daily outside their windows, but the reasons leading to hunger and famine have not gone away. The economic condition of most African countries continues to worsen, and the next drought could make this past one look like a warm-up exercise to the real tragedy of starvation and death for millions.

Despite the outpouring of generosity by Americans in relief aid to Africa in 1985, Africa is not a priority for the U.S. To me there is little doubt that Africa is on the bottom of priorities for the U.S. generally, whether it is our foreign policy, the media, the educational institutions, or most of the Christian churches. Historically the United States had little to do with Africa, except for buying slaves and some minerals. Africa was a European concern. While the United States is quickly becoming the major outside actor politically, economically, and militarily in Africa, there is little awareness of this in the United States beyond specialized groups that profit by such involvement.

I have come to the conclusion that there are cultural limitations in the United States that make it difficult for us to become interested in any sustained focus on Africa, besides the historical reasons and the normal selfishness of human nature. First of all, it seems that reality for the average American is what is presented on television. Since Africa has slid off our television screens, it no longer merits attention.

In addition to the television mentality, there are two cultural presuppositions that color our perspective about Africa and much of the Third World. Americans generally see the Third World in terms of East-West, that either the capitalism of the United States or the communism of Russia is going to dominate and control the Third World countries. Since we are the ones with the white hats spreading freedom and democracy, it should be us. A few innocents may get hurt when we have to shoot up the bad guys, but that is how life is. The people of the Third World see the global scene in terms of North-South - the wealthy and powerful nations of the Northern hemisphere, including the United States, Europe and Russia, versus the poor and powerless Southern hemisphere. The perspective of the world as North-South does not enter into the picture for the United States, not only in our foreign policy but also on the popular level of street talk.

The other cultural limitation we deal with in the United States is that we are victims of our long history of dualism. Reality is seen in terms of good and bad, right and wrong, the evil empire seeking to overcome the virtuous one. The movie "Star Wars" does not seem foreign for those of us who grew up with Flash Gordon. If we combine the East-West and dualistic mentality in looking at Africa, we have a formidable unconscious morass to counter.

Another problem in dealing with Africa is that Africa is caught up in the racism still prevalent in many Americans. I have encountered this with many people.

TENTATIVE INITIATIVES

There are several realities facing Africa about which we can do something as individuals and as members of groups. It seems to me that the two most important are the development debate and peace.

The development challenge is crucial for most of the countries of Africa at this time. The debt crisis, the militarism of countries, and the prices on the world market are all part of the problem for developing countries. For my part, I think I can take a slightly different tack because of my experience working and living with the peasants in rural Africa for twenty years.

From the meetings and conferences I have attended, little attention seems to be paid to those for whom development is a matter of life and death - the peasants, women, and urban poor. While anthropologists and small NGO's speak to this issue as a primary focus in some instances, there is usually little connection made by them to the national and international realities involved. I plan to return to work in Africa in late 1986. One of my tasks will be to explore what can be done to let the peasants, women, and urban poor have a greater voice in their future, and to encourage local indigenous experts to join with them in articulating what is full human integral development. Hopefully, those ideas will filter back to the major donor groups, the NGO's, and even the Western academics of good will concerned about Africa's future.

The second reality about which I have become deeply concerned is warfare and militarism. While I make no pretensions that I or Maryknoll will bring peace to the African continent, we can help raise consciousness here in the U.S. Most of the countries severely affected by hunger in 1986, as mentioned above, cannot even consider the possibility of development at this time. Even donor groups and NGO's which claim to have re-directed their efforts from relief aid to development cannot make much of a difference at this time.

How can you do development in war zones? In January, 1986, Maryknoll hosted a conference on war, militarization and hunger in Africa. At this meeting, a resolution was passed unanimously to do a tour in the U.S. on the need of peace in Africa and the role of the U.S. in the militarism of this continent.

Perhaps the most important result of the Peace Tour is bringing together people who are anti-hunger - peace people, and academic people. The initiative for this tour has come out of the conference held at Maryknoll involving people primarily from the East Coast. Similar conferences should be held in the Midwest and West. Only if there is a concentrated and unified effort made throughout the U.S. is there any hope of changing the U.S. foreign policy for Africa's betterment.

SECTION V

AFRICAN-AMERICANS AND AFRICA

CHAPTER 15

THE LEGACY OF FRANTZ FANON AND BLACK POLITICS IN AMERICA

Edmond J. Keller

The political thought of Frantz Fanon was not introduced to black Americans until 1964 when the first English translation of his seminal work, *The Wretched of the Earth,* found its way into the American literary market. Initially, the power of this brilliant and insightful theorist was perceived only by American intellectuals. However, through the endorsement of Fanon's ideas by black political activists such as Huey P. Newton, Bobby Seale and Eldridge Cleaver of the Black Panther Party and Stokeley Carmichael of the Student Non-violent Coordinating Committee (SNCC), Fanon's analysis and prescriptions began to be disseminated to the black American "grassroot". Dan Watts of *Liberator Magazine* once commented to Jimmy Breslin, a journalist with the *Chicago Sun Times* at the time, "...every brother on the rooftop can quote Fanon (Sutton: 1971, p. 60). 1

Admirers of Fanon have termed him "a man of his times", a throwback to the romantic nationalists of the 19th century, "the Marx of the African Revolution" (Burke: 1976, p. 127). Indeed, after his death, the mystique of Frantz Fanon seemed more profound than ever in the minds of black intellectuals and activists throughout the world who had been searching for a model which allowed them to explain the terms of their oppression at the same time that it provided them with the keys to their liberation and empowerment. Nowhere was the impact of this man and his ideas more felt than in the Black Power Movement in the United States in the late 1960's and early 1970's. G. Louis Heath, for example, quotes former Black Panther Party Minister for Information Eldridge Cleaver as asserting:

> Not until we reach Fanon do we find a major Marxist-Leninist theoretician who was primarily concerned about the problems of black people, wherever they may be found. It is because of the fact that black people in the U.S. are also colonized that Fanon's analysis is so relevant. After studying Fanon, Huey P. Newton and Bobby Seale began to apply his analysis of colonized people to black people in the U.S. They adopted a Fanonian perspective but they gave it a uniquely Afro-American context (Heath, 1976, p. 75).

The Black Panthers came to describe black Americans as a segment of the international lumpenproletariat, "those who have no secure relationship or vested interest in the means of production and institutions of capitalist society" (Heath, 1976, p. 75). Of course, Fanon's own definition of the lumpenproletariat referred to landless peasants in pre-industrial third world societies who migrate to the cities only to find there is no work there either. Thus, they became a potentially revolutionary underclass in urban areas. The Panthers suggested that the black underclass in America was analogous to and not the same as the third world lumpenproletariat. This adaptation of this key Fanonian concept was necessary to make his ideas relevant to the situation of black Americans.

The Wretched of the Earth became no less than the "bible" for black American leftists who wanted to accept the Marxist-Leninist methodology but found it wanting in terms of how it virtually ignored the power of racism and the interaction of racism with capitalism. The formative impact of the discovery of Fanon and his ideas upon the Black Panther Party is repeatedly attested to by the Party's former leaders. Bobby Seale, for example, in his book, *Seize the Time,* clearly details the connections between the "coming of age" of the Party and the reading and reinterpretation of Fanon's *Wretched of the Earth* by Huey P. Newton (Seale: 1970). Eldridge Cleaver notes that:

> The feelings and thoughts and passions that were racking us were incoherent and not connected until we read Fanon. Then many things fell together for us, harmonizing our attitudes and making it possible for us to organize into a political organization (Hansen: 1977, p. 5).

For a brief few years, the Black Panther Party, armed with its Fanonian perspective, asserted itself as a leftist alternative to some of the more traditional civil rights organizations. However, in retrospect, the Party and the guiding light of Fanon's ideas were relatively short-lived. Today, Fanon's works are hardly referred to in the rhetoric of black politics. Students in university courses on African Politics or Third World Revolution may be assigned passages from Fanon's major works; but then only those dealing with the social psychology of colonialism, violence, or the revolutionary potential of the peasantry. Seldom are they asked to identify and to understand the universal implications of the model Fanon advanced in *The Wretched of the Earth.*

There are numerous possible explanations for the failure of the black political left to take Fanon's ideas further than they did. They seemed not to have progressed further than recognizing that Fanon's description of colonialism and its social psychological impact was analogous to the institutional racism and black identity conflicts found in America. No new theory, informed by Fanon but based on the objective conditions in the United States, was articulated or applied by a clearly defined black political leadership. Malcolm X (without apparently being influenced by Fanon's work) only months before he was assassinated formed the Organization for Afro-American Unity (OAAU), indicating to some observers that the struggle for black liberation in America had to be taken to another level. He abandoned his former Black Muslim belief that black Americans could only be completely free from white racism and exploitation if they acquired their own land on which to reconstitute an independent black nation. By the mid-1960's Malcolm had come to believe that black empowerment was possible even in the context of racist America, if only the masses of black people were guided by a national party such as the OAAU. They could seize political power especially at the grassroots and this would lead to economic empowerment. This approach, of course, was similar to the role Fanon envisioned for the most ideal type of nationalist parties in the Third World (Fanon: 1967).

Some observers contend that the disappearance of Fanon's political ideas from the lexicon of black politics in America had more to do with those ideas themselves than with anything else. Aristide and Vera Zolberg, for example, suggest that the attraction of black intellectuals and leftist activists to Fanon was little more than a passing fad (Zolberg and Zolberg: 1967). The Zolberg's go on to argue that the ideas expressed in *The Wretched of the Earth* are extremely situational rather than universal. Fanon, they contend, is weak on theory and high in utopian vision. He analyzed the African colonial and immediate independence experience. He made only passing reference to the plight of black Americans.

Peter Geisman, on the other hand, tries to draw a picture which portrays Fanon as having at least thought of the American situation. He refers to a speech given by Fanon at a 1956 Paris meeting of the Congress of Black Writers and Artists. In the speech, Fanon considered the oppressed blacks of America in the same light as other oppressed peoples of color in the Third World. Geisman claims that, "In 1956 he (Fanon) suddenly began to map out the future course of the Black Power Movement in the United States, the resurgence of cultural nationalism, the resurrection of an African style" (Geisman: 1971, p. 150). While this is an interesting notion, it is not convincing. It does little to silence those critics who assert: "Fanon's ideas were written from an African experience, for the African people; the reason they did not endure as a guide to political action for black Americans was because they were irrelevant to the American context".

The substance of Fanon's work indeed was informed mainly by his personal experience in Africa and the Caribbean. His model, however, was informed by Marx, Lenin, Mao, Hagel, Sartre, Freud, Adler and others (Seigel: 1968-69, p. 93; and Martin: 1983, p. 182-190). He eclectically fashioned a Marxian model which was sensitive to the interaction between race and class in a capitalist society. It seems reasonable to assume that Fanon's model, then, could be adapted to fit a non-African situation where race and class are intertwined. For one reason or another, this logical connection was virtually ignored in black American political thought after the brief fascination with Fanon's ideas (Marable: 1980). 2 The question is: "Why?" Was it because the black American leftists who endorsed Fanon's ideas were flawed and lacked the intellectual and organizational capacities to generate a Fanonian strategy uniquely suited to liberate and empower black America? Was it because the objective conditions existing in the United States at the time Fanon's ideas were introduced were not conducive to such a radical transformation of the social, political and economic fabric of American society?

The purpose of this essay is to critically assess the reason why Fanon's ideas failed to have a lasting impact upon black politics in America. The discussion is divided into two parts. First, I briefly outline why Fanon and his ideas were so appealing to some black American intellectuals in the 1960's and early 1970's.

Second, I consider the various actors in the black political movement of that era, their contending positions and finally, the current situation in American politics as it relates to the prospects for a rediscovery of Fanon's ideas by black American intellectuals.

FRANTZ FANON AND THE BLACK AMERICAN CONDITION, 1964-1972

Edmund Burke III has described *The Wretched of the Earth* as a "utopian work, a mighty hymn to the advent of the new man, freed from colonialism, racism, national chauvinism and class oppression" (Burke: 1976, p. 131). The book is written in a secular salvationist style and aimed at oppressed people of color throughout the world. It was natural, then, for black American activists and scholars alike to be attracted to Frantz Fanon's analysis on the heels of the Civil Rights Movement. Between the 1950's and the early 1960's thousands and thousands of blacks and their allies confronted first-hand the raw oppression and brutal repression of the system of racism in the American South. Millions of others watched on television screens on a daily basis individual and institutional racism in action and read about its excesses in the print media.

The net effect of the witnessing of such confrontations was to heighten the consciousness of millions of black Americans who, until then, had more or less resigned themselves to their inferior "proper" place in American society. The courage of those black people who engaged in non-violent protest against a violent and entrenched status quo during the Civil Rights Movement inspired them (as well as others) to have pride in their black heritage and to demand their rights as citizens. It also rekindled in many a sense of black nationhood. In some cases, black activists and intellectuals envisioned the creation of an independent "Republic of New Africa" (Morris: 1975, p. 106). In others, the goal was merely respect and social justice for blacks within the context of a renewed America. This was the climate in which the revolutionary ideas of Frantz

Fanon were first introduced to black Americans.

Fanon's notions of the social psychology of colonialism; the cathartic effect of ritual, symbolic violence against an oppressor; and the creation of a new black identity through struggle were all thought to be elements essential to insure the ultimate empowerment of the Black Nation.

In order to apply Fanon's concepts to the situation of blacks in America, his model had to be adapted to fit objective circumstances. Rather than the 20th Century being characterized by classical colonialism, black American scholars and activists fashioned the concept of "internal colonialism" or "domestic colonialism", and stressed that all varieties of colonialism have similar effects on Third World peoples (including black Americans) wherever they are found. At a meeting of Latin American Revolutionaries in Havana, Cuba, in 1969, for example, Stokeley Carmichael proclaimed:

> Our people are a colony within the United States; you are colonies outside the United States. It is more than a figure of speech to say that the black communities in America are victims of white imperialism and colonial exploitation (Allen: 1970, p. 7; and Blauner: 1969, p. 393-408).

In contrast to classical colonialism, the domestic colonialism being described at this time did not involve the domination of a people in their traditional homeland by a foreign colonial power thousands of miles away from its home base. In the case of black Americans, it was argued, they were forcibly uprooted by the colonial power from their traditional territory and colonized in a new territory. J. H. O'Dell maintains, "In defining the colonial problem it is the role of the institutional mechanisms of colonial domination which are decisive" (Allen: 1970, p. 8). In other words, the colonial territory is nothing more than the arena of exploitation and oppression. The fundamental essence of colonialism, then, is the particular kind of institutionalized relationship which grows from the process of domination.

In describing the particular character of internal colonialism in America, Carmichael stated:

> There are over thirty million of us in the United States. For the most part we live in sharply defined areas in the rural black belt and shantytowns of the South, and more and more in the slums of the northern and western

> industrial cities ... In the cities we do not control the land, the houses or the stores. These are owned by whites who live outside the community. These are very real colonies, as their capital and cheap labor are exploited by those who live outside the cities. White people make the laws and enforce those laws with guns and nightsticks in the hands of white racist policemen and black mercenaries (Allen: 1970, p. 7).

Fanon's notions of the colonial experience and its impact upon the colonized were seen as particularly relevant to black American analysts because his model was based on the interaction between race and class in the colonial context. Not only was this theoretic contribution recognized by activists but also by scholars. Robert Staples employing a version of the domestic colonialism model, for example, examined the relationship between race and crime within the political-economic context of American society (Staples: 1975, p. 14-22). To devise his analytical framework, Staples relies specifically, although not exclusively, on Fanon's model. The study presented empirical evidence that black Americans were generally victimized by judicial and law enforcement institutions rather than being protected by them. They were more likely than whites charged with similar crimes to receive stiffer penalties, longer jail terms, and even the death penalty.

Staples also found that the colonial analogy could be applied to the traits of those who enforced the law. Black policemen tended to be underrepresented in the police force. Major black urban areas tended to be patrolled by white policemen who behaved like an army of occupation. Staples asserted, "The law itself constitutes the basis for colonial rule; and the ideology of white supremacy shapes the police force, the courts, and the prisons as instruments of continued colonial subjugation" (Staples: 1975, p. 7).

Although Staples endorses the colonial model suggested by Fanon, he does not entirely endorse his prescription. Staples ignores consideration of the use of violence on the part of the oppressed which Fanon suggests is necessary for the creation of the "new man" (Fanon: 1967b, p. 36). Instead, he calls for: community control of the police and trial by juries of one's peers (Staples: 1975, p. 22). Similar alternatives were offered by other American scholars at the time (Blauner: 1969).

Henry F. Jackson was more directly influenced by Fanon in his application of the colonial model to the plight of black America. Jackson, employing Fanon's model, suggests that "black liberation requires a fundamental restructuring of the status quo, a *social revolution* (Jackson: 1972, p. 483). Rather than concentrate on the reversal of the racial order, Jackson focuses on economic and political transformation. He argues that under the system of domestic colonialism, American blacks are politically and economically powerless and this keeps them from attaining full empowerment. To become liberated, Jackson contends, blacks must acquire both economic and political power through active participation in those systems. This power requires the presence of a clear sense of "nationalism" on the part of the black leadership. In articulating this argument, Jackson refers to Fanon's prescription that the revolutionary struggle must crystallize out of the "national movement" (Jackson: 1972, p. 483-89). Indeed, at the time Jackson wrote, there was a growing sense, particularly in black student and intellectual circles, that "national consciousness and solidarity was the end product of the Civil Rights and Black Power Movements. Jackson defined nationalism, in this instance, simply as a 'state of mind' which people of common origin, culture, religion and/or heritage hold regarding an actual or potential nation" (Jackson: 1972, p. 488). He argued that national liberation could be realized within the existing system; and in doing so, Jackson like other black American scholars seemed to reject Fanon's argument that:

> In decolonization, there is therefore the need of a complete calling into question of the colonial situation. If we wish to describe it precisely, we might find it in the well-known words: The last shall be first and the first last (Fanon: 1967b, p. 37).

Like other black American intellectuals as well as politicians, Jackson accepted the need for black liberation, but suggested that it could come about by better political organization within the context of American pluralist democracy rather than by violence. He contended that, "On the question of revolutionary black nationalism ... Fanon's analysis tends to lose its relevance to the black American situation" (Jackson: 1972, p. 488-89). The reason he offered was that black Americans had simply not completely rejected the myth of American pluralist democracy. Even the black American lumpenproletariat, Jackson argued, continued to believe in the system; and therefore, the objective conditions did not favor a violent revolution.

What seems to have initially attracted black American scholars to Fanon's work was his description of the colonial domination of whites over blacks and the assumption that black nationalist consciousness and cohesion could grow out of a struggle against racial economic oppression. From this scholars like Staples could suggest policy reforms designed to empower black communities. Others like Jackson could lay out the problem and suggest a solution which necessitated blacks determining their own destiny. Still others, such as Nancy Clasby, used Fanon's work to attempt to establish a case for home-grown black American heroes. Clasby, for example, described Malcolm X as "the American prototype" of an emergent black American consciousness similar to that found in Fanon's work (Clasby: 1974, p. 191). She attempted to show how Malcolm generated a new consciousness among black Americans not only of their worth but also of their potential power.

Fanon not only suggested an apt characterization of the situation of American institutional racism, but also a route to the political empowerment of *the world's* oppressed people. The blueprint offered might be different from place to place, but wherever they were found, according to Fanon, the oppressed held the keys to their own liberation. Malcolm X believed this as well, and after his assassination his idealism was carried on by black activists *cum* intellectuals like Eldridge Cleaver, Huey P. Newton, leaders of the Black Panthers, and Stokeley Carmichael of SNCC and later of the Panthers.

To a large extent, these young black American leftists were attracted to Fanon because of his humanism. Indeed, Fanon's ideas went beyond a narrow conceptualization of cultural nationalism which tends to be backward rather than forward looking. Fanon constructed an image of a black people with a unique culture that fit neatly into the composite culture of humanity. J. E. Seigel suggests, "Fanon sought to delve into blackness, to make it yield up the painful reality behind the masks it wears in the world, and finally to overcome it, to find the means by which blackness could be made irrelevant by merging it in the larger fact of humanity" (Seigel: 1968-69, p. 86; and Fanon: 1967a). Moreover, Fanon suggested that the oppressed had the duty to struggle to have their humanness accepted by those who oppressed them. They had an obligation to believe in their own humanness.

The notion of *struggle* - indeed, *violent struggle* - was also what attracted many young black activists, including the Panthers, to Fanon. Eldridge Cleaver, the Black Panther Minister for Information until he was forced into exile while attempting to evade imprisonment in California in 1968, suggested:

> Violence in the United States is inevitable. I think what Fanon will do is make that violence more intelligent and more directed and therefore more specific and probably less than it might have been, because it won't be wasted. It will be controlled violence (Sutton: 1971, p. 60).

Indeed, the Panthers were never committed to non-violence. The organization often found itself in violent armed conflict with the authorities because of its militant stance. The death of Martin Luther King at the hands of an assassin only seemed to give the Panthers an occasion to justify their dictum: "black liberation by any means necessary". In his essay, "Requiem to Non-Violence, written at the time of King's death, Cleaver wrote:

> Malcom X prophesied the coming of the gun, and Huey Newton picked up the gun, and now there is gun against gun (Cleaver: 1969, p. 78).

Many who joined the Black Panthers in the mid to late 1960's understood what Fanon had to say on violence in its literal rather than figurative sense, and like Fanon, they saw the lumpenproletariat as the urban spearhead of the revolution. This class had nothing to lose and everything to gain. The lumpenproletariat for Fanon were landless peasants forced to move to the cities in search of work. Once there they came to compromise a "horde of starving men, uprooted from their tribe and from their clan ... classless idlers [who] will by militant and decisive action discover the path to nationhood" (Fanon: 1967b, p. 124-30). The Panthers considered the black underclass to be the lumpenproletariat of American society. Moreover, rather than the lumpenproletariat being the parasites of the working class as some Marxists contend, the Panthers, like Fanon, considered them to be progressive as compared to the reactionary working class. In the absence of a black peasant class in America, the Panthers portrayed the lumpenproletariat as the holders of the noblest of "the peoples" values (Cleaver: 1967).

Contrary to the requirements of Fanon's model, although the Black Panthers saw themselves as the vanguard of the black revolution, they were never able to harness the spontaneous violence of the black American lumpenproletariat and to shape it into a constructive revolutionary force. They did much to improve the lot of ghetto residents where they operated. In 1968, the party initiated four community programs which addressed some of the most immediate problems of the local black poor in northern California. The Panthers began a free breakfast program for needy black children; initiated a petition campaign for community control of the police; and set up free health clinics and liberation schools. Soon such programs were exported to other parts of the country, and this as much as the Panther's ideology contributed to a growth in their following.

The Panther ideology was centered around the themes of black nationalism *and* class conflict. Consequently, the organization was able to secure support from more orthodox Marxist groups. As the organization grew, its appeal became more international. Yet, its following remained almost exclusively young black Americans who were born and lived in urban ghettos.

Apart from the core of the Black Panther following, few black leftists attempted to apply Fanon's ideas to America. Some cynical observers have argued that simply reading Fanon and spouting his ideas does little to bring about black liberation. Roy Innis, for example, contended that for many Fanon was nothing more than a romantic escape:

> You don't have to take action, all you have to do is walk with a couple of Fanons under your arm. That's your badge of courage. That becomes your gun and your revolt. You can go home to your living room and fight the battle right there. Or go see *The Battle of Algiers*. That's really doing it. And maybe if you're a little bit psychopathic, then maybe you'll knock off somebody and be on trial in New Haven, or maybe you knock some guys off in Harlem, but then you have to be more than romantic, you have to be a little bit stupid and also a little bit psychopathic (Sutton: 1971, p. 60).

Indeed, Fanon's major contribution to black American political thought and action should not have been his thoughts on violence. Black Americans who reject his notions on the subject as well as those who endorse these ideas, often misinterpret Fanon. Fanon did not glorify violence for violence sake; nor did he suggest that violence perpetrated by the oppressed against the oppressor would cause all problems to be solved. The violent rejection of all forms of domination and exploitation, however, was for him the key to true liberation. According to Fanon, the form of this violence would have to be determined by objective conditions.

The value of the Fanonian model lies in its explication of the relationship between racism and capitalism; and, in what it has to say about how that relationship contributes to a sense of powerlessness among the oppressed. Once the oppressed realize the source of their problems they inherently have the means to solve them. Fanon correctly perceived that empowerment can only be achieved through struggle and rebirth.

PROSPECTS FOR A REDISCOVERY OF THE FANONIAN MODEL IN BLACK AMERICA

With the virtual demise of the Black Panther Party and other black leftist groups by 1972, Fanon's ideas all but disappeared from the lexicon of black American politics (Thompson: 1972, p. 46-53). In part this was due to the shallowness of his appeal among black leftist groups, and in part it was due to the adaptation of the American economic and political systems as a result of the Civil Rights Act of 1964, the Voting Rights Act of 1965, and the policies which grew out of these laws.

In 1968, the Black Panther Party drafted Stokeley Carmichael to become its Prime Minister. He left the Party a year later because of his disapproval of its growing tendency towards alliances with white leftists. For Carmichael the beauty of Fanon was in how he wedded race and class into this model for black liberation. Carmichael accused Eldridge Cleaver and other Panthers of being preoccupied with trying to be accepted by the New Left. Manning Marable has noted that in response Cleaver charged Carmichael with being involved in a "skin game", and asserted that white leftists who were familiar with Fanon, Malcolm X and Marcuse were more suitable allies in the fight against racism and capitalism than narrow nationalists like him (Marable: 1981, p. 429). Huey Newton in the same vein described the goals of the Black Panther Party in 1972 as "Revolutionary Communalism" which was supposed to negate "the outmoded concept of nationhood" (Thompson: 1971, p. 53). Thus began the debate among black intellectuals - which has continued ever since - over whether race or class is more important in analyzing the black American condition. This development must be considered in light of the transformation in the American political economy after the Civil Rights Era.

The Civil Rights Movement gave way to the Black Power Movement. At the purely ideological level, Black Power referred to black pride and self-determination (Carmichael and Hamilton: 1971). These are values which are indeed central to the Fanonian model. However, even as the content of the ideology was being fleshed out, it was being reinterpreted and co-opted by would-be black capitalists and their white patrons in the political and corporate establishment (Allen: 1970, p. 167-82). Black Power came to be equated with "Green Power" or "Dollar Power" and with blacks getting their share of the capitalist economic "pie". Whereas Fanon had seen capitalism as one of the major obstacles to black empowerment, in an atmosphere of new opportunities to play the capitalist game, many black American intellectuals who were so desperately needed to take the struggle to another level, abandoned the course. This is quite understandable since Fanon's ideas had appealed to young black leftists who represented only a small segment of black activist organizations at the time. Sociologist Harry Edwards in a 1972 interview asserted:

> There is ... no 'Black Left'. What we've seen since the early 1960's were activist children of black Democrats and Republicans (Thompson: 1971, p. 48).

Civil Rights organizations such as Martin Luther King's Southern Christian Leadership Conference (SCLC), CORE (Congress of Racial Equality), and the NAACP (National Association for the Advancement of Colored People) basked in the glory of their victories following the passage of the Civil Rights Act. They seemed confident that they had proved non-violence was the only viable unconventional form of protest strategy open to the poor and the weak.

Even after the passage of the Civil Rights Act and the Voting Rights Act, King's SCLC and the NAACP dominated the black political scene. Cultural nationalism in the United States was reduced to mere slogan and symbolic ritual, as were varying strands of Pan-Africanist ideology. The Black Panthers were harassed and eventually liquidated. Once federal and local authorities recognized the explosive potential of the Panthers and their appeal to the black underclass, their fate was sealed. On December 4, 1969, in Chicago, Illinois, for example, police raided the home of several Black Panther Party members in the dead of night, killing Fred Hampton and Mark Clark while they slept, and arresting others. This sort of tactic was repeated in other places with similar results until the Panthers ceased to be a significant political force.

Simultaneously, the administration of President Lyndon B. Johnson, in response to widespread and severe urban riots in black ghettos throughout the late 1960's heralded his *War on Poverty* and *Great Society* programs. The federal government came to be intimately involved in financing and administering welfare and educational programs designed to facilitate some measure of black empowerment. The "buzz words" at the time became "community action" and "community control". Consequently, many blacks came to see the federal government as flexible and concerned about their interests.

A part of Johnson's reforms included federally mandated "affirmative action". He pledged to use the full weight of the federal government's authority to make sure that blacks and other minorities were afforded equal educational and economic opportunity. By doing this, Johnson and other politicians and corporate leaders who endorsed his plan clearly hoped to diffuse black discontent. Over the years, the tactic worked.

Fanon warned that the initial success of the nationalist movement could be rendered meaningless if the nationalist bourgeoisie, the black middle class, simply replaced the oppressor and continued his ways (Fanon: 1967b, p. 148). In effect, this is what happened to the movement towards black liberation in America by the 1970's. To be sure, black liberation - on purely objective grounds - would have had to have entailed something less than a total reversal of the racial order. However, some have argued that there was no apparent reason why its pursuit should have been abandoned before all black Americans were guaranteed an equitable share of society's benefits. Fanon recognized the need for the people to hold the nationalist leadership accountable, and he cautioned them not to be lulled into false consciousness by partial liberation.

Fanon did not have the opportunity to become intimately familiar with the situation of black Americans, but other observers could well have been speaking on his behalf when they described the adaptive strategies on monopoly capital and how black Americans are affected.

Paul Baran and Paul Sweezy, for example, have argued that a combination of vested economic interests, socio-psychological needs and technological trends - all deeply rooted in monopoly capitalism - have served to prevent blacks as a group from advancing very far in American society in spite of legal protections and compensatory programs (Baran and Sweezy, p. 268-71). Baran and Sweezy contend that the black bourgeoisie or middle class, the critical actors needed to advance the cause of black people's empowerment, were co-opted by mere tokenism. Fanon surely would have said the same. They were allowed access to a material stake in the existing social order. If their loyalty to the system (as opposed to their own people) could be secured, the establishment would neutralize their potential for revolutionizing the black movement. Affirmative action and civil rights laws were necessary to secure the allegiance of the black middle class to the system. They needed to be provided with greater access to the dominant institutions of society (corporations, government bureaucracies, the universities, the suburbs) in order to ensure their loyalty to the system. In the end, Baran and Sweezy contend, few blacks can take advantage of such opportunities for upward mobility. In some cases it is because they lack the skills to do so; in others it is because of the persistence of individual as well as institutional racism.

Baran and Sweezy argue that the essence of tokenism is the slight and selective upward mobility of minorities (Baran and Sweezy: 1966, p. 174-78). Those who make it come to view themselves as special because they have mastered the system. They quickly abandon any thought they might have had that their advancement was due to the imperatives of tokenism. They come to rationalize their dependence on the white establishment for favors and support, saying, "That's how they've (whites have) been doing it all along. Now, I belong to the Club". Baran and Sweezy go on to suggest that, if co-optation fails, the system attempts to destroy the independent black leader by branding him a Communist or a troublemaker and by subjecting him to legal harassment.

One of the main purposes of tokenism, Baran and Sweezy maintain, is to disconnect the best and the brightest of the black middle class from their people, and thereby to make them unavailable or unwilling to play leadership roles in the liberation movement (Baran and Sweezy: 1966, p. 148). They tend to concentrate more on personal advancement and on the advancement of their immediate families.

Even though they might not benefit directly from the newfound opportunities for upward mobility, many blacks take pride in the accomplishments of those who do advance. They come to believe that the system is now open, and that their children - or their children's children - may have similar opportunities. There are those who claim that Baran and Sweezy are much too cynical, but their argument represents a view which I feel would have been close to Fanon's if he was alive.

The War on Poverty, the Great Society, and affirmative action programs were all created with "white backlash". Average whites came to believe that blacks wanted too much too quickly. This conservative trend in white America began to become manifested in the late 1960's, and much of this sentiment represented in the Presidential campaign of former Alabama governor George C. Wallace. But it did not burst fully into view until Ronald Reagan became President in 1981. By then, it was clear that the Great Society was over. Reagan immediately made it known that he was opposed to vigorous government intervention in the pursuit of affirmative action.

By the late 1970's the black leadership class was severely split. Black leftists like Eldridge Cleaver, Stokeley Carmichael, H. Rap Brown, Robert Williams, and Huey P. Newton were either in exile, in jail, or maintaining a low political profile in order to avoid becoming victims of a system which by then was involved in an active campaign against all radicals. In their place, there emerged opportunistic black conservatives, usually intellectuals who had entrenched themselves in the establishment. For the most part, these individuals have in common their disdain for affirmative action programs. These are often talented men who in a color-neutral society would probably have made it anyway. Indeed, they might well have secured their current positions on their own merits. They seem to feel, however, that the emphasis on affirmative action for blacks minimized their individual accomplishments. As a group, black conservatives tend to downplay the need for the federal government to insure equality of opportunity or equality of condition for minorities. They do not see race as being as important as it once was in determining economic opportunity.

The tendency among many black conservatives is to blame the black lower and underclasses for their own condition. The argument is that the opportunities are there if only blacks are willing to seize them. Affirmative action, they say, has a double effect on blacks: (l) it stigmatizes them and minimizes the achievements of the ones who succeed and, (2) it creates a dependency complex among those who feel they cannot do without affirmative action. Both points have a ring of truth to them, but what is equally true is that racism continues to exist in America, and it continues to be intertwined with social class.

Although some blacks have prospered since the 1960's, in relative economic terms the majority of black people have not progressed much. In 1984, two out of every five black families were below the poverty line as compared to only one out of every ten white families. The median family income for blacks stood at only $13,471, while the median family income for whites was $23,647. The ratio between white and black median family incomes in 1984 was about the same as it was in 1967. By 1983, the unemployment rate for blacks was more than double (20 percent) that of whites (9 percent). In 1984, 33.8 percent of all black families earned less than ten thousand dollars per year and thus were below the poverty line. Only 11.5 percent of all white families were in that category. Less than 15 percent of all black families earned more than $35,000, while almost twice as high a percentage (29.6 percent) of white families were in this bracket (Statistical Abstract: 1986).

The illusion of black success has neutralized the discontent of many blacks who themselves may not be doing so well, and it has encouraged many of those who are successful to claim that they are because of personal qualities rather than as a result of the design of the status quo. Many blacks who "make it" rationalize their divorce from those who have not "made it" by saying, "The opportunity is there for all who will take it, and it's too bad for those who don't see this and who don't help themselves".

Even some black conservatives recognize the negative implications of such a trend for the advancement of black Americans as a group. Sociologist William Julius Wilson, for example, argues that the problem of black America today is the problem of the black underclass (Wilson: 1987). However, the black underclass, he contends, are not the source of their own plight. Nor is the problem a result of institutional or individual racism. Instead, Wilson contends that this dilemma is rooted in: (1) natural shifts in the American national economy and, (2) the widening class divisions among blacks as a group.

Over the past two decades, Wilson argues, the national economy has come to be characterized by an increase in the demand for service and white collar skills and by a simultaneous decline in the availability of low-skilled, high-paying industrial jobs. Consequently, the educationally disadvantaged (a class in which blacks are disproportionately represented) tend to be the most negatively affected. The problem is compounded by the continued miseducation and non-education of black youth. Many of the black youth, then, are relegated to permanent underclass status.

Regarding the widening gap between those blacks who have made it out of the ghetto and those who remain, Wilson argues, as do some leftists, affirmative action has contributed to this rift. He notes that prior to the reforms which began in the 1960's, blacks of all classes were forced to live and work in the same communities and to rely on the same social institutions. Now, however, the black middle class can escape the ghetto and leave its problems behind. Wilson's solution is not more welfare, nor is it as Fanon might have prescribed, black middle-class "class suicide" in the cause of "nationhood". His solution is better public policies which seek to serve the needs of all equally. By taking this position, Wilson, like so many other black conservative intellectuals who mean well, totally ignored the continued profound effects of racism and the need to tackle this cancer as vigorously - if not more so - as ever before.

Wilson merely notes the widening gaps in the black class system. He applies no value judgments to this development. It is clear, however, that the stagnation of black progress in America can in large part be laid at the feet of many of the black middle class who have physically and emotionally disconnected themselves or who have by chance become disconnected from the black masses.

In a recent interview, black advertising executive Frank Mingo asserted, "I don't mean it in a derogatory way, but a black family that moves into a higher socio-economic level inevitably develops a new and different social agenda" (Williams: 1987, p. 37). Mingo went on to emphasize that the first obligation of the black middle class is to survive, and the second is to take care of its offspring. "I don't think," he said, "we should put the burden on individuals in the black middle class to turn around and help the underclass" (Williams: 1987, p. 38).

This line of thinking is representative of the burgeoning black conservative middle class whom Manning Marable labels the "new accommodationists" and "black Reaganites" (Marable: 1981, p. 430). In 1980, blacks gave Ronald Reagan more than 15 percent of their votes, the highest percentage they have given a Republican presidential candidate since 1960. Black conservatives have subsequently been rewarded with high level government positions and prestigious appointments for their loyalty and are frequently turned to when Reagan wants a black opinion. Consequently, the old civil rights leadership has been put on the defensive. They feel that there is much more to be done in the cause of black liberation, but they find difficulty in gaining the support of white liberals who are also on the defensive from the conservative onslaught. Moreover, they cannot rely much on black conservatives in positions of power because the conservatives feel that racism is no longer a problem and that blacks should do more to help themselves.

Perhaps the most dynamic and sensitive black leader on the scene today is Jesse Jackson. Jackson harps on some of the same themes as black conservatives, but with one difference. He feels he has a mission to make sure that black people - black youth in particular - are proud of their heritage and respect themselves. Without openly endorsing Fanon's ideas, Jackson's appeal is rich in the same kind of humanism which pervades the work of Fanon.

Jackson has pressured corporations like Coca Cola, Coors, Kentucky Fried Chicken, and Major League Baseball to open up their executive ranks to blacks and to reinvest some of their profits in black communities. At the same time he has pressured federal, state and local governments to keep up their efforts to alleviate the problems of poverty, homelessness, poor education, and unemployment. What he has not seemed to be able to do is to build a national black political movement capable of playing the role Fanon assigned to the nationalist party in the Third World.

Jackson has emerged as the charismatic spokesman for the left in American politics, but that left is only slightly left of center. In 1984, he fashioned what he termed the "Rainbow Coalition", despite opposition from old guard civil rights leaders and regular members of the Democratic party, and he ran in the Democratic Presidential primary. This coalition included poor and dispossessed people from all races as well as liberals and leftist intellectuals. People supported Jackson not because they thought he could win, but because of what he stood for.

Jesse Jackson, however, is no Fanonist. He believes that the system can be made to work. The one individual who comes closest to being disposed to applying Fanon's ideas to the contemporary black situation in America is Kwame Toure (Stokeley Carmichael). After his return from exile in Conakry, Guinea, in the late 1970's, Toure set about organizing the All-African People's Revolutionary Party. His message is a blend of Marxism and Pan-Africanism, and he appeals mainly to mature black college students and radical black intellectuals who seek alternatives to the established political parties. Toure's movement, however, does not have any appeal to speak of at the black grassroots. Except in a few localities, the same could be said for other black groups, like the National Black Political Convention and the National Black Independent Political Party, which have attempted to pursue third party options in recent years.

Fanon correctly noted that once the goal of national independence is achieved, the nationalist party must be prepared to adapt for the purpose of pursuing the social revolution. It could be said that in the United States the end of the Civil Rights Era marked a watershed akin to national political independence in the third world. The next step, according to the Fanonian model, would be for the nationalist party to lead the social transformation. This party must, however, be held accountable by the people. Clearly, no party such as this exists for black Americans at this time; therefore, it is understandable that the liberation movement has stalled. To be sure, America is not Africa, or Asia, or Latin America. Objective conditions vary from place to place. Perhaps "national liberation" in the sense that Fanon meant is not a realistic goal for black Americans.

Black success in electoral politics since the mid-1960's has done much to neutralize any prospect for a vigorous liberation movement of nationwide proportions. The average black citizen has come to believe that the system does work for him at least part of the time. In 1969, there were only about 300 black elected officials nationwide. By 1986, that figure climbed to almost 6,500, and there were almost 300 black urban mayors (*Black Elected Officials,* 1986, p. 15). The symbolism represented in the steady increase in black elected officials at the local level has a profound effect on the political consciousness of most black Americans. Most see this as a significant sign of progress, and pay little notice to the continued disproportionate representation of blacks at all levels of elective office. For example, in 1987, out of 100 U.S. Senators not one was black; only 20 of 435 U.S. Representatives were black; and although blacks represented about twenty percent of the South's population, they accounted for only three percent of all the elected officials in the region. Clearly, there is no real reason to lessen the drive for meaningful black empowerment. However, the urgency of the matter seems to have escaped all but a few in the black community.

CONCLUSION

Although "national liberation" in the sense that Fanon meant it for Africa is beyond the reach of black America, meaningful political empowerment is a realistic goal for many black communities. This would call for the formation of black political movements at the grassroots, guided by enlightened and committed members of the black middle class, and characterized by a following which is politically and culturally conscious. The black middle class has the resources to contribute to this renewed struggle - money, talent, time. Somehow, they must come to accept their mission.

The lumpenproletariat of black America, the underclass, presents problems for any attempt to form such a movement (Wilson: 1987; Glasgow, 1980; and Auletta, 1982). Indeed, even Fanon realized that in the Third World this class can just as easily be a force for good or ill. They can be mobilized in the cause of revolutionary change, but their allegiance is not guaranteed unless material rewards are forthcoming.

In America, the black underclass is large and growing. These are the chronically unemployed undereducated, and miseducated, predominantly young blacks who are destined to remain outside of the economic, social, and political mainstream throughout their lives. They are apolitical, but not politically unconscious. The black underclass realizes that it is in a hopeless situation, and that it above all is politically powerless.

The writings of Frantz Fanon seem to indicate that he would have been undaunted by this situation. He would no doubt have argued that in spite of their wretched condition, the black American lumpenproletariat must be mobilized if the goal of the empowerment of the black American nation is to be consummated. Fanon's discussion about the need for a rebirth of national consciousness among the oppressed still has relevance to black America. It seems that such a consciousness is needed to accentuate the continuing significance of race and class in determining the black condition. Consciousness of this sort could open the way for the creation of the "new souls" that Fanon talked about to lead the struggle for black empowerment in the United States to another level. This could happen only if significant numbers of the black middle class recognize and accept their leadership roles, and if the black underclass is made to recognize its self-worth. Leadership may take many forms. It does not necessarily require highly visible political activism. Leadership might simply mean utilizing one's talents consciously and to the fullest on behalf of the progress of the group. Those blacks in positions of power and wealth have a special role to play, if only they recognize and act on it.

REFERENCES

Allen, Robert L. Black Awakening in Capitalist America: An *Analytical History*, New York: Anchor Books, 1970.

Auletta, Ren. *The Underclass,* New York: Vintage, 1982.

Baran, Paul A. and Sweezy, Paul M. *Monopoly Capital,* New York: Monthly Review Press, 1966.

Black Elected Officials, 1986, Washington, D.C.: Joint Center for Political Studies, 1986.

Blauner, Robert. "Internal Colonialism and Ghetto Revolt", *Social Problems,*

Vol. 16, No. 4 (Spring), p. 393-400, 1969.

Burke III, Edmund. Frantz Fanon's *The Wretched of the Earth*, Daedalus, Vol. 105, No. 1 (Winter), 1976.

Carmichael, Stokeley and Hamilton, Charles V. *Black Power: The Politics of Liberation in America*, New York: Vintage, 1971.

Clasby, Nancy. "The Autobiography of Malcolm X: A Mythic Paradigm", *The Journal of Black Studies*, Vol. 5, No. (September), 1974.

Cleaver, Eldridge. "On the Ideology of the Black Panther Party, " San Francisco: Black Panther Party, 1967.

_____ , *Post-Prison Writings and Speeches*, New York: Vintage, 1969.

Fanon, Frantz. *Black Skin, White Mask*, New York: Grove, 1967a.

_______ , *The Wretched of the Earth*, New York: Grove, 1967b.

Geisman, Peter. *Fanon*, New York: The Dial Press, 1971.

Glasgow, Douglas. *The Black Underclass,* New York: Vintage, 1980.

Hansen, Emmanuel. *Frantz Fanon: Social and Political Thought,* Columbus, Ohio: Ohio State University Press, 1977.

Heath, G. Louis, ed. *The Black Panther Leaders Speak*, Metuchen, New Jersey: The Scarecrow Press, 1976.

Jackson, Henry. "Political and Social Ideas of Frantz Fanon: Relevance to Black Americans" , *Pan-African Journal*, Vol. 5, No. 4 (Winter), 1972.

Marable, Manning. *Through the Prism of Race and Class: Modern Black Nationalism in the U.S.,* Dayton, Ohio: Black Research Associates, 1980.

_______, "Toward a Black Politics: Beyond the Race-Class Dilemma," *The Nation* (April), 1981.

Martin, Tony. *The Pan African Connection*, Dover, Massachusetts: The Majority Press, 1983.

Morris, Milton. *The Politics of Black America,* New York: Harper and Row, 1975.

Seale, Bobby. *Seize the Time,* New York: Vintage, 1970.

Seigel, J. E. "On Frantz Fanon" , *American Scholar* (Winter), Vol. 38, No. 1, 1968-69.

Staples, Robert. "White Racism, Black Crime, and American Justice: An Application of the Colonial Model to Explain Crime and Race", *Phylon*, XXXVI, No. 1 (March), 1975.

Statistical Abstract of the United States, 1986, Washington, D.C.: Department of Commerce, 1986.

Sutton, Horace. "Fanon: The Revolutionary Prophet," *Saturday Review* (July), 1971.

Thompson, Walt. "What's Left of the Black Left?", *Ramparts*, Vol. 10, No. 12 (June), 1972.

Williams, Juan. "Moving Up at Last", *Harpers* (February), 1987.

Wilson, William Julius. *The Truly Disadvantaged: The Inner* City, the Underclass, and Public Policy, Chicago: University of Chicago Press, 1987.

NOTES

1. Watt's assertion, however, is disputed by the conservative leader of CORE, Roy Innis, who is quoted as saying: "I have my doubts whether that Fanon-reading crowd was on any roof. I'm sure they weren't in the streets [during the urban riots of the late 1960's], that's too close to reality."

2. Exceptions to this can be seen in the work of Manning Marable, Throuqh the Prism of Race and Class: Modern Black *Nationalism in the U.S.* (Dayton, Ohio: Black Research Associates, 1980); and in the political work of Rwame Toure (Stokeley Carmichael) as he attempted to form the AllAfrican People's Revolutionary Party beginning in the mid1970's.

CHAPTER 16

COMMON THEMES IN THE HISTORY OF AFRICANS AND AFRICAN- AMERICANS

Vincent G. Simiyu

By origin and probably by destiny, Africans and African-Americans are a slice of Africa. The massive forced migration across the Atlantic in the era of the Atlantic slave trade transported part of African history and culture to the Americas. That history and culture, modified in the capitalist crucible of North America and South America including the West Indies and other islands, has nonetheless stoically maintained some of the most striking aspects. The destiny of capitalist accumulation based on the use of Black people, whether in the Americas or on the African continent, has sealed the common themes of African and African-Americans embracing the entire societal spectrum in the two spheres of the African peoples.

There has been a kind of accusing finger-pointing by African-Americans at their African brothers and sisters: "You sold us!" Caught off guard, the African brother or sister has apparently no answer. It is important to transcend that pedestrian level and rise to the pedestal level of a historical discourse. Africans on both sides of the Atlantic have contributed a great deal to the rise of the modern world in the last three hundred years and African-Americans and Africans should see themselves not as mere victims of history but as part and parcel of shareholding in the stakes of the modern world. A close critical look at the internal dynamics and development of African societies at that time and during the period shows the underpinnings of slavery in those societies.

Several factors are significant: 1) the African/African-American contribution to the rise of the world capitalist system; 2) the political and cultural sensitization of the African-American at the end of the 19th century leading to the early sensitization of Africans through political Pan-Africanism during the first half of the 20th century, and finally, the recurrent aspects of African culture among African-Americans, especially those of the sea islands of South Carolina and Georgia. In this context, the preservation of culture through oral tradition, not to mention material culture, is one of the most fascinating common themes.

AFRICANS AND AFRICAN-AMERICANS AS CONTRIBUTORS TO THE MODERN WORLD ECONOMIC SYSTEM

Studies done by many contemporary scholars today point out the contribution of the peoples of the African continent to the rise, not only of the North American economic system, but of the entire western hemisphere during the last three hundred years or so. J.E. Inikori argues that the:

> export of slaves trade from Africa in world history is . . . tied up with the problem of understanding and explaining the historical origins or the contemporary world economic system (a) (Inikori: 1992: 75).

Africans contributed to the economic system in the early part of the modern period from the 16th to the 19th century as consumers. In the second part Africans contributed to the economic system as both producers of primary commodities for the world market and consumers of Western manufacturers. Africans in the Americas also contributed to the economic system in the sugar triangle (including the Southern United States) during the rise of the Northeastern American capitalist system in the first half of the 19th century. African-Americans also shared the common consumer role with Africans in the 1750-1820s; they bought the English checked cotton cloth.

With regard to the figures of slaves transported across the Atlantic, Inikori points out that only partial research has been done since Philip Curtin published his findings in 1969. More recent works show that the estimates are in the range of 19.6 million people who were forcibly transported across the Atlantic.

Inikori further argues that the early mercantile system in Western Europe, starting from the end of the Medieval period with Christopher

Columbus' arrival in the Americas and based on the Spanish-American bullion, plunged into a deep crisis in the seventeenth century. New opportunities for Europeans' profitable investment shrank. Europe had to look elsewhere and share the new opportunities within the plantation agriculture in the Americas, reducing mineral production in South America to a relative position. This restructuring took place in the 18th century on the basis of the now well known triangular trade. This triangular trade involved the transportation of slaves from Africa to the Americas to become a labor force on the plantation farms of sugar cane (Latin America and Caribbean), tobacco and cotton in North America, and agricultural produce and precious metals - gold and silver from the Americas (South) to Europe. European manufacturers traveled from Europe to Africa, especially Western Africa, for the purchase of more slaves.

> The eighteenth century can be truly called the Atlantic stage of European economic development. Foreign trade, and especially trade with the Americas, was the most dynamic sector of the whole economy (for instance, French colonial trade increased tenfold between 1716 and 1787), and furthermore the demand from overseas was stimulating the growth of a wide range of industries as well as increased specialization and division of labour. (F. Couzet: cited by Inikori [b]).

The wide range of industries stimulated by this overseas trade included the English import substitution industry which began in the second half of the 18th century - the cotton industry to replace the Indian cotton in the English home market (Inikori (b): 1992). Through a series of laws passed by the House of Commons on the prompting of the local textile merchants, the English established an effective protectionism that shut out Indian cottons completely. Checked cotton manufacturers became so popular in Africa and among the African-Americans on the plantations in America that this branch alone made the fortunes of the English textile industry at that time. Africans and African-Americans had a common role of consumers.

> ...this branch of the industry provided a preponderant share of total English cotton textile exports from 1750 to 1774, varying between 48 percent and 86 percent during the period." (Ibid:157)

Every European nation - French, Dutch, Portuguese, you name it - fully participated in this lucrative West African trade, realizing enormous accumulation of financial capital. When England was at war during the American Revolution, European nations benefitted the more. Between 1750 and 1807, the value of East India and English cottons exported from England to West Africa rose from £7, 839 to £270, 274 (Inikori, Ibid: 175- 176).

With regard to the British North American colonies, African slave labor enabled them to move from a subsistence to a flourishing economy in the 17th century because of plantation agriculture in the South, producing rice, tobacco, and cotton, first for the European (British) industries, then for the Northeastern industries in America. In the decades after the Revolution, African slave labor enabled the British North American colonies to industrialize.

At the beginning of the nineteenth century, North American capitalism flourished on the basis of the African Southern slave labor - a restructuring that led to an internal division of labor whereby the South specialized in plantation agriculture, the North specialized in industrialization, and the Midwest specialized in the food industries. The South became the 'internal third world', so to speak, of the United States with surplus value of the African-American's labor in the South invested not in the South but in the North, especially the Northeast. Slave-based agriculture in the Southern colonies of America was tied up in the regional triangular trade between the future United States (distilling rum), the West Indies (supplying molasses) and Africa (supplying slaves).

It was the development of the textile industry in the United States at the beginning of the nineteenth century that best epitomized the contribution of the African-American in the rise of North American capitalism. This contribution has a running parallel with Africa's contribution, a century later, to the enhancement of a maturing world capitalism through colonial forced labor.

> Far more important than the number of Africans taken from their homeland and sold into slavery are the labor of African peoples and the profitability of their products in the various sites where they were enslaved and exploited (Bailley: 1992: 206-9).

The cumulative net migration into the Americas was overwhelmingly of Africans rather than Europeans who by 1820 were totally outnumbered in the ratio of three to one, of 8,399,000 Africans compared to 2,365,000 Europeans (Ibid, 208). In Brazil in 1798 out of a population of 3.29 million, 1.988 were of African origin, of whom 1.5 million were slaves. The proportion had not changed much by 1872 when peoples of African origin were 9.9 million (58%) of the total Brazilian population (Inikori (a): 96).

It was the textile industry, dependent on cotton produced in the South by slave labor, that first entered into the Atlantic system and then into the rapidly developing internal market of the United States. The textile industry sparked the industrial revolution the industrial revolution of the United States from the beginning of the nineteenth century. The number of people employed in the textile industry in New England rose from 5,000 people in 1816 to about 100,000 people by 1840 (Ibid.).

> This remarkable explosion of industrial activity was dominated in every sense by the expansion of the cotton textile component of manufacturing. The cotton industry was the only major New England industry to expand steadily in the earliest years of the period from 1816 to the early 1820's. In the late 1830's cotton textiles accounted for two-thirds of the value added in all large-scale New England manufacturing (Zevin 1971: 123 - quoted by Bailley: Ibid - 221).

By 1860, the United States had become the world's biggest cotton producer with 60% of the world production. The great pioneer families in the American textile industry, e.g. Moses Brown, Samuel Slater, and Francis Cabot Lowell, either directly traded in African slaves or dealt in business directly linked to the Atlantic-West Indian slave trade and slavery. During 1768-1772, New England merchants dominated the shipping between British and foreign West Indies and the various regions of the United States (Ibid: 214).

New England merchants also dominated the internal shuttle slave trade supplying slaves to South Carolina, Savannah and other planters in the South. At the same time, they supplied the West Indies with a variety of goods. The West Indies were, therefore, both producers of molasses and consumers of manufactured products, just as Africans on the African continent were suppliers of slaves and consumers of European and later American manufactured goods.

The contributions of Africans on the continent to the modern world economic system did not, however, reach the optimum until the advent of twentieth century formal colonialism. Without getting into the details of the colonial economy of Africa, it must be pointed out that the political economy of European colonialism in Africa revolved around massive land alienation dispossessing Africans for white settlement as a ruthless strategy to force Africans into colonial labor.

In Southern Africa one can say the struggle through formal colonialism over land between Africans on the one hand and Europeans and/or their descendants on the other throughout the nineteenth and early decades of the twentieth century epitomized colonial political economy in its expropriation mechanism. In the 1906 Zulu revolt, that nation lost virtually all its land. By subsequent legislation in South Africa and Rhodesia, Africans lost tracts and tracts of land in the name of colonialism.

In Zimbabwe alone (Southern Rhodesia) by 1925 as much as 35 million acres of prime land, including all land 900 m. above the sea level and all land within 40 km of the rail track, was alienated from Africans for European settlement (Kaniki, 1985). Furthermore, 50.8% of land in the colony was reserved for white settlement while Africans (over 90% of the colony's population) had only 22.4% of land left for them, most of it being poor land (Ibid). In South Africa by virtue of the Native Land Act (to mention only that one) passed in 1913, 88% of the land was reserved for whites (20% of the total population) while only 12% of the land was left for Africans.

In Kenya the appropriated land was simply called white highlands. By virtue of the 1915 Crown Lands Ordinance, the white highlands were under 999 year leases. The highlands themselves constituted a small fraction of the total land in Kenya, but, by 1930 75% of the total African population lived on these lands. Reserving those lands for white settlement meant that by 1929 nearly 75% of the African population had been displaced in favor of some 16,600 Europeans. Land alienation was not a uniform phenomenon throughout Africa during the colonial period. There was little, if any, land alienation in British West Africa precisely because the African elders and early elite mobilized resistance which went up to the British Privy Council for formal litigation and this British "Supreme Court" ruled in favor of Africans.

In French and Belgian Africa, land alienation took the form of large concessions to exploitation companies and sometimes private individuals. The concessions were for wood exploitation in the dense forests of central equatorial Africa or for the exploitation of rich minerals (Coquery-Vidrovitch: 1985).

The land alienation in itself does not constitute a common theme in the history of Africans and African-Americans. However, the objective does. Africans were to supply free or near-free labor to work the land or mine the rich minerals through various legislations (in S.A. Apprenticeship Act, 1922; Native Urban Areas Act, 1923; Native Adm. Act, 1927; Native Services Act, 1932; in Kenya, Master Servant Act, 1916; Native Registration Act, 1919; in French, Portuguese and Belgian colonies, the Indigenats, and so on). In Southern Africa from 1867 up to the 1930's, Africans were literally forced through various legislations and the trappings of the colonial political economy to bring out the underground wealth for the world capitalism market. Migrant labor became, throughout the entire colonial period to the present day, the hub of the mineral industry in this region of Africa (V.G. Simiyu: 1991). Gold has been the central nerve of the world finance system; during the last century gold has been the pivot of the world economic order. It is African labor that has given it the value.

Other minerals in Southern Africa, and elsewhere - diamonds, copper, cobalt, platinum, chrome, uranium, phosphates, iron, manganese. . . you name it - all have entered as critical elements of the world economic order thanks to the cheap labor of Africans throughout the colonial period and today. The brutalities of forced labor in the French equatorial Africa (Suret-Canale: 1971) or of the migrant workers in South Africa have a parallel in the brutalities of the slave plantation economies in the American Southern colonies and the West Indian sugar plantations.

Africans produced and continue to produce other primary commodities for the world market, not for their benefit but for the world economic order. These commodities whose proportion of world trade today has dwindled to a pittance, were very important in the first half of the twentieth century - cocoa, palm oil and palm kernels, cotton, coffee, tea, pyrethrum, natural rubber. They were part and parcel of the world accumulation system.

Africans and African-Americans share this destiny of having been the labor (though not sole suppliers) in the rise and development of the modern world economic system. Even though they have also been consumers, because of the exploitative nature of the system, their consumption has led to their underdevelopment rather than to development.

OTHER AFRICAN AND AFRICAN-AMERICAN COMMONALITIES

There are other areas of commonality between the history of Africans and that of African-Americans. At the end of the last century there were what one historian has called the nostalgic movements of African-Americans to go back to Africa. African-Americans like Bishop Henry McNeal Turner and Jamaican Marcus Garvey conceived the solution of the problems of Africans and African-Americans in terms of emigration of African-Americans back to Africa. Once there, a vigorous evangelization process would salvage Africans from their misery, body and soul.

The evangelization work took Methodists to Southern Africa and elsewhere. Apart from early Christianization in those areas, the major point to underscore was the opening up of education opportunities for African youth in the Black American institutions of higher learning including universities. That is how the first generation of educated African nationalists like Namdi Azikiwe of Nigeria, Hastings Banda of Malawi, Kwame Nkrumah of Ghana, to name only those, came to receive their university education in the Black institutions in America.

The migrationist movement became so powerful under the leadership of Marcus Garvey that even heavyweights like W. E. B. DuBois and Booker T. Washington (who in 1928 hosted Garvey) were convinced that it might be a solution to problems of African underdevelopment. Booker T. Washington, a marvelous agricultural researcher and scholar at his world-famous Tuskegee Institute, was convinced that Africans needed a vocational practical education to uplift themselves rather than theoretical education. Colonists saw in this a perfect matchwith the role of the African in the colonial political economy as that of a skilled worker for the settler. Dr. Washington was appointed to several education commissions in central and eastern Africa in the 1920's. Washington's book, "Up From Slavery" (1899), galvanized the young Marcus

Garvey into action, and he was later (1914) to launch the Universal Negro Improvement and Conservation Association and African Communities League, (UNIA) with a grandiose agenda and mission. The work of Marcus Garvey should be put into proper perspective.

It was under these circumstances that the ideas of political Pan-Africanism were born and it was none other than Booker T. Washington who hosted the first Pan-African Conference at Tuskegee Institute in 1900, inviting Black delegates from all over the world. It was, however, the launching of the first Pan-African Congress under the dynamic leadership of Dr. DuBois that took the limelight and has continued to do so. It forms a vibrating political linkage between Africans and African-Americans. The birth of African nationalism partially ties into the work of these Pan-Africanists from the United States.

Their enthusiasm for a sovereign Africa free from economic exploitation and political oppression, a united Africa where African-Americans would feel at home and live with dignity, spoke volumes. DuBois personally carried to Geneva the resolution and the recommendations of the first Pan-African Congress which was held simultaneously with the Versailles Peace Conference. Africans and African-Americans have never been more united and motivated than they were during the 1900-1945 period when the Fifth Pan-African Congress was held in Manchester to launch the modern African nationalist political parties; these parties intended to press for the end of colonialism and for independence. Even if the Organization of African Unity (OAU) stands today as the legacy of the efforts of more than a half century of Pan-Africanism, by the time of its creation (1963) Africa was already once again a divided house and African-Americans' dream of a return to Africa was shattered. Lone voices of Kwame Nkrumah, P. Admore, Makonnen and others as the flag bearers of Pan-Africanism were being submerged into regionalisms and, in some cases, parochialism. Nonetheless, this is yet another common chapter in the history of Africans and that of African-Americans.

Last but not least is the field of culture. It is in the field of culture that African-Americans have shown a remarkable resilience as a part of Africa. First of all, in the domain of oral history African-Americans have kept oral traditions over the centuries and generations that today constitute in some cases virtually the only source of their history. At any rate, the history of African-Americans cannot be fully written without the use of their oral traditions, and this is exactly the same case with African history.

These traditions face many dangers, including the underpinnings of modernity, not to mention the hostility of the cultural environments of the two peoples on both sides of the Atlantic. Just like some scholars, particularly European scholars, continue to denigrate or to reduce to the minimum the usefulness and validity of oral traditions in favor of written documents in European languages about African history (Henige: 1987; J.D. Fage: 1987; Beatrix Heintze and Adam Jones: 1987, and so on), few scholars have attempted to use oral traditions even partially in the reconstruction of the history of African-Americans. In one study, "The Coe Ridge Saga, William Lynwood Monteil has revealed how precious oral traditions can be in the reconstruction of the history of some of the African-Americans because they may be, as in his case study, the only source available (William L. Monteil: 1970)". In "The Coe Ridge Saga" the author has shown that this source of history is by no means limited to Africans and African-Americans. He has also shown the immediacy of the danger threatening oral traditions per se. The custodians have either died out as in this particular case when the "Negro Colony that was nestled in the foothills of the Cumberland Mountains in Cumberland County, Kentucky, near the Tennessee line" (Monteil: 1970; vii) was destroyed in the late 1950's after a dogged existence of about two centuries. The same danger faces the African oral traditions on the African continent, and in other parts of the United States, especially the Sea Islands of the Carolinas and Georgia. The collection of these traditions among African-Americans in the U.S.A. and the Caribbean is an urgent program, just as it has now been established on the African continent.

What are some of the contents of those traditions and written materials that are shared between Africans and African-Americans? The late Patricia Jones-Jackson demonstrated in her study the striking similarity of some cultural aspects between the inhabitants of the sea islands and the peoples of the West African coast, particularly among the Igbo of Nigeria, where she did her field study (Patricia Jones-Jackson: 1987). The themes explored include folk literature - storytelling whereby the variations due to time and space are so slight that they fall within the normal range of variations in that genre.

Prayers, mode and content of praying, invoking the ancestors or even within the Christian paradigm, the clapping of hands - all are very similar and reflect the resilience of African cultural traits in the cultural *mouvance* of African-Americans (Evalyn Baker Dandy: 1991).

Analyzing the Gullah tales with the African parallels, Jones-Jackson writes:

> The evidence of literary continuity is most apparent in the handling of traditional themes and characters. Both cultures (Gullah and Igbo) delight in imbuing physically insignificant and seemingly helpless creatures with extraordinary acumen. Their superior intelligence and discretion make these small beings not only godlike in powers but models for much stronger creatures to emulate. The "helpless" animal may take the form of the spider of the Gold Coast, the turtle of the Slave Coast, the rabbit (hare: change added, V.G.S.) of the Sierra Leone, or the *hlakanyana* of South Africa. Regardless of the region, these animals are heroic figures in the same tradition as Brer Rabbit in Gullah and inland black literature, or Ananse the spider in Caribbean Literature (Jones-Jackson: 1987: 111- 2).

The author concludes that the Gullah or Geechee language is a merger of English and languages used along the Western African coast from Mandinka in Senegal across Ewe, Fante, Efik, Ibibio, Igbo, Yoruba, Twi, Kikongo (Ibid: 113).

Evalyn Dandy argues that the dialect spoken by African-Americans today is a full-fledged language that has developed with specificities whose roots lie deep in the continental African cultures, and it must be recognized as such in the educational curricula and education psychology in the United States instead of its being denigrated as bad English.

The resistance to African culture and the hostility it continues to suffer on the continent and in the Americas is yet another common theme. African culture has survived probably nowhere else more than in the Caribbean, where it has given birth to a whole array of modern cultural manifestations that are worldwide, whether in music, art, philosophy or religion. Dr. Ben Lewis of the Sapelo Island off the Georgia Coast says that not very long ago while he was a child in the 1930's, and 1940's, his people used to place the plate and a little dish of the preferred food of the deceased on the grave of the deceased as a sign of the continuity of the ancestral spirit with the lives of the living. This still goes on in rural Africa, but on Sapelo Island, graveyards are now marble and concrete. However, Christians, as the Sapelo people are, still secretly resort to ancestral worship or to talismans in their supplications for a good life in this world.

Traditional medicine is another area of common ground manifested by Africans on both sides of the Atlantic Ocean. The African practice of medicine and health care was denigrated as primitive atavistic witchcraft for a very long time. However, its persistence has won it a place in the European format of our health programs. First of all, African practice of medicine combines both the chemical drugs (herbs) and the psychological environment of the patient for optimal healing. The validity of African practice of medicine was recognized by the World Health Organization (WHO) at its conference in 1972 held in Cairo. The WHO recommended incorporation into the health policies and programs of African countries (alongside European-type medicine) of: 1) herbal drugs wlth an emphasis on research using modern scientific methods to determine the efficacy and dosage of those drugs supplied by African medicine men and women; 2) gynecology and mother-child care where the role of the rural traditional midwife has continued her practice; 3) psychiatry; and other areas. Since African societies like the Gusii of Western Kenya successfully practiced neurosurgery long before the advent of colonialism and have continued today in virtually every African country, modern medicine should include research in African traditional practice in collaboration wlth African rural doctors.

Some studies have been carried out on the practice of medicine among African-Americans. At one time in the history of the United States, both colonial settlers and African-Americans in some regions relied entirely on the medical knowledge of African-Americans. In a study on the healing practice in South Carolina, Tom W. Shick has demonstrated that although the African-American practice of rural root medicine was suppressed as evil, it survived. He cites a case whereby a certain Gullah by the name of Jack was charged in a court of law with the practice of root medicine as a doctor to induce others into rebellion. He was sentenced to death and hanged in 1822. Ten years later in 1833, Henry Wilkins, member of the American Association, published a guide for planters called "The Family Advisor: Do It Yourself for Treatment of Illness." In that publication he listed over four hundred plant species with the description of their medicinal properties and the diseases they cured. In virtually all of them, the authorities he quoted for the authenticity and seriousness of his recommendations were African-American sources who had related to him that African-American "ròot doctors" were using those drugs. Since they were effective, therefore, they were good for white planters too (Tom W. Shick: 1986).

More recently, Patricia Jones-Jackson recounts her own experience in 1970 or thereabouts, when her asthmatic child had a crisis in the dead of the night while Patricia was carrying out her field research. The child's medicine had run out. They were then staying with her host, Miss Myma, about seventy years old, who was also her informant. After Miss Myma had scolded the young Patricia for not telling her that the child was asthmatic when they first came, she dug out some roots, brought them in, cleaned and boiled them. When the liquid was cool, Miss Myma took the child and gently administered it in small doses by spoon. Patricia Jones-Jackson writes:

> Twenty minutes later my daughter lay asleep and breathing peacefully on her lap (Jones-Jackson: 1987).

This is an area that needs urgent attention and research on both sides of the Atlantic before the expert men and women join the ancestors with all their treasures.

John Michael Vlach has demonstrated in his study entitled "Afro-American Tradition in Decorative Arts" (1978) that there is a direct linkage between the African material culture (he enumerates the material culture of peoples as varied as the Wolof and Bambara, the Mandingo, Akan, Kongo-Bushongo and the 0vambo) and that of African-Americans in areas such as basketries, musical instruments, wood carving, quilting, pottery, boat building, blacksmithing, architecture and graveyard decoration. In basketry, similarities cut across the entire sub-Saharan African subcontinent and those of African-Americans especially those of the sea islands of South Carolina and Georgia and, we should add, of the Caribbeans. The shotgun house architecture that has been very popular on the American continent is of African origin, introduced by African-Americans (Vlach: 1978). Dale Rosengarten has shown that long before the rise of capitalist agriculture, Africans brought the agricultural technology and techniques of rice cultivation that were so vital for the survival of the colonies and settlers in the early decades of the seventeenth century. Africans also brought the material culture that went with that particular form of agriculture - especially sea grass basketry. That material culture has continued to our day, and many people are still making a living out of the industry on the sea islands of South Carolina and Georgia.

SUMMARY

The common themes are endless, and can be summarized by saying that African-Americans are part and parcel of the African cultural *mouvance.* However, African culture is now under enormous pressure to change. Much of it has already disappeared among African-Americans under the double blows of Christianity and Anglo-Saxon culture.

There is an urgent need to collect and record the traditions which still remain, as these will be the only point of departure to guide any future archaeological and documentary study of African-American history. Such attempts are being made in Southeastern Georgia involving African-American elders, and they should be encouraged to spread to other areas. In Africa too, the agenda has been on for more than two decades but a lot still remains to be done. It is a challenge to all of us.

REFERENCES

Curtin, Philip D., "Africa Remembered by West Africans from the Era of the Slave Trade," University of Wisconsin, Madison, 1967.

Dandy, Evalyn B., "Black Communications: Breaking Down the Barriers," African-American Images, Chicago, Illinois, 1991.

Fage, J.D., "Guide to Original Sources for Precolonial Western Africa - Published in European Languages." African Studies Program, University of Wisconsin, Madison, 1986.

Heintze, Beatrix and Jones, Adam, "European Sources for Sub-Saharan Africa Before 1900, Use and Abuse." Paideuma 33, 1987, Federal Republic of Germany, 1987.

Inikori, Joseph E. (a) "Africa in World History: The Export Slave Trade from Africa and the Emergence of the Atlantic Economic Orders", in B.A. Ogot (Ed.) General History of Africa, Vol. V., Heinemann, California, 1992.

Inikori, J.E. (b) "The Atlantic Slave Trade: Effects on Economies, Societies and Peoples in Africa, the Americas and Europe.", Duke University Press, 1992.

Jones-Jackson, Patricia, "When Rooks Die - Endangered Traditions on the Sea Islands," The University of Georgia Press, Athens, 1987.

Knight, F.W. (with a contribution by Y. Talib and Philip D. Curtin), "The African Diaspora," ln General History of Africa, Vol. Vl, ed. J.F.A. Ajiayi, (Africa in the Nineteenth Century until the 1880's).

Monteil, William Lynwood, "The Saga of Coe Ridge: A Study in Oral History," The University of Tennessee Press, Knoxville, 1970.

Rosengarten, Dale, "Sea Grass Baskets of the South Carolina Low Country," McKissick Museum, University of South Carolina, 1986.

Simiyu, V.G., (Unpublished Monograph), "Migrant Workers ln Southern Africa," YMCA-Africa Alliance Study, August 1990, 98 paper.

Vlach, John Michael, "The Afro-American Tradition in Decorative Arts," The Cleveland Museum of Art, University Circle, Cleveland, Ohio, 1978.

CHAPTER 17

THE PALAVER: A SYSTEM OF CONFLICT MANAGEMENT

Yeno Mansoni Matuka

Africans have an intuitive but nonetheless elaborate system of peace distribution and preservation. This system of conflict management will be illustrated by describing what the Bakoongo of Zaire do to provide a solution to the problem of disputes.

This Bantu ethnic group of approximately six million people live on the West coast of equatorial Africa. Before the nineteenth century, they constituted the Koongo kingdom which was split into three by the former colonial powers, namely Belgium, France and Portugal. Today, the Koongo people (or Bakoongo) cover respectively the Western Zaire region called Bas-Zaire (or Lower Zaire), the Southwest of the People's Republic of Congo known has Bas-Congo, and the Northwest of Angola located in the San-Salvador district. The latter region, which is historically known as Mbaanza Koongo, is the homeland of the whole ethnic group.

The Bakoongo identify themselves with reference to the anthropological concepts of clan *(kaanda)* and lineage or womb *(yumu)*. The numerous clans that spread throughout the old Koongo kingdom are all believed to have originated in the Kingdom city of Mbaanza Koongo. The Kakoongo, then, recognize a distant female ancestor who, probably assisted by her powerful brother or maternal uncle, might have contributed to found the original clan.

To acknowledge the male ancestors, however, authentic Koongo people socially describe themselves in a triangular type of relationship. They claim to be chief of their mother's clan; this stands as their primary or "chiefship" clan. They also acknowledge their patrilineal descent by considering their father's clan as their secondary or "childship" clan. Last, they acknowledge their mother's patrilineal descent, which they also consider their tertiary or "grandchildship" clan. In addition to this direct kinship, they locate themselves with respect to affinity by marriage contracts.

Whenever a serious dispute arises in any of the clans - their chiefship, childship and grandchildship or even in-laws clans - the Bakoongo feel socially and culturally obliged to attend a gathering and take an active part in dispute settlement.

THE PALAVER

The historical and rhetorical concept of palaver, according to Lafage (1986:154-55), is an important speech event in the life of an African village. Because this sociocultural activity is rarely studied by Africanists, scholars may fail to understand and defend the underlying organization of traditional Africa.

African scholars who have a negative view of palavering activity are called "black white men" or "white black men" by the Bakoongo (Mindele-Ndome). Such people are considered to have had a dose of Western acculturation which has caused them to ignore the organizational impact of a palaver upon traditional Africa, a "Time of Communication, time of collective discussion (in the village square, under the 'patam' or the 'palaver tree')."

The definition of the term palaver, according to Webster's *Third New International Dictionary of the English Language* is "an often prolonged parley usually between persons of different levels of cultures or sophistication (as between a 19th-century European trader and natives of the African West coast" or "a parley between European explorers and representatives of local populations, especially in Africa" *(The American Heritage Dictionary, 1982).* Both dictionaries give a negative characterization of the concept, palaver, and this is the connotation often seen in this term.

Lafage has suggested an extended meaning of the palaver as a form of "conference," "discussion," or even "conversation." It may be "an extended conversation" conducted publicly by wise and caring speakers in order to resolve a serious conflict. The audience may experience a palaver-conversation as a dialogue of "give and take" (Bublitz, 1988:140) which the disputants produce to contribute at a high level in the organization of their society. The ultimate role of the disputants is that of agents of "conflict prevention and reduction" (Bublitz, 1988:140).

A palaver is an expression of formal speech behavior which has an institutional value not only among the Bakoongo but also among Africans in general. Conceived in this positive sense, palavering may be considered one of the oldest forms of public speaking aimed at settling disputes. In this perspective, it can be studied from the point of view of its setting, interactants or disputants, audience, and the affair to be settled - all belonging to a *customary court* in Africa. The historical perspective of the palaver is connected over time from Greco-Roman antiquity to modern Africa [(.Jarrat (1990) and Finnegan (1970:445)], or from African antiquity to Greco-Roman rhetoric (Bernal, 1987), with land affairs which have had the functional characteristics of legal disputes with sociopolitical implications. Land disputes constitute the most complex palavers with which the Koongo people deal with quite regularly.

Such disputes, often not handled successfully by government courts, have fostered the art of public speaking. This is an art because native Bakoongo who are close to their culture learn it by just living within the group, or better, by attending palavers. In other words, there is no formal training yet in this art. The westernized system of schooling to which we are addicted has had no room to accommodate it.

This speech behavior, however, has survived the colonial rule, and it is the core of the Koongo system of conflict management. It is a process realized under a rigorous application of the pragmatic mechanisms of oral exchanges, namely "the principle of turn-taking and the maxim of agreement" (Leech, 1983 and Carlson, 1983) or "the cooperative principle" (Grice 1975) which implies what Van Eemeren and Grootendorst (1984) call "Code of Conduct for Rational Discussants."

A palaver, than, is an event made of ways of communication geared toward a resolution of a number of serious issues. Put together to be treated, these issues culminate into the Koongo term, maambu, "affairs or conflicts." The maambu, then, may be social, economic, cultural or even political "disputes." The anthropologist, Frake (1969:210), defines the term, maambu, as "disputes," namely "events such as wedding ceremonies, bereavement gatherings, and land litigations."

The treatment of problematic events engenders a high level of organization. The anthropologist, MacGaffey (1970:103), studied these particular events and quotes Henry Richards, an Anglo-American missionary (1879-1919), who said about the Bakoongo:

> They are accustomed to hold frequent assemblies for the public consideration of every question which in any manner affects the general interests.

This art of verbal exchange held in public has made it possible for the Bakoongo to co-exist with practically no stories of belligerence. (In the first twenty years of my life spent in or around the village, I never watched a fight involving adults. I believe that this coexistence has been made possible by the fact that these people could interact most systematically with one another to resolve their conflicts.)

SYSTEMATIC INTERACTIONS OF PALAVERING

Social harmony is defined as a collective state of well-being that any kind of dispute may contribute to break. The mending of the broken equilibrium, then, generates a network of systematic interactions realized under the activity of palavering. Marriage ceremonies, bereavement gatherings, and land litigations stand out as the main occasions of cooperative speech production. They constitute three of the ways in which language is used to organize sociocultural institutions in Africa in general, and in Koongo society in particular. The participants of the events bring their skills in verbal negotiations to solve the disputes which often interest them in one way or another and at various levels. In other words, these people exhibit different degrees of involvement related not only to the nature of the dispute but also to the role and status of a Koongo person in the context of the three clans discussed above.

As a system of dispute resolution, a palaver requires the formation of two parties supervised by two benevolent spokesmen, people who are often invited by the heads of the extended families whose members caused the dispute to be settled publicly. Unlike the Western system of conflict management, there is no judge at a palaver site. The gathering itself provides or constitutes the judges. In this respect, the people follow and listen attentively to what the spokesmen are saying as they exchange speeches directly and publicly. Any good speaker can participate at appropriate moments provided by the code of conduct at a palaver.

But each of the spokesmen leads the palaver by making his points or else refuting the argument put forward by the previous speaker.

A Mukoongo considers a palaver a socially inviting business. In a litigation palaver, a spokesman introduced the rationale for the gathering by saying:

> Spokesman: "But the issues keep on getting more serious, indeed. They started with two people. Then, they involved three people. Today, they are for many people.
> People: "many (people)." (Matuka, RP. 207:4-9)

This extract is also informative of the way a palaverer is expected to speak. He has to pay attention to the audience which includes the direct addressee (the antagonist) and the members of both sides of the palaver. He does this by inserting what is referred to as response elicitation in the language of palavering - pseudo-turns of talk. (The closest equivalent of response elicitation is found in an African - American preacher who expects the audience to respond with him). Response elicitation is just a rhetorical strategy by which the speaker involves the audience to make sure they are still following his line of argumentation. The main speakers also have a systematic way of introducing subtopics in the palavering processes. Real turns of talk are those which give way to a change in the main speaker, i.e., the spokesman.

Indeed, depending on the nature of the dispute being settled, any move or introduction of the main topics coincides with a change in the turn of speech. The move is marked by drink offering. A demijohn of palm wine or a keg of beer which will be served in due time is presented to articulate the main palavering moments. In marriage and bereavement ceremonies, a gathering can use up to 14 demijohns of palm wine to introduce the main topics or subtopics of a palaver. However, in the case of a litigation palaver which is often loaded with emotive moments, the Bakoongo are wise enough to avoid using alcoholic beverages in large quantity. In any case, the refreshment is served after the dispute has been settled.

CONCLUSION

The Koongo system of conflict management works as follows. Spokesman

A exposes the motives of the palaver, paying attention to the people and the sociocultural norms of respect and the norms of public speaking. Spokesman B summarizes what A said to make sure they are talking about the same subject. He, too, minds the code of conduct for rational discussants. After reviewing A's presentation, B logically formulates his own response, using proverbs, anecdotes, and, of course, the strategy of response elicitation to involve the audience. Both speakers use language efficiently, signaling the change in turns of talk explicitly and verbally, with body language and wine offering. The body language (or gestures that prolong speech) is basically a systematic set of hand clapping that signals addressees and change in turns of talk.

In turns of talk, the spokesmen formulate their speeches as truthfully as possible and according to the information they have. However, sometimes they are short of information. In this case, they ask for a systematic pause translated as "Bed Time." At this moment, the spokesman confers with the members of the clan he represents.

The systematic aspects of a palaver as a speech event could be conceived from the point of view of the terms or jargon that exists in Kikoongo. The setting or palaver place is called *mbazia maambu*. The actions related to the palaver are components of palavering as an activity. The speakers or *banzoonzi*, for example, are said to "be taking a bite at the palaver" when they argue (*ta_kinzoonzi*). The gathering or the audience is known as *n'kaangu* and it is made of "fathers, mothers, and folk, "*bataata, ye maama, ye bampaangi* , which are generic terms for "ladies, gentlemen and relatives. " The palaver itself or *maambu* is "a number of affairs" (*minsamu*) to be settled publicly *(va ntenda nkoongolo)*. The public discussions or verbal exchanges (*kinzoonzi*) which take place during the palaver are real "conversations" (*ngyambila)* . The end is an "agreement" (*ngwiizani*), which is the ultimate objective of a palaver. The spokesmen's task is to try hard to understand one another. They try to reach a compromise (*nqwaawani*) which is a serious attempt to "come toward one another" (*wiizana*).

The resolution of the affairs or disputes may be seen as a tug of war whose cord "has been cut off" (*zeenguka*) rather than "broken" (*tabuka*). The breaking of the cord, or rather, the cutting of the cord, is thought of as a positive incident which implies that the conflict has been resolved (*maambu ma zengokene*); in other words, the conclusion has been drawn. The gathering has followed the thread leading to the resolution of the affair implicitly get the feeling that the collective mind is unified or else the broken social equilibrium is restored (*ngwiizani yi vutukidi*).

Organizing palavers in this African society is a systematic way of conflict management which deserves encouraging. Compared with the Western system of court trials, it minimizes the expenses and the emotional hurts or after-trial traumas. Whenever a palaver is organized, the gathering seeks more the collective welfare than personal interests. The palaverers believe that their action must lead to reparation of the social, economic, political, or even metaphysical equilibrium that has been upset by the disputing parties. They do not work to seek retaliation against whomever has been found guilty of breaking this state of the collective mind. Fines, which are sometimes paid, have only a symbolic value.

REFERENCES

The American Heritage Dictionary. 1982. Second College Edition. Boston: Houghton Mifflin Company.

Bernal, Martin. 1987. *Black Athena: The Afroasiatic Roots of Classical Civilization*. New Brunswick, New Jersey: Rutgers University Press.

Bublitz, Wolfram. 1988. *Supportive Fellow Speakers and Cooperative Conversations*. Amsterdam: John Benjamin Publishers.

Frake, C. 0. 1969. "Struck by Speech: The Yakan Concept of Litigation." In John J. Gumperz and Dell Hymes, eds. 1972. *Directions in Sociolinguistics: The Ethnography of Communication*. New York: Holt, Rinehart and Winston, Inc. p.106-129.

Gove, Philip B. ed. 1966. Webster's *Third International Dictionary of the English Language*. Unabridged. Springfield, Massachusetts: G. & C. Merriam Company.

Jarratt, Susan C. 1990. "The Role of the Sophists in Histories of Consciousness." *Philosophy and Rhetoric*, Vol. 23. No.2. University Park and London: The Pennsylvania State University Press.

Lafage, Suzanne. 1986. "Outline of a Practical Frame of Reference for a Sociolinguistic Analysis in an African Context." In George Huttar and Kenneth Gregerson, eds. *Pragmatics in Non-Western Perspective.* The University of Texas at Arlington: The Summer Institute of Linguistics.

Finnegan, Ruth H. 1970. *Oral Literature in Africa.* London: Oxford University Press.

MacGaffey, Wyatt. 1970. *Custom and Government in the Lower Congo.* Berkeley: University of California Press.

Matuka, Yeno M. *Three Koongo Palavers: Wedding, Bereavement and Reconciliation.* In Appendix to "The Pragmatics of Palavering in Kikoongo." Ph.D. Dissertation: Ball State University. (1991)

CHAPTER 18

AFRICAN/AFRICAN-AMERICAN DIALOGUE: TOWARD A NEW DIASPORA

Anthonia C. Kalu

Reference to a New World denotes the existence and acknowledgement of an old world. For the descendants of the people who 'discovered' the New World and subsequently settled it, there was never any question as to whether the old should be overtaken, let alone be forgotten or discarded. In spite of (or because of?) the often-remembered and discussed religious intolerance and other social ills that contributed to the relocation of the Mayflower pilgrims, it was never thought necessary for either the pilgrims or their descendants to forget or reject the traditions of their ancestors. Instead, at the famous White Chapel sermon, the ambassadors to the new settlement were exhorted to remember the injunction, given Abraham by God, to keep the race pure.

The predominant message disseminated by the 'daring' moral messengers and traders from the West always emphasized the West's need to initiate the colonized peoples, by fire, into Western beliefs and traditions. No other ideas were allowed to stand in the way of the mission to conquer and control, to attain economic dominance. The most unfortunate recipients of the implied and overt messages included in this package have been people of African descent.

For three hundred years, Africans in various parts of the world have listened to, accepted and even believed that the West was superior to Africa, and Westerners superior to Africans. Not only has this been true on both sides of the Atlantic, where most people of African descent are found, but the extent of the acceptance of inferiority continues to stand in the way of unified positive action within African communities all over the world.

For Africans in North America, considerable research work has been conducted by scholars without effecting much change in the conditions or experiences of African-Americans because research has tended to look at problems from the 'outside in' or at specific sections of the population defined by current interest groups. Conclusions may reflect the successes of African people despite the odds; but the successes have been so few in number that most Africans have come to identify with the idea of mere survival as part of their heritage.

There have been leaders who have come from the masses and spoken the will of the people. However, the works of such leaders, rather than gaining recognition in support of the peoples opinions, have become included among works labelled successful by Anglo-American standards. Since success in the last few centuries has meant compliance with Western thought and lifestyle, the net result of this upward movement has been a lack of voice identifying a basic decision-making culture or tradition for people of African descent. This lack of voice implies absence of a viable mechanism, within the traditional or modern African experience, for the organization or unification of Africans in the diaspora. This erroneous view is the outcome of several centuries of devaluation by the West and research conducted by white liberals and members of the black middle class.

Since most of the research has implicitly been based on the African's condition, and this is negative at best for the masses, the findings have tended to confirm the African's lower status vis-a-vis those of other peoples. On the part of the masses of African people everywhere, the absence of authentic African participation in progressive research has facilitated estrangement with Africa through erosion of African thought. This continues to manifest as absence of knowledge about persistent positive action by African communities everywhere.

In the seventeenth century, the argument used to justify continued domination of Africans was that the heathen African should be enslaved to enable the Christian West to save the African soul. However, neither baptism nor references to the intentions of the Christian God made the African eligible for equal participation in the economic advancement that the West was pursuing with energy derived from the blood and sweat of the African. Concurrently, through the teaching of the works of eminent Western biologists and physicians and the conjectures of profit-seeking land-owners and aristocrats, slavery became the African's 'natural' heritage. In place of free-will and the promised domination of the rest of creation, Africans became heirs to forced labor and bondage. This new heritage has taught Africans while the rich African heritage was declared inferior, primitive and pagan.

However, these teachings would not have been effective if they had not been accepted and implemented over the years by Africans on the continent and in the diaspora, [1] a process requiring that the modes of thought of ancient African civilizations be attributed to other groups of people, ignored, or irretrievably lost. For instance, scholars do not agree on the origins of aspects of the Judeo-Christian tradition as presented by Moses to the Israelites [2] (who had lived in bondage in Egypt for many years). By the same token, some African peoples and traditions have been studied such that to possess Jewish/Christian origins rather than vice versa tends to put them in the position of claiming superiority among neighboring groups. [3]

The interference and intervention of Western civilization in Africa and the subsequent teacher/pupil, master/servant relationships denied Africans the ability for profundity in any aspect of life. This paternalistic approach helped to promote dependence in the past and continues to disapprove attempts to establish equitable relationships and communication. As a result, Western/African relationships stagnate and the formation of alliances between Africans on the continent and those in the diaspora either never begin or do not go beyond certain boundaries. These limitations, usually manifested as economic or political realities, are sustained by the often ignored abyss created by lack of communication and interaction between Africans everywhere. The result has been the placement of people of African descent, as a group, in a category where it has been difficult for them to claim their due as visible participants in the advancement efforts of the twentieth century. Scholars of African origin, raised within the remnants of a rich but vanishing heritage, now have the responsibility of rediscovering and remodeling African thought to enable equitable recognition of African contributions toward the achievement of balance in all aspects of human advancement.

Previous efforts at unification through ordered communication have been difficult because survival has constituted a major factor in the African's life. In the effort to survive and adapt to the new Euro-American world, the African had to shelve the old African world and, in time, Euro-America, for instance, became a part of the everyday way of life. In the case of the African-American, the extent of the adaptation was so pronounced that Frazier and others declared that the

African had indeed lost all. [4] But W.E.B. DuBois and Melville Herskovits had also gone back, separately, to the shelves and found some valuable remnants of Africa in African-American and other New World sub-cultures. Based on findings similar to DuBois' and Herskovits', African peoples could have proclaimed a day of reaffirmation of their ancestral roots. Instead, Africans in the New World engaged in discussions about how much of the old had been retained. Africa had to be justified all over again since the New-World-African was being asked to pick up a forgotten heritage in modern times.

When E. Franklin Frazier was writing about the demise of African ways in African-American life and culture, the Pan-African Movement had been in existence for three decades and DuBois had been advocating the elevation of African traditions for even longer. Also, Marcus Garvey's great mobilization of the African-American masses had come and gone.

Nothing convinced the African in America to unequivocally declare Africa a heritage worthy of pride. Rather, many bought into Euro-America's concept of an Africa with no history, culture, tradition, or rights which the West felt obliged to respect. For many Africans, traditional Africa was unable to evoke the same degree of pride and commitment that Western concepts and traditions had.

Within the continent, contact with the West and colonization resulted in dispersion of cultural thought and transaction. This was followed by sporadic attempts at merging the West with African traditions or complete replacement with traditional African thought or complete rejection of both. This latter reactionary approach has been at the root of underdevelopment, political chaos, and other problems that have come to be identified as peculiar to African peoples and countries. The subsequent cultural stagnation has resulted in social and political disfunction because Africans have had to take time to learn and understand Western traditional thought before they could apply it. However, the situation has been compounded by the fact that while African scholars continue to imbibe and disseminate traditional Western thought in the diaspora and on the continent, the West continues to employ the blood and sweat of the people to build new technologies resulting in new Western traditions that the African scholar has to learn.

Scholars of African descent, the modern source for African leadership, have become locked into a cycle of scholarship on issues that are not directly relevant to the people's reality. This has resulted in the much-studied African or African-American condition. For African communities in the New World, it is manifested as economic dependence on the system; on the continent it fosters dependence on the West even after the achievement of political independence. Recognition of this cycle is the first step toward the maintenance of continuity in the efforts of African leaders and scholars to evolve a unifying and unified approach to Africa's problems. However, the authenticity of African thought and the necessity for African unity, though often acknowledged, have yet to be explored or used beyond the symbolic level.

In the early years, African identity was legitimized through association with Egypt and Ethiopia. At the same time, within the religious experiential level, both were seen as part of the Biblical and therefore, Western reality and experience. Often, Egypt especially was portrayed as the land of bondage from which the African, enslaved in America, sought freedom to a spiritual promised land, thereby reinforcing, psychologically, a non-commitment to Africa. African-American folk literature and songs are filled with references that present Egypt and Ethiopia in such light. [5] Symbolic perception of Africa was especially prevalent among African-Americans for whom circumstances made symbolism a necessary element for survival; however, the relationship seemed to stagnate at the symbolic level. For the most part, the conflict was resolved in favor of the spiritual experience since Africa was physically unattainable.

For generations, most Africans in the New World had no knowledge of the extensive land mass that is Africa, and the myth of the insignificance of Africa continued. According to Roy Ottley, the American black nation first became aware of the modern black nation of Ethiopia in 1919 when Ethiopian dignitaries arrived in the United States on a diplomatic mission. [6] Before that, most African-Americans perceived Egypt and Ethiopia only as Biblical phenomena, reinforcing their relevance in Western Christian ideology. The set of images evoked through this symbolic reference and relationship became a barrier to the achievement of meaningful relationships in the real world between Africans from the continent and African-Americans when, for various reasons, Africans began to voluntarily emigrate to the United States after Emancipation.

Scholars like Essien-Udom [7] and Louis Lomax [8] who have studied this relationship have not arrived at a decisive conclusion regarding its nature. [9] The range of relationships is vast but may be subdivided into three main groups. The first group consists of African-Americans who have bought into the stereotypical Western/Euro-American concept of Africa and Africans. This group does not want such a relationship and does see any reason to revive an old problem. The second group wants a relationship based on the conventional Western/Euro-American concept of the African. During the early period of contact, members of this group went to Africa as missionaries. Bernard Magubane asserts that this is part of a "process of social regeneration" based on an "emotional consciousness which (was) a legacy of the pre-civil war era. [10] According to Magubane, this regeneration process, expressive of black-American interest in Africa, has been demonstrated in varying degrees in Garveyism and DuBois' Pan-Africanism. [11] The third group is made up of those who want all Africans in the New World to become African citizens. This group has always favored mass deportation of Africans from the New World to the homeland.

In the three centuries of African peoples' quest for their dispersed and misplaced heritage, there have always been supporters of the view that Africans in America do not need relationships with Africa to contribute to their American reality. However, history books show that, either through blatant omission or calculated indifference, the African in America has, from the beginning, lacked a point of reference that would have made equitable recognition of the African presence in the New World possible. Three centuries of prejudice and discrimination based on skin color would not have been so effective if the reality forced on the African-American did not include a concept of numerical minority within that for intellectual inferiority. Other groups of Americans, for instance, Jewish-Americans, Mexican-Americans, Japanese-Americans constantly find reasons to maintain ancestral roots and are supported in their efforts. Euro-American culture continues to extol its rich heritage from Greece, Rome, Britain and other white and European cultures. In each case, the ancestral homelands have been and continue to be clearly visible, resulting in a definite sense of community in those aspects of life that are not pertinent to New World realities. Thus, it has been easier for these groups to succeed in situations in which African-Americans have been less able to cope as a group.

The fact that there are people of African descent who believe that the African heritage was completely lost or replaced by other cultures in the New

World illustrates the extent of Western/Euro-America's success in the degradation of African peoples and cultures. The process of misinformation achieved a great deal of success because of the silence imposed on Africans by the West along with slavery and colonization. When African peoples were exported to the New World, it became necessary to keep secret from the Africans the extent of progress being made on both sides of the Atlantic ocean. Thus, the 'person in the middle' [12] was not only able to come between siblings during the process of 'commercial deportation' [13] but was able to extend that role to being an intermediary between the African groups on both shores of the Atlantic. As the sole source of information regarding activities in both places, the 'person in the middle' became teacher and interpreter of all affairs about Africa and the severed relationships. The result was that Africans were kept ignorant of each other's existence long enough for alienation to take place. Those who left African coasts were taught that since Africa was primitive and pagan, it was worth nothing. On the other hand, those who were left behind were not told, during the process of Westernization, that their cousins had survived and were alive and well.

A good example of this selective transfer of information is seen in the miseducation of Africans in Africa during and after colonization. Chinweizu cites the ways in which Africa's universities, established to serve colonial interests, have become roadblocks to the development of Africa's culture and future. [14] For instance, until recently, the education of African youth up to the university level consisted of lessons on European history (termed World History), Europeans in Africa, and European Christian humanists' efforts to enlighten the rest of the world. The African educational curriculum did not contain materials about Africa or Africans in other parts of the world. Until a few years ago most Africans arriving in the West, especially the United States, were shocked to see people of African descent, black people, speaking nothing else but the white man's language. The initial shock was usually followed by a genuine move toward the establishment of kinship. This, in turn, was and often still is quickly replaced by estranged feelings resulting from linguistic barriers.

To the ears of the African-American, the African who usually has learned the English language from the British speaks 'with an accent' and is 'foreign.' The African, on the other hand, has to deal with the problem of how to form ties with another African who cannot claim ownership of an African language and to all intents and purposes is non-African. More often than not, a second surprise awaits the African who is usually unaware of Africa's reputation as 'dark and primitive,' and of other nonwhite peoples as inferior rather than different.

The tensions that arise between the New-World-African and the newly arrived African usually require mediation, but few avenues are as yet available for such services of reconciliation. For Africans who arrive in the United States as students, initiation into American society may be through an Anglo-American family working within the host-family system. In her work, *Blood and Flesh,* Josephine Moikobu asserts that African students she interviewed reported their white friends stated they were different from their African-American cousins and should stay away from them. [15] Initial introductions into society may keep the average African visitor away from the African-American community. On the other hand, the African-American, unaware of the motivation behind the African visitor's reluctance toward involvement may label the African unapproachable.[16]

The two groups are, therefore, kept apart through the reinforcement of perceptions undermining each other's image. In this situation, lasting perceptions of the other are reformed through journalistic evidence and the results of research conducted by the 'person in the middle' whose motivation has been commercial exploitation of the dispersed communities. The resultant conflicts within the African-American/African community have generally not been acknowledged or confronted. The lack of knowledge of each other's culture coupled with a reluctance to learn arising from prejudices already mentioned have served as barriers for people from both sub-groups.

In order to facilitate consistent and viable participation of people of African descent in the reinstatement of Africa's and Africans' contribution to modern advancement, it is necessary to study the continent, the diaspora and the people more systematically. Such commitment in scholarship will allow the establishment of durable, balanced communication based on the core of a heritage that has harmonized individual African communities despite the divisive forces of dispersion and colonization. Development of the people's consciousness toward ordered and persistent utilization of concepts known to work for centuries entails studying and using African resources effectively for the enhancement of the people.

AFRICAN SCHOLARS, EDUCATORS AND ELDERS

Over several centuries of participation in the various processes of human advancement, Africa has produced a formidable number of excellent modern thinkers. Most of these have not been recognized or used in any way. Those who have been recognized in this century have had to spend their energies on urgently needed reactions to injustice. For example, it has been the task of great African thinkers like W.E.D. DuBois, Nkrumah, Nyerere, and Martin Luther King Jr., and others to initiate strategies and maintain processes for liberation from bondage and exploitation. These reactions are still necessary, especially in South Africa where the activities of the black African majority have been reduced to that of mere survival in a part of the world that continues to be noted for its natural beauty and wealthy resources.

As the dawn of the twenty-first century approaches, communities on the continent and in the diaspora should begin to use scholars of African descent to reeducate people about the rich African heritage and to stimulate participation in retrieving African thought from African traditional cultures. Scholars of African descent should conduct viable, long-term research on (1) Africa's rich material and abstract resources and so (2) the problems of the African continent and diaspora. Resources should be evaluated on the basis of potential use to enhance the people's existence. Scholars should have the capability to reach conclusive recommendations based on research findings and to develop implementation procedures for originating groups and/or countries.

Within the new dispensation, modern African scholars who have been assuming the various leadership roles of traditional chief priests and priestesses and of traditional medicine men and women have become Africa's modern sages: they should be given due recognition to enable the modern world to use their wisdom in the same manner that traditional Africa used their traditional counterparts to maintain harmony and advance the communities.

EXCHANGE PROGRAMS

Additional African Exchange programs should be initiated between the continent and the diaspora. These programs should begin in high school and continue through the university and other higher-level educational institutions and activities. Over the years, many Africans have been educated through old and new exchange programs that placed them in universities renowned because of their consistently successful participation in the dissemination of Western thought. African and African-American graduates of these institutions often have to be re-introduced to their traditional cultures. [16] The problem of the white-African, or the African-American Oreo-cookie has been discussed for a long time. In both instances, the alienation is such that it is often impossible to reverse the process. On the other hand the institutions that contribute to the condition often do not acknowledge the contributions of these and other Africans toward the advancement of humanity. A broad-based exchange program that starts early to teach African youth of their heritage, will foster positive self-concept, drastically reduce the number of disoriented Africans and enable increased participation in the advancement of Africans everywhere.

YOUTH INVOLVEMENT

Children were wanted and respected in traditional African communities. As a result, organized and informal socialization processes that helped youth to become responsible adults evolved in these communities. This does not imply that traditional Africa did not produce irresponsible or passive adults. However, the rate at which the number of African youth without goals and/or ambition has soared in the second part of this century is not consonant with traditional or modern African thought. The difficulties that scholars of African descent have had with resolving the various conflicts discussed here usually emanate from their inability, when they were young, to reconcile the gaps produced during the formative years of education. The gaps, due to the benign neglect inherent in the selective transfer of information, usually became problematic for the majority of youths of African descent because few elements in their reality were and are consonant with the real world. Consequently, the traditional African family is at a disadvantage in most communities. The new community of scholars and elders must evolve viable new concepts that will ensure the future.through empowering the youth, a revolution of expectations shall occur in African and African-American youth under the concerned supervision of the modern community of involved and committed scholars and elders.

WOMEN

In his keynote address during the Seventh Annual Pan-African Congress, Professor Ali Mazrui referred to the role of women as custodians in traditional Africa. 17 In most African communities, women began to lose their rights as full and active participants in the decision-making, educational and sociological advancement of the people during Western intervention. During this period the conscious elevation of the African male in African society by profit-seeking Western traders, missionaries of a one true male God, and other messengers from Europe and, later America, almost succeeded in completely undermining the female in Africa. However, pockets of female identification as necessary participants in the African cosmology still exist in most African cultures. It has become imperative that the modern community of scholars and elders evolve programs that will facilitate the reinstatement of African women in the new order. Of all the recommendations here, this may be the most difficult to implement because of extensive loss of culture, alienation of women themselves through acceptance of Western religious and other thought, and the fact that the modern African man has become accustomed to being the sole head of the rapidly emerging African nuclear family.

THE FAMILY

Scarcely any discussion about the survival of Africans on the continent and in the Diaspora is considered complete without reference to the imposing role played by the family. Thus, any community of scholars that participates in these Africa centered, awareness-based projects has to include the family. The family, here, as in most traditional African communities, means a group of people of the same bloodline supervised by a female or male. Family members within this concept may or may not live under the same roof, but each member acknowledges their relationship and importance to other members of the group. Since most traditional African activities found initial and ultimate expression in the family, the various aspects of the community discussed in this section should take the family into consideration. For instance, African university personnel should make African family life more available and accessible to the exchange program between the continent and the diaspora discussed above.

Conversely, African-American families should be encouraged to become more involved in the host-family programs that include African students and faculty. The community of scholars should conduct research or re-evaluate the results of existing systematic research to identify the people's world view with the objective of isolating those survival mechanisms that can be duplicated. Careful instruction in strategies for survival will increase the number of achieving youth from families in dead-end situations as well as improve community interaction and family welfare.

Although education in the Western sense is one of the keys to effecting change in this area, the case of Africans should, as much as possible, be resolved according to African history and experience. The denial of Africa at different levels - as a culture - and history-rich environment - by Africans an the continent and in the New World facilitated the continued subjugation of Africans by slave-traders, slave-owners and colonists. The internalization of the inferiority doctrine during those periods of overt domination is understandable, but continued acceptance of those ideas should be inexcusable. Internalization here does not only refer to active or passive acceptance of the Anglo-European/American perception of the African but includes the African's continued reactionary attitude in the fact of protracted racism, oppression and neocolonization.

NOTES

1. Diaspora is used here to refer to exiled and dispersed people who have formed stable communities with or without the acquisition of nation-state status. For detailed discussion of this idea, see: Ben Halpern, "Exile Abstract Condition and Concrete Community;" in "Negating the Diaspora," *Jewish Frontier.* 47, 10 (December, 1979):9; and Elliot P. Skinner, "The Dialectic Between Diaspora and Homelands;" in Joseph E. Harris, ed., *Global Dimensions of the African Diaspora.* Washington, D.C.: Howard University Press, 1982.

2. See, for instance: Ali Mazrui, "The Semitic Impact on Black Africa: Arab and Jewish Cultural Influences;" *Issue: A Journal of Opinion* . 12 (1984) 3-8; Hailu Habtu, "The Fallacy of the 'Triple Heritage' Thesis: A Critique;" *Issue* 12 (1984) 26-29.

3. G. T. Basden. *Niger Ibos.* New York: Barnes and Noble, Inc., 1966, 411-413.

4. E. Franklin Frazier. *The Negro Family in the United States.* Chicago: The University of Chicago Press, 1939, 21-22. 5. See, for instance, the lyrics of Negro spirituals like: "Go Down Moses;" "Oh Mary Don't You Weep," in which Egypt is depicted as the land of bondage and the Africans enslaved in America become symbolically 'the children of Israel;' 'Swing Low Sweet Chariot," in which Jordan is 'home;' and some celebrated folk sermons. The psychological impact in favor of the West was made mostly through the African's need for salvation from bondage through religion and the emphasis on liberating influences outside Africa. Similar techniques obtained in Africa during colonization.

6. Roy Ottley. *New World A-Coming.* Boston: Houghton Mifflin Company, 1943, 80.

7. E. B. Essien-Udom. *Black Nationalism - A Search for Identity in America.* Chicago: The University of Chicago press, 1962, 8-9.

8. Louis Lomax. *The Negro* Revolt. New York: Harper and Row, 1962. 249.

9. Bernard E. Magubane. *The Ties That Bind: African-American Consciousness.* Trenton, New Jersey: Africa World Press, Inc., 1987, 185-187. 10. Magubane, 186. 11. Houston Baker, Jr. *Blues. Ideology and Afro-American Literature: A Vernacular Theory.* Chicago: The University of Chicago Press, 1984, 31. 12. Baker, *Blues*, 31-56. 13. Chinweizu. The West and the Rest of Us. New York: Vintage Books, 1975, 134, 322-340. 14. Josephine Moraa Moikobu. *Blood and Flesh: Black American and African Identification.* Westport, Connecticut: Greenwood Press, 1981, 118, 131-133.

15. Moikobu, 127. 16. Chinweizu, 324, 333-334; Houston A. Baker, Jr., *Afro-American* Poetics: *Revision of Harlem and the Black Aesthetic.* Madison: The University of Wisconsin Press, 1988, 11-16. 17. Ali Mazrui. "Cultural Power in North and South Relations: Pan-African Perspective;" Keynote Address, Seventh Annual Pan-African Conference, Indiana State University, April, 1989. 1962, 249. 9. Bernard E. Magubane. *The Ties That Bind: African-American Consciousness.* Trenton, New Jersey: Africa World Press, Inc., 1987 , 185-187.

10. Magubane, 186.

11. Houston Baker, Jr. *Blues. Ideology and Afro-American Literature: A Vernacular Theory.* Chicago: The University of Chicago Press, 1984, 31.

12. Baker, *Blues*, 31-56.

13. Chinweizu. *The West and the Rest of Us* . New York: Vintage Books, 1975, 134, 322-340.

14. Josephine Moraa Moikobu. *Blood and Flesh: Black American and African Identification.* Westport, Connecticut: Greenwood Press, 1981, 118, 131-133.

15. Moikobu, 127.

16. Chinweizu, 324 , 333-334 ; Houston A. Baker, Jr., *Afro-American Poetics: Revision of Harlem and the Black Aesthetic.* Madison: The University of Wisconsin Press, 1988, 11-16.

17. Ali Mazrui. "Cultural Power in North and South Relations: Pan-African Perspective;" Keynote Address, Seventh Annual Pan-African Conference, Indiana State University, April, 1989.

SECTION VI

NEW CHALLENGES

CHAPTER 19

PETER - PAN SYNDROME : AN ANALYSIS OF AFRICA IN WORLD AFFAIRS

Bamidele A. Ojo

Current research on African politics and international relations agrees through their findings that Africa, as usual, is plagued with poverty, corruption, maladministration, decadent political situations, coup d'etat, inept leadership, debt crises, political instabilities, ethnic conflicts, and dependent and neo-colonial relationships with the major countries of Europe, America, Asia, and the Pacific (and with international financial institutions). There are clientelist and patrimonial relationships between leaders and their followers, and total disregard for fundamental human rights. These characterizations have remained evident since independence. However, there are changing dynamics in the international political system whereby major powers are more preoccupied with their domestic economic problems.

In the obvious reordering of the major power's foreign policy priorities, Africa appears to be on the endangered list. This situation has been characterized as the inevitable marginalization of Africa in the politics among nations (Callaghy: 1991).

There is a pattern of relationship between African leadership and their counterparts in the developed world which contributes to the problems facing African States and which is indicative of a lack of accountability and responsibility on the part of African leaders vis-a-vis the performance of their duties. Protecting the interests of their African constituents is an important duty which needs more attention. The problems characterizing African politics are a product of many factors among which are the Colonial heritage, prevailing domestic situations, the economy, and the socio-political predispositions of the leadership. The importance of the roles assumed by African leaders cannot be overemphasized in the search for socio-political and economic development on the continent. An examination of policy orientation and content demonstrates an ever increasing dependence on the developed world even in these post-Colonial times. It is this pattern that is characterized as the *Peter-Pan Syndrome.*

Peter-Pan, a fictional character, is a boy in a state of perpetual adolescence who will never grow old. He is always in conflict with the evil one-eyed pirate, Captain Hook, who dominates and is the most powerful leader in the land. Captain Hook controls and exploits Peter-Pan and the never-never boys by all possible means. Peter-Pan is immature, lacks any sense of responsibility, and remains dependent on the promises held out by the fairy situation of the never-never land.

In African leadership's relations with the developed world there is an apparent lack of independence, especially on major policy options critical to the well-being of their African constituents. The African leaders have not appeared to accept responsibilities for their domestic and foreign policies, and they blame everybody but themselves for the political and economic problems. The African leaders have acted like children who need to be spoonfed, assisted and tutored. They are so scared of losing their power that they will do anything they think is necessary to hold on to it. They personalize power, suppress opposition, corrupt the administration and mismanage the economy. There is no sense of accountability. Yet, whose who are political leaders are in a position to make productive use of the resources at their disposal for the benefits of all.

LEADERSHIP

In a relationship between two sovereign states, there are many variables determining eventual outcomes. Most studies of political leaders have emphasized their importance in the critical development of social, economic and political changes (Bienen and deWalle: 1991). Under normal circumstances, political leaders with skills, resources and goals formulate strategies under conditions of constraints and must then try to build support through policy formulations and implementations. Skills, styles, resources, policies, constituencies, luck and external constraints interact in complicated ways and are difficult to isolate. It is these variables that determine the role and performance of leaders in the decision-making process.

Roles mean leaders act according to what they think others expect of them as well as what they expect of themselves. Roles also involve leaders' views about their countries' proper place and conduct in the world and the leaders part in meeting those expectations.

Leaders have some moral responsibilities toward their constituents. These moral responsibilities depend upon the extent of the leader's ability to perform acts which have positive and/or negative effects upon the welfare of constituents and also to foresee the extent to which these acts are beneficial and/or detrimental to constituents. Ideally, leaders should act so as to promote the greatest possible happiness in the greatest possible number of present and future persons who can be affected by their acts (Blumenthal: 1975; Singer: 1991).

The reference to moral responsibility may sound far fetched but historical records give abundant reasons for wanting particularly close moral scrutiny of our leaders.It is a fact that exploitation of political positions for personal profits is strongly disapproved in many cultures, and this is very true of Africa too. Against this must be set the fact that political leaders are thought to have special obligations to their nations, their constituencies, their party, their faction and even their race. In the relationship between leaders and followers, exemplary leaders do not wield power without paying attention to the goals of their followers. Leaders are, ideally , inseparable from follower's "needs and goals" (Lawson: 1993; Burns: 1978).

The quality of governmental leadership has considerable bearing on the power of a country. Leaders in a national government set the priorities and determine the allocation of resources. They should not only have the national interest at heart but also the ability to turn good intentions into good programs. Leaders must be able to gain public support for proposed programs and policies. Strength and wisdom in leadership help to produce a stronger country, and the well-being of a nation often depends on the capacity of leaders to choose wisely and act prudently.

AFRICAN STATES AND THE DEVELOPED WORLD

Many African leaders emerged after the Second World War, loomed large in the anti-Colonial struggle, and had key roles to play in the formation of their independent nations. While observers differ in their assessments of the qualities of specific leaders, it is prudent to relate these to a general pattern apparent in the foreign policy posture of African states.

The Colonial heritage and the historical linkage of Africa to the developed countries have influenced the roles and performance of African leaders in the relationship of African states with other nations. There are existing domestic variables peculiar to Africa which conflict with the adoption of Western institutions and values. These cultural values include the extended family system, a collective rather than individualistic view, and anti-government sentiments (a carry-over from the colonial period.

In the neocolonial situation following independence, elitist groups were organized, sometimes after education and training abroad, who also saw themselves as the only viable leadership capable of solving African problems. Yet, African leadership has for decades demonstrated their inability to generate progressive economic growth on the continent and their inability to individually or collectively solve some of the problems facing Africa - unless the United States, Europe, or the United Nations stepped in to help them out. African leaders have appeared to stand back and do nothing. Meanwhile, there has been continuing peripheralization of Africa in the international economic system while internally there has been a lack of institutionalization resulting from instabilities, coup d'etat, and/or political engineering.

Each of the aforementioned variables could be extensively analyzed to illustrate their importance as determinants of Africa's international relations. But this does not preclude the dominant role of leadership. In the first years of independence, African leaders sought to legitimize their power by restructuring the inherited institutions toward either suppressing opposition, satisfying their perceptions of how things should be, or maintaining themselves in power perpetually. African leaders have needed external actors such as former colonial countries and other developed countries as guarantors of their power; they have sought external support by "opening up" their countries and seeking policy guidance and economic initiatives. Their continued search for aids and technical assistance and absence of domestic initiatives or alternatives is a demonstration of this dependence the Peter-Pan syndrome. Just as in the case of an adolescent, many of the African leaders would never admit they are still dependent on their foreign mentors for security, guidance and support.

African leaders do not acknowledge that they have "sold out" to actors from more developed countries. Beneath the rhetoric of loans, trade agreements, and cooperative development is the reality that the distribution of benefits from an agreement between a more developed country and a less developed one usually reflects the underlying inequalities in political and economic power. External economic and political actors are allowed by national elites to pursue their interests under economically favorable conditions because of benefits the national elites will derive from such cooperation. Among such benefits are technical and military assistance to suppress opposition and to maintain their political survival. Leaders like Mobutu Sese Seko of ZaiIe and Leon M'ba of Gabon among others have benefited from these types of arrangements. The French commitments to Houghouet-Boigny in Cote d'ivoire and Leopold Senghor and his successor in Senegal, undoubtedly have raised the stakes for would be opponents and made military coups less probable. Soviet and Cuban military personnel also legitimized the leadership of men like Mengistu Haile Mariam of Ethiopia.

Profit sharing between African leaders and their Western counterparts and the open-door policy of African states are characteristics of this dependency syndrome. Other examples include developmental programs initiated from abroad especially through international financial institutions such as the International Monetary Fund (IMF) or the World Bank or through Western countries and their multinational corporations. The dependency syndrome can also be recognized by the absence of a sustained democratic process and the presence of authoritarian leadership, nepotism, coup d'etat and personalization of power. Examples are numerous over Africa, i.e,Kamazu Banda of Malawi, Arap Moi of Kenya, Housni Moburak of Egypt, Babangida of Nigeria, Paul Biya of Cameroon, Eyadema of Togo, Hissene Habre of Chad, Omar Bongo of Gabon, Dauda Jawara of Gambia, Siad Barre of Somalia, Mattieu Kerekou of Benin, Blaise Compore of Burkina Faso. Despite the nature of the leadership, Western countries have continued to support them, contrary to professed democratic values.

African states became independent with hopes and expectations but shortly afterward the economy in many states went into a decline. The continent has witnessed decades of falling per capita incomes, increasing hunger, and accelerating ecological degradation. African states are as poor today as they were thirty years ago (World Bank: 1989). As a result of the debt crisis,the economies have been characterized by a weak agricultural growth, a decline in industrial output, poor export performance, climbing debt, and deteriorating social services. In the 1970s, to maintain income and investments, governments borrowed heavily from abroad. Africa's long-term debt has risen 19 fold since the 1970s and is now equal to its gross national product (GNP). The impact of the crisis is enormous in several countries with expenditures on social services sharply down, school enrollments falling, nutrition worsening and high infant mortality rates. Unemployment in the towns (especially among educated youth) threatens Africa's long term productive capacity. Population pressures on the land are accelerating, desertic lands are increasing, and forests are becoming depleted. Institutional decay is symbolized by the poor conditions of universities which were once world class, the disintegration of paved highways and the collapse of the judicial and banking systems. Many governments are wracked by corruption and are increasingly unable to command the confidence of the population at large.

There is no doubt that the responsibility for African economic crises must be shared (in fact, they are traceable to the Colonial policy on the continent) but Africa's future can only be decided by Africans with external agencies in supportive rather than dominant roles. Post independence development efforts failed because the strategies were misconceived. Many leaders were acquiring wealth and stacking millions of dollars away in foreign accounts while continuing to borrow and pan-handle around Western capitals for technical assistance and loans. Given the above crises, African leaders have failed tremendously. Their continued dependence on loans and aids from Western countries as the only way out has resulted in the IMF and other Financial institutions taking the place of internal African finance ministers. International corporations are in Africa to make profits, not to help Africa, and they are ready to milk the uncomprehending leadership. It is difficult to imagine that these leaders are totally unaware of the dynamics of the issues involved. Maybe they did not believe it was necessary for them to protect the general interests of their constituents.

CONCLUSION

In Ethiopia, Liberia, and again in Somalia, the Organization of African Unity (OAU) which is the collectivity of African leadership failed to respond to the needs of their people. It is questionable whether any of the contemporary African leaders has the power or moral aptitude to assist their fellow Africans. The more economically affluent states could not offer any help until the United Nations and, of course, the United States step in. This dependency syndrome between Africa and nations in the developed world can be demonstrated by examination of the governmental structures (the presence or absence of democratic processes); the policy-making processes and the extent of foreign involvement in domestic affairs (i.e. IMF or World Bank guidelines); the implementation of progressive developmental programs as alternatives to foreign induced plans; and attention (or lack of attention) to the preservation of African civil liberties and human rights.

There is a need for domestic African initiatives to demonstrate *real* independence. African leadership should be held accountable to their African constituents through establishment of democratic processes, selection and change. The democratization process now going on in Africa may be the signal needed to create the necessary political stability and stimulus for economic growth. However, long range strategies are needed as bases for sustained economic development. Programs should be aimed at making African economies less vulnerable to external shocks, and efforts to accelerate industrialization must go hand in hand with agricultural expansion to minimize risk and increase self reliance. Sub-regional and regional trade and coordination of development plans and strategies are important for African economic growth.

To be sustainable, an adjustment program must be designed to fit local conditions and involve indigenous institutions rather than external ones. The weak bargaining positions of African governments and ineffective use of existing capacity for policy formulation continue to undermine ongoing efforts to achieve economic growth. International organizations have been setting the agenda for policy reforms on the continent. However, African leaders should propose alternative and viable approaches.

Capable African political leadership is crucial to ensuring the sustainability of African economic growth. The accountability of African leadership and the need for an independent and dominant role in the formulation and implementation of Africa's international relations will be determined by the ability of the African population to take control of their African governments and to institute democratic processes that determine the allocation of resources within various African states.

REFERENCES

Ajay, Chibbers, S. Fischer, (1991). *Economic Reform in Sub-Saharan Africa* (Washington DC, World Bank.)

Bel, Balassa, (1982). "Structural Adjustment Policies in Developing Countries,*World Development* 10/1.

Bienen, Henry, Nicolas Vard de Walle, (1991). *Of Time and Power: leadership Duration in the Modern World.* (Stanford. CA., Stanford University Press) pp. 4.

Blumenthal, Albert, (1975). Moral Responsibility: Mankind's Greatest Need (Santa Ana, CA., Rayline Press).

Burns, James, MacGregor, (1978). *Leadership* (N.Y. Harper & Row, 1978) pp. 18.

Callaghy, Thomas, M. (1991). "Africa and the World Economy: Caught between A Rock and A Hard place", in John W. Harbesons & Donald Rothchild (1991) *Africa and World Affairs* (Boulder,Co., Westview Press).

Chapter 3.

Chazan, N., (et.al) ed. (1992). *Politics and Society In Contemporary Africa* (Boulder, Co., Lynne Rienner Pub.).

Danziger, J.N., (1991). *Understanding the Political World* (N.Y. Longmans).

Deger, S., (1986). *Military Expenditures in The Third World: The Economic Effect (London: Routledge & Kayas Paul).*

Erikson, Erith H., (1968). *Identity: Youth and Crisis* (N.Y. Norton).

Husain, Ishrat, Ishac Duvai, (1990). *Dealing With The Debt Crisis* (Washington, D.C., World Bank).

Hussain, I., Underwood, J. *(1991). African External Finance In 1990s* (Washington, D.C., World Bank).

Jackson, Robert, H., Carl, G. Rosberg, Jr. (1982). *Personal Rule in Black Africa* (Berkeley, CA., University of California Press).

Johnson, T., et al (1984). "Explaining Africa's Military Coup d'état 1960-1082" *APSR* 78 (1984) pp. 622-40.

Lasswell, H., (1958). *Politics: Who Gets What, When, How,* (N.Y. Meridian Books).

Lawson, Kay, (1993). The Human Polity: A Comparative *Introduction To Political Science* (3rd. Ed.) (Princeton, N.J., Houghton Mufflin Co.) pp.305

Magstadt, Thomas, M., P.M. Schottes (1993). *Understanding Politics: Ideas, Institutions and Issues* (n.Y., St. Martin Press).

Mullus, J.A.F., (1987). *Born Arming: Development and Military Power in New States* (Stanford, CA., Stanford University Press).

O'Kane, Rosemary, H.T. (1981), "A Probabilistic Approacl to the Causes of

Coup d'étât"*British Journal of Political Science* (2)(1981) pp .287-308.

Ribe, Helen, (et.al) (1990). "How Adjustment Program Can Help The Poor", *World Bank Discussion Paper*, 71, 1990.

Rourke, John T. (1993). *International Politics On the World Stage* (Guilford, CT., The Duskin Publ.) pp. 120.

Shils,E. (1975). *Center and Periphery: Essay in Macro-Sociology* (Chicago, University of Chicago Press, 1975).

Singer, Peter, (ed) (l991). *A Companion to Ethics* (Cambridge, Mass., Blackwell Ref.).

Turker, R.C., (1981). Politics As Leadership,(Columbia: University of Missouri Press.).

Walker, Stephen, G., (1987). "Role Theory and the Origin of Foreign Policy". In Charles F. Hermann (et. al) (ed.) *New Directions In the Study of Foreign Policy* (Boston, Mass., Blackwell Ref.).

Winter, R., Herbert, (et al.) (1992). Conflict and Compromise: *An Introduction To Politics* , (NY. Harper & Collins),

World Bank (1989). *Sub-Sahara Africa: from Crisis to Sustainable Growth* (Washington, D.C.,The World Bank) pp.1.

Wriggins, H., (1969). *The Rulers' Imperative* (N.Y. Columbia University Press).

CHAPTER 20

THE 1990'S: A DECADE OF CHALLENGE FOR THE OAU

Assefaw Bariagaber

Even though some international organizations appeared during the nineteenth century, the post-1945 period may reasonably be characterized as an era in which proliferation of various international organizations occurred. Depending on the needs of national and supranational actors, international organizations with varying purposes - some for security, some because of economic motives, and others for environmental reasons - were formed to facilitate the realization of a set of specific goals which otherwise would have been immensely difficult for a single entity to accomplish. It is not, therefore, surprising to see that the newly independent countries of Africa, Asia, and the Caribbean were quick to join the United Nations Organization and form other regional groupings. The Organization of African Unity (OAU) is one such regional organization formed to promote the unity, independence, and well-being of the African peoples.[1] It was especially germane for the African states to form a Pan-African organization for the following reasons:

1) Most of them were newly independent countries that did not have any previous experience with the intricacies of international diplomacy. Dealing as a block would further enhance their interests.

2) All of them had no developed social, political, and economic infrastructure.

3) A portion of the continent was still under colonial rule.

4) Most of them were small states that could easily be destabilized by a few hundred mercenary forces.

5) Due to their degrading experience under colonialism, it was pertinent to build continental unity in order to regain their dignity and build what was known as "African Personality."[2]

The OAU was thus formed to enable all African countries to face these challenges collectively. As broad as these objectives were, the OAU had an immense task ahead. Since the continent was balkanized by different powers, it was not easy to accommodate the different interests of African countries in a single organization. In addition, the post-1945 era was characterized by global ideological struggles from which Africa was not immune. These ideological struggles between the West and the East and their impact on the OAU are especially relevant because they indicate the nature of the evolving organization and suggest reasons for the OAU's apparent inability to live up to many of its declared objectives.

Prior to the formation of the OAU in 1963, there were essentially two groupings - the Monrovia and Casablanca groups. The former stressed cooperation between independent African states and, if any, a gradual and cautious approach to continental political unity. The latter consisted of countries that believed in a socialist United States of Africa as the only alternative to poverty, weakness and disunity. Its leaders, such as K. Nkrumah, favored quick political unity and the disbanding of all colonial boundaries. The "moderate" leaders, such as W. Tubman, viewed this socialist leaning with suspicion and equated it to the loss of freedom. Thus, as early as 1960, before many African countries became independent, ideological rivalry in the form of "Marxist-socialism" and "liberal-democracy" was apparent. It is within this context that the efforts of the OAU are to be analyzed.

"In numbers, population, and total geographical area, the Monrovia Group had more weight than the Casablanca Group, whose strength was the strength of ideas."[3] Thus, when Emperor Haile Selassie of Ethiopia, himself a "moderate," called for the founding conference of the OAU, it was evident that the forces of compromise would prevail. [4] Indeed, while recognizing the need for African political unity, the OAU constitution sanctified the respect for sovereignty and territorial integrity of each member state and bestowed a de facto as well as de jure recognition to the so-called artificial borders. [5]

No compromise was made on the issue of sovereignty and no program of continental unity was issued, which, incidentally, almost all countries agreed would be the goal of the OAU. Thus, even after the OAU was formed, no serious effort was made to achieve this goal. No meaningful solutions to the economic and social issues were found. Problems of international borders continued to be the main source of inter-African conflicts. Apart from a united stand against the racist regime of South Africa and the wider issue of decolonization, no cause, apparently, was worthy enough to warrant consistent and united effort.

This is not to belittle the achievements of the OAU. Indeed, the liberation of Zimbabwe and the former Portuguese colonies, and political pressure to ostracize the racist South African regime from the world community of nations are but some of the accomplishments of the OAU. However, very serious problems remain to be tackled.

This paper will address the following questions:

1) Why did the OAU fail to achieve or, for that matter, fail to attempt bringing about the much aspired continental unity?

2) Why are issues of human rights and inter-African conflicts persistent problems of contemporary Africa?

3) What were OAU's responses to the economic problems of the continent?

4) How should the OAU face these challenges in the next decade?

Even though adequate solutions to some of the problems may be beyond the reach of the OAU, a fundamental deficiency appears to lie within the structure (constitution) of the OAU. The paper explores and makes suggestions for radical changes in the OAU constitution.

THE NATURE OF THE OAU

As noted earlier, the OAU was an organization born out of compromise. Those leaders that were influenced by western liberal tradition and those that saw their position at stake in the future United States of Africa were very reluctant to accept the unity proposal of the "radicals" who, at the time, became very influential because of their outspoken and persistent attack on European colonialism [6] and their immense organizational ability. Indeed, some of the "moderate" leaders were members of the French National Assembly and had close ties with France. Because of their suspicion of the OAU, they formed the *Organization Commune Africaine et Malagache* (OCAM), a regional organization of most French speaking African countries, in 1965. [7] Thompson (1969) observed that, "As long as such a regional grouping exists, the suspicion remains that its [that is, the OAU] retention is symbolic of the reluctance of most of the gradualist states to make African unity a reality." [8]

Thus, it is not an exaggeration to state that the OAU was not only an organization where the ideals of immediate unity were compromised but, indeed, the OAU was also deliberately limited as an organization, even with respect to gradual unification. Secondly, the OAU constitution adopted in 1963 was very broad and multi-purposed. It undertook to solve the political, social, cultural, economic, and other problems. On the other hand, the member countries themselves were very poor and could not provide the necessary resources for the smooth functioning of such a broad-purposed organization. This disjuncture between the enormity of the purposes and the scarcity of the resources seems to have contributed immensely to the inability of the OAU to confront these problems.

Many African countries have been accused by international organizations and fellow African countries of showing utter disregard for human rights. Indeed, reports of indiscriminate shooting that killed about 500 peaceful demonstrators in the central African Republic, [9] the public execution of President William Tolbert of Liberia, [10] and the systematic killing of more than 100,000 Hutu in Burundi are all disheartening. [11] In 1977/78, the military government of Ethiopia executed many Eritreans and Ethiopians in what was called the "red terror." [12] Similarly a sizeable number of Igbos were massacred in Northern Nigeria. [13] Over 40,000 Kenyans and Tanzanians from Uganda and Ghanians from the Ivory Coast were among instances of expulsions where the victims had to leave their property behind. [14] The presence of millions of refugees in the continent is still a source of great frustration.

A few African countries openly condemned these flagrant violations of the dignity of African peoples, which, incidentally, each state had agreed to respect. However, the OAU has failed to express even the mildest concern. The non-interference clause included in the constitution was invoked time and again by any state that infringed on individual and collective rights. [15] This clause, ostensibly included at the insistence of the "moderates" primarily to prevent political interference from the "radicals," was invoked indiscriminately by the "moderates" and the "radicals" alike in their attempts to suppress legitimate opposition to their respective regimes. Clearly these acts of unilateral expulsions cannot be regarded as domestic. Indeed, they affect other countries in terms of draining the meager economic resources and creating other political problems. The main problem thus rests on when an issue stops being internal and becomes a matter of concern for the OAU and other African countries. As to human rights and the dignity of the individual, it was only in 1979, more than 15 years after the establishment of the continental organization, that "serious efforts have been undertaken by the OAU itself to establish a formal human rights machinery."[16]

The record of the OAU in its attempts to solve inter-African political problems is equally in question. Borders that did not take into consideration the ethnic configuration of regions have always been a source of significant frustration for the OAU. Indeed, from its inception, the OAU has not been able to extricate itself from this menacing problem. The Ethio-Somalia border dispute is still unresolved after two border wars, one in 1964 and the other in 1977/78. The Kenya-Somalia dispute lingers on. Claims and counterclaims for the same strip of land between Chad and Libya are but a few examples of the inability of the OAU to come up with some acceptable solutions. These problems may be said to have occurred contrary to the expectations of the "founding fathers" of the OAU. They had hoped that the maintenance of the European-created boundaries would, in terms of stability, be better than the revision of the territorial status-quo. However, the persistence of border conflicts should have alerted subsequent leaders to the enormity of the problem. To fail to provide some legal mechanism for the settlement of border problems threatening the very existence of the organization is beyond comprehension.[17]

The problem of civil wars is another area which has incapacitated the OAU. The civil war in Chad is a vivid example that has continued for about 20 years. In the Ethio-Eritrean conflict, the OAU did not intervene, ostensibly because the problem was entirely Ethiopian. In the Sahara Arab Democratic Republic (SADR)-Morocco, the OAU faced a problem that threatened its very existence.[18] In other words, the OAU could not function properly because it appeared that its primary intentions were to satisfy each conflicting party.

The withdrawal of one or more countries from the organization is seen as a prelude to the disintegration of the organization - a precedent that must be fought at any cost, even if it means the paralysis of the OAU. It is high time that the well-phrased words of African solidarity and brotherhood be based on principles of justice. The discrimination of right and wrong should necessarily entail reward and punishment for any member state.

As was mentioned earlier, the OAU was formed by the newly independent countries, many of which were small states comprising pieces of land with economies that were meant to provide raw materials for industries in Europe. What is still worse is that each country had only one cash crop, usually at the mercy of international market forces. The infrastructure was such that it enhanced the smooth transfer of raw materials to overseas industries. Roads, railways, and telecommunication facilities were to be found in coastal regions and in some isolated mining regions of the hinterland. Because one of the purposes of the OAU was to "coordinate and intensify cooperation and efforts to achieve a better life for the peoples of Africa,"[19] an economic and social commission was established to facilitate the integration of African economies. However, the commission was unable to effect meaningful changes. Sesay, Ojo, and Fasehun (1984) give three possible reasons:

1) The annual summit, by becoming a substitute for the commission, passed resolutions that were not amply discussed and debated; that is, it was not a proper organ for detailed and purposeful examination of Africa's development strategies;

2) The leaders were preoccupied with political issues such as stability, national security, and territorial integrity; economic and other issues that required careful and timely decisions did not receive needed attention;

3) The disparate political and ideological beliefs of member states were wide enough that a collective stand on important issues could not easily be reached.[20]

Another fundamental source of weakness for the OAU was that the technological expertise which each state or even the whole continent could supply was so meager that it could not conform with the various resolutions of the annual summit. In fact, the Economic Commission of Africa, one of the specialized agencies of the United Nations, was comparatively more organized and well-staffed to undertake various ventures than the OAU commission. Thus, the disjuncture of resources and the immensity of economic issues rendered the OAU incapable of solving any substantive problem.

Despite the material constraints and the diversity of the political, ideological, and economic structures of the member states, the OAU has succeeded in projecting itself as a "forum to which African issues should first be referred before recourse to any other international organization."[21] Once the OAU was formed, even contemporary "radical" leaders never opted for another organization, in spite of their disillusionment. Indeed, it would be improper to suggest the dissolution of the OAU. However, one should be objective as to what the OAU can and cannot do.

Two main sources of weaknesses may be identified: 1) the organizational structure of the OAU; and 2) the broadness of the purposes the OAU strives to achieve and the limited resources at its disposal. With respect to the first, the OAU "founding fathers" were very apprehensive of the powers of the Secretary General. Their desire for a weak apolitical secretariat, as stated by one influential leader, was that it "would be an administrative body and not a political one; a body which implemented decisions but did not make them."[22] The summit meeting, normally held once a year for three days, was the main source of all resolutions. However, without ample pre-summit deliberations, the kind of decisions that could be reached in a three day meeting punctuated by elaborate festivities could not be as meaningful and relevant as much as they were well-phrased demagogy. As Meyers (1976) stated, "In contrast with the United Nations Secretariat, which is considered as equal to the other principal organs, the OAU's Secretariat is subordinate to both the Council of Ministers and Assembly of Heads of State and government."[23] The OAU charter emphasized that the secretariat was administrative and not executive. [24] Even the personnel serving in the secretariat were appointed by their governments which tended to make them loyal to their respective countries rather than the organization. This legal-structural restraint within the constitution seems to have been the main cause behind the powerlessness of the office of the Administrative Secretary General.[25]

The second important feature that may account for the inability of the OAU to solve some outstanding problems is the disjuncture between the resources and the broadness of the goals. In view of the intractable problems inherited from colonialism and other contemporary systemic restraints, two possibilities are that the OAU could scale down its objectives or else create specialized agencies that would address different aspects of current problems. Both suggestions do not seem to be plausible due to the following:

1) In a situation of multiple problems, narrowing down the purposes would apparently deprive the organization of its noble causes and this may be construed as a defeat, or retreat at best. In Africa and all over the world, the OAU is seen as a vital organization that has gained respect for its ability to survive in the face of diverse and often highly conflicting interests.

2) Creating specialized agencies like those within the United Nations would fragment the limited resources at the OAU's disposal.

CONCLUSION

A natural question to ask is, what should be done under the prevailing circumstances? Various scholars have suggested recommendations ranging from strengthening the OAU executive office to making changes in the clause pertaining to domestic jurisdiction. Others suggest a general revision of the constitution in light of new developments without, however, making clear what kind of changes are needed. In my view, carrying out these suggestions would not make much difference because they do not seem to take into account the human, material, and technical resources the OAU has at its disposal. Any change would have to take place within the context of the restraints. If the OAU is to be a viable organization in the decades to come, some structural changes of the kind described below seem to be imperative.

The OAU is a 50-state organization with broad purposes but meager resources. Its history, as in any multi-purposed organization with a large number of members, shows that there was a tendency of progressive dilution of commitments. Thus, altering the constitution to embrace a lesser number of purposes, drastically increasing the budget of the secretariat, or bestowing more power to the executive office may increase the effectiveness of the organization.

Another possibility, which in my view is preferable, is to add a clause in the constitution by which regional organizations with memberships of about ten states could be formed. These organizations would effectively substitute for the OAU in their respective regions. In other words, the OAU would be an umbrella organization of these regional groupings which, due to their limited and less diverse membership, would be in a better position to address political, social, and economic problems.

The OAU, due to its stature in African and world politics, should continue to exist because it is a symbol of the desire for African unity. As an umbrella organization, the OAU should be in the strongest possible position to exert pressure on South Africa in the United Nations and other international organizations. In the future, the OAU may be called upon to settle problems arising between two or more regional organizations. Such an arrangement could generate, hopefully, increasing cooperation and commitment to African unity among the various regional organizations, thus giving a much needed dynamism to the effort of changing Africa.

NOTES

1. See A.Sesay, O. Ojo, and O. Fasehun, *The OAU After Twenty Years* (Boulder and London: Westview Press, 1984), p. 4.

2. The concept of "African Personality" was emphasized by radical leaders such as K. Nkrumah and S. Toure and was an outcome of increasing self-awareness and race consciousness. For more information, consult V. Thompson, *Africa and Unity: The Evolution of Pan-Africanism* (New York: Humanities Press, 1969), p. 170.

3. Thompson, *Africa and Unity*, p. 181.

4. Ibid, p. 182.

5. Ibid, p. 371.

6. For more information, consult K. Nkrumah, *Revolutionary Path* (New York: International Publishers, 1973), p. 235.

7. Thompson, *Africa and Unity*, p. 192.

8. Ibid.

9. Welch cited this from a report of Amnesty International on the violations of human rights in Central Africa. See C. E. Welch, Jr., "The OAU and Human Rights: Toward a New Definition." *Journal Modern Africa Studies* (New York), Vol. 19, No. 3 (September, 1981), p. 401-20.

10. Ibid.

11. U. O. Umozurike, "The Domestic Jurisdiction Clause in the OAU Charter," *African Affairs* (London), Vol. 78, No. 311 (April, 1979), p. 197-209.

12. For more information on the "red terror," consult P. Schwab, *Ethiopia: Politics, Economics and Society* (Boulder, Colorado: Lynne Reinner Publishers, Inc., 1985), p. 40.

13. Umozurike, "The Domestic Jurisdiction Clause in the OAU Charter," p. 201.

14. Ibid, p. 199.

15. A full text of the OAU Charter may be obtained in Thompson, *Africa and Unity,* p. 369-374.

16. B. Ndiaye, "The Place of Human Rights in the Charter of the Organization of Africa Unity," in K. Vasak, *The International Dimension of Human Rights,* Vol. 2 (Westport, Connecticut: Greenwood Press, 1982), p. 601. For a full text, see p. 616-30.

17. A Sesay et al, *The OAU After Twenty Years,* p. 35.

18. Strictly speaking, the Ethio-Eritrean and the SADR-Morocco problems are not civil wars. Both Eritrea and SADR claim their right to independence (as any other African country) because of their experience under European colonialism.

19. Thompson, *Africa and Unity,* p. 370.

20. Sesay et al, *The OAU After Twenty Years,* p. 65.

21. Ibid, p. 92.

22. B. D. Meyers, "The OAU's Administrative Secretary General," *International Organization,* Vol. 30, No. 3 (Summer, 1976), p. 509-20. The leader was President Léopold Sedar Senghor of Senegal.

23. Ibid, p. 511.

24. Ibid.

25. Ibid, p. 519.

CHAPTER 21

THE DEMOCRACY MOVEMENT IN AFRICA TODAY

G. N. Nzongola

Africa today is a continent in crisis. There are civil wars in Liberia, Mozambique, Rwanda, Sudan, Somalia, and conditions approaching civil war in Algeria, Burundi, Chad, Djibouti, Ethiopia, Mauritania, South Africa, Uganda, Zaire. There is continued illegal occupation of Western Sahara by Morocco, a U.S. ally, even in the wake of the Gulf War. There are increasing economic crises and insecurities as millions of very poor people are destitute, having fallen into a deplorable state of physical want.

The consequences of all these events are, among others, social unrest, proliferation of religious sects and the rise of Islamic fundamentalism with its institutionalization of Islamic law into civic governance.

On the positive side, a new political awakening has occurred--*the rise of a new democracy movement.*

With the widespread recognition that there is a close relationship between Africa's crisis and the lack of democracy, the struggle today thus centers on the democratization of political structures and processes in such a way that national leaders will become accountable to their own people rather than to external patrons and allies.

In its popular content, the new democracy movement is just another phase of the national liberation struggle, with its Pan-Africanist ideals of total independence and economic development.

SOURCES OR DETERMINANTS OF THE MOVEMENT

The first major source or determinant of the democratic movement in Africa today is our people's *permanent aspiration for democracy*, an aspiration manifested in (1) precolonial democratic traditions such as the democratic principles of governance in African societies, the *palaver*; (2) the anticolonial struggle all over the continent, beginning with the ANC of South Africa in 1912; and (3) "second independence" movements (Zaire, Chad, Uganda).

The *economic crisis* associated with the worldwide recession that began in 1975 is the second major factor in peoples' dissatisfaction with governments that seem to care little for their welfare. Discontent has been aggravated by austerity measures imposed by external donors like the IME and the World Bank.

A third factor is the end of the Cold War. The fall of Stalinism and one-party dictatorships in Eastern Europe and the former Soviet Union have given Africans added hope that the Western powers will stop supporting African dictators.

THE DYNAMICS OF THE MOVEMENT

Popular struggles for democracy against single-party and military dictatorships have taken the form of either armed struggles (Ethiopia, Eritrea, Sudan, Somalia, Liberia, Rwanda) or urban rebellions and strikes (Algeria, Benin, Cote d'Ivoire, Gabon, Zaire, Mali, Madagascar, Cameroon, Congo, Zambia, Togo, Niger, etc.). Responding to domestic and external pressures, a number of governments have reluctantly agreed to face political change by holding national conferences and/or national elections.

National conferences are democratic forums of all relevant sectors of the society convened to take stock of what went wrong in the past, to give vent to sentiments and feelings hitherto suppressed, and to chart a new course for the future with decisions that are binding on all, hence their sovereign character. They are also meant to function as a national catharsis in the tradition of the African *palaver*. National conferences have taken place in Benin, Gabon, Liberia, Congo, Ethiopia, Togo, Niger, Mali, and one is currently being held in Zaire.

National multiparty elections for parliament and for president have also taken place in a number of countries, including some countries that did not hold national conferences (Cape Verde, Zambia, Cameroon). They have varied greatly on a continuum ranging from government controlled and rigged elections (Cote d'Ivoire, Gabon) to free and fair elections with international monitors (Zambia). In Algeria, a military-backed government has nullified the 1991 parliamentary elections and banned the winning party, the Islamic Salvation Front (FIS).

POLITICAL CONSEQUENCES

A relatively successful transition has taken place in Sao Tome and Principe, Cape Verde, Benin, Zambia, and, apparently, in Mali. It remains to be seen, however, whether these new regimes will go beyond formalism to genuine democracy.

There are ongoing transition programs in Ethiopia, Eritrea, Togo, Niger, Nigeria, and Congo with some encouraging signs, particularly in Eritrea and to some extent in Ethiopia, but disturbing signs in Togo and Congo.

Of great concern is the open resistance to change in Cote d'Ivoire, Gabon, Zaire, Cameroon, Togo, Madagascar, Kenya, Sudan, Uganda, Tanzania, Algeria, and so on, but such resistance can only be short-lived. In the long-run, the sovereign people will prevail. Why? There has been a loss of fear on the part of the masses, and there is reluctance on the part of external patrons to openly back their African clients.

CONCLUSION

The current struggle for democracy will be won by the people waging it on African soil. However, international solidarity is needed, particularly in the United States, the only superpower in the world. The best hope of democracy in Africa and elsewhere in the countries of the South is a U.S. foreign policy based on the democratic principles of fairness, equality, and freedom supported by a well informed public capable of promoting the practice of democratic principles around the globe.

CHAPTER 22

PAN-AFRICANISM IN THE NEW WORLD ORDER

Edward Boyle, Wendell Stills and Arun Elhance

Since 1990 many world leaders have suggested that a new paradigm of world order has emerged. [1] Although a myriad of elements have been combined to suggest such a new paradigm exists, the more important elements highlighted in this new paradigm are the changes in communism and the greater integration of the global economy, elements which have a largely Western bias. Largely ignored in this concept of new order is the role of the Third World, ethnicity, and the post-colonial state.

During the Cold War era, intense interest in the Third World by the superpowers was limited to ideological control rather than economic development. In fact, it could be suggested that interest in Africa by superpowers contributed more to war than to development. These superpower wars should not simply be reduced to proxy wars and ideological conflicts, since they contained within them many elements which yet remain to be analyzed in the post-Cold war era.

Much of the Third World, but Africa in particular, stands on the cutting edge of geopolitics, geo-economics, and global order in the paradigm of a new world order. That Africa has such a role to play in this new order has largely been ignored by the powers of the Western World. Since Africa or much of it falls into the category of post Colonial states, we need to explore this issue before we can look at ethnicity or Pan-Africanism in the context of its Colonial past. We will then determine whether or not any states have reached the stage of a post Colonial state in the sociological sense or whether the post Colonial state is simply a political westernized conceptualization without any sociological foundation.

STATE, ETHNICITY, AND NEO-MARXIST THEORY IN AFRICA

It has been suggested that much of the Third World is made up a series of 'soft states', a notion which we feel should be at the center of any debates on Pan-Africanism, ethnicity and the global economy. While we agree that such states exist, we would suggest that they are 'soft' in a very different sense from that used in the Myrdal (1968) concept of a soft state. The Myrdal soft state concept adopts the Marxist perspective that institutions, government agencies, dependence on state structures, and the class divisions created under colonization were the molding blocks in this solidification process. A soft state in our context is the nature of a state which has not been solidified through its socialization of ethnic groups to their past and how that past can be translated into a newly independent state.

Such a notion of solidification lies within the Cold War framework. The solidification processes are part of the physiological, sociological and psychological adjustments required to be undertaken by a state in the advent of independence. Thus, the solidification processes under the Marxist ideology were not permanent and tended to do little more than create a control within a state which legitimized a certain number of elites. Among these elites were those who had the foresight to understand the framework within which a legitimate government could operate regardless of the ideology followed by that government.

Hyden (1973a) suggests that the Myrdal type of soft state was the result of the 'peasant mode of production' which resulted in a lack of dependence on the state for material and social reproduction, rendering it impossible for the state to capture the system. As a result, those who controlled the state did not control society. While agreeing with Hyden that the post Colonial state was as foreign to the peasantry as the Colonial state and that many African countries are societies without states, we would suggest that his reasoning for arriving at this conclusion is rather misconceived for the simple reason that it suggests a deliberate action on the part of the peasant. Nor does his explanation attempt to analyze the emergence of indigenous elite power structures which developed within the state in the advent of independence. These power structures had been put in place in the Colonial period as processes through which independence might be achieved or at the very least to facilitate independence agencies.

Hyden's notion of 'clientelism', while pointing out a distinct relationship between many governments, their agencies, and constituencies of a given communal or ethnic nature, tends to suggest it was the dimensions of the mode of production which encouraged this 'clientelism' rather than any reciprocal relationship to be derived by those in power. Yet, certain ethnic elites or regional power brokers maintained power at the expense of the state. While pointing out that the state "sits suspended in mid air over society and is not an integral mechanism of the day to day productive activities of society," Hyden fails to draw on the impacts of Colonialism in the post-Colonial period when describing the processes leading to the formation of government and society in the post-Colonial state, thereby failing to suggest either forms of continuity from the Colonial period or an entire breakdown of the Colonial legacy.

Hyden also argues that 'clientelism' produced a set of core-periphery relations forced on the state by a system which is ethnically structured, resulting in the "elevation of the informal redistributive principles of the economy of affection to official policy levels" and in doing so "reduced the dangers of ethnic confrontation in most African countries" (1983b). Murphree (1988) suggests that in a core-periphery relationship the state/core intrudes on the peasant/periphery, but not in a mode which evokes any initiative from the peasant/periphery to act on such intervention. It is suggested that these interventions are "seen as obstructive intrusions to be neutralized, diverted or if possible, to be manipulated for the benefit of individual or communal interests" (Murphree 1988:132).

The example applied to support this argument is that the state tells the peasants where they can live, fish, cultivate, and what taxes they pay on goods and services. The peasants obtain other services in return. The services negotiated in return never exceed the simplest needs of survival, and all other services and goods can be obtained within the peasant community. Thus, there is never a dependency on the state by the peasant community. Hyden presents this as the notion of dominance of the 'economy of affection', where the community is friendly and central while the state foreign and peripheral. (The terms, central and peripheral, are used here in a diametrically opposite concept to that used by Hyden or Murphree). Hyden, therefore, suggests that while ethnicity may be one criterion for core-periphery relations, the 'economy of affection' being broader cuts across ethnic and tribal boundaries and is thus a better explanation for core-periphery relations.

Murphree (1988) notes that ethnic salience is rarely operationalized since ethnic homogeneity is neutralized within the 'economy of affection,' that ethnic heterogeneity intrusions/potential conflicts are regarded as acceptable interfaces with the state, and that, as such, they are defused by a combination of demographic and communal histories. Except for an aside caveat, the possibility of ethnic conflict is regarded as unlikely except where the state directly impinges on a homogenous group in such a manner as to disrupt their normal existence. Examples might be the taking tribal lands endowed with natural resources or the exploitation of natural resources likely to result in immigration of other peoples. Dilution of the homogeneity and integrity of a group may destroy the principle of the 'economy of affection.' In a final caveat, exclusion from the state political system of ethnic groups may result in the creation of two separate histories, that of nation building and that of state building, the paradox being that if ethnic groups are included in the political system as ethnic groups then the impact of 'clientelism' could produce conflicts of interest within a heterogeneous secular form of government. Thus, we are left with a zero sum game.

GEO-POLITICAL DIMENSIONS OF THE POST-COLONIAL STATE IN THE COLD WAR ERA

A state should be secure with itself before it takes its place in the community of states and is ready to begin the long road toward prosperity and economic well-being. If this process has been undertaken there should be little in the way of conflict or of upheaval regardless of the nature of ideological upheaval in other parts of the world. In such a context it is worthwhile to examine the nature of nationalism and the forces of nationalism in the face of major changes. Nationalism can take on at least two very different and opposing directions - nationalism which is singular and nationalism which is pluralistic. Historical evidence demonstrates that nationalism often takes on both phases; in the case of many post Colonial African nations, this means wars of independence and civil wars.

Young (1976) points out that nationalism is not simply the rejection of colonial rule. Nationalism also involves the positive goals of cultural regeneration and the escape from poverty and exploitation. The positive goals of nationalism as suggested by Young are by no means mutually inclusive. The emphasis of the newly formed government is to gel into a new state as the most serious issue, leaving the other for later unless ideological conflicts stemming from the war of independence make this impossible. States have taken two directions both of which ultimately lead back to ethnic issues and ethnic conflict. With the fall of Communism, this has left Africa in a rather precarious position. Many African states are being torn in two directions at the same time.

The Cold War, as Hogan et. al. (1992), Cox (1990), Mearsheimer (1990), and O'Loughlin (1987) have noted, had a stabilizing effect on the world. Even where proxy wars were being fought, an equilibrium existed which has now disappeared. Proxy wars may be viewed from a variety of perspectives, especially where several ethnic groups were involved. They might have been ideological conflicts, but they had their ethnic dimensions. As a result, these ideological divisions were more often than not proxies for the real nature of many of these Third World conflicts which had an ethnic base to them. Westerners all too often forget that the colonial powers did not create the history of Africa; they simply arrived in the middle of it and altered its direction, thus leaving many unfinished conflicts in limbo and creating others by the unnatural division of Africa in the 19th and early 20th centuries.

van den Berghe (1983) notes that there are clear ethnic traits in all states, regardless of whether they are nation-states or multi-ethnic states. In the case of the multi-ethnic state, it began as a powerful ethnic state and through conquest became larger and more powerful economically, often encouraging migration from other regions to sustain its base for expansion. The nation state for the most part tends to be a proto-version of this process, a process curtailed by some geographic barrier. Ethnicity is based on kinship, but as the ethnic group increases in size, the bond of common descent is diluted to the point of being unimportant from a kinship perspective, although the sociological/myth characteristic of attachment remains within the psyche of a group at some removed level.

Thus, larger ethnic groups do not maintain the same level of solidarity to ethnicity and belonging as smaller ethnic groups. As a result, it is possible to see a pattern in which ethnic groups increase in size and evolve into larger and larger social groups, often encompassing other groups and creating societies which become increasingly more technologically complex and politically centralized (van den Berghe 1983). However, large ethnic groups can often be divided into a series of smaller groups based on locality and ending with kinship groups. This is an important point when we tie such kinship relations to regional power brokers in areas such as Somalia, Nigeria, Ethiopia, South Africa, Senegal, and Egypt.

Ethnicity and class can both be manipulated for individual gain, especially in a state in flux "where the sheer multiplicity and complexity of competing affiliations gives the individual considerable scope to shift allegiances opportunistically" (van den Berghe 1983: 231).

In larger more complex state level societies, ethnic groups tend to be larger, ethnicity is diluted and class formation becomes more important; there is the tendency for ethnicity to wane as class waxes. However, this says little about the opportunistic behavior of the individual actors. Nepotism or 'clientelism' tends to act less in an ethnic sense than it may in the narrower kinship sense.

A priori predictions as to the importance of class or ethnic salience in a given society is impossible to determine without understanding the sociological, psychological and physiographical details of the given region. Furthermore, any analysis for a region cannot be transferred to the continent as a whole or even the black African part of it.

Clearly class and ethnicity overlap, but the degree to which they do is determined by the make-up of each region. As class structures or ethnic homogeneity become rigid over time, the analytical distinction between class and ethnicity is blurred. The 'clientele' relationship can cut across ethnic barriers undermining ethnic solidarity, but alternatively 'clientelism' can be used to reinforce it. Clientelism has the ability to activate the individual to maximize opportunity according to the opportunity presented.

Traditional African societies tended to have certain quasi ethnic-class feudal systems where societies managed to dominate regions for considerable periods of time and used quasi-class structures to encompass other peoples within their society. Only where Islamic or Christianized societies developed do we see a distinctive Western class order emerge, societies which have influences from civilizations which had managed to dominate and enslave a variety of peoples and had used some means of maintaining control over subjected peoples.

What emerges in the post Colonial state is the simultaneous continuation of two separate societies, an ethnic society and a class society. Each is from a different legacy of African history, using the opportunities available to them to survive in the post Colonial state. (This state of being may fail to satisfy the needs of either society.) Colonial Africa was divided into a myriad of multi-ethnic states created by dividing ethnic groups through the use of created boundaries such as lines of longitude or latitude. The collapse of the Colonial state left a legacy of artificial boundaries, artificial states, and artificial state institutions running them.

van den Berghe rightly points out that African nationalist movements were shamelessly misnamed, since they were:

> fragile class based movements, led by a Western educated intelligentsia often drawn from several different ethnic groups who formed loose opportunistic coalitions, often with the support mostly from the emergent urban proletariat (which was in itself in a privileged position viz-a-viz the rural masses), and who sought to inherit the mantle of colonialism......They came to power because of their command of linguistic, cultural and educational traditions foreign to Africa, not because they were owners of the means of production. Thus, by class position they were intelligentsia not a bourgeois. Nor were they nationalist because in most cases they led political movements which were loose, multi-ethnic united fronts, eclectic in ideology, opportunistic in tactics, and diverse in ethnic membership. The new ruling class in Africa thus represented mostly their own class interests as a foreign trained intelligentsia, and the neo-colonial interests of the capitalist (and in a few cases the communist) world system (van den Berghe, 1983: 233-4).

Thus, the post Colonial state represents little more than a new mandarinate, a politically correct way of exploitation by the former Colonial powers. To a large degree it was the ability of the elite leadership to remain stable which kept the state from collapsing as an entity. The elite operate to maintain themselves, and we see that most of the leaders of the post Colonial states were little more than 'god kings' who had led rebellion against Colonial power through education and knowledge which impressed the masses.

Given that post-colonial African states were created by fragile institutions which were regarded as alien by the majority of the people within these states, the leaders were subject to incredible pressures from the former colonial masters or from those influences which had aided them in the road to independence.

Therefore, we can see two core peripheries in operation. Core-periphery has inherent within it a relationship-dependency function to it. In immediate post Colonial Africa this core-periphery can be noted in the following manner. There was no real core-periphery relationship between the state institutions and the ethnic-rural population, but there was a dependency by the state on outside aid; thus, the state had little contact with ethnic groups in the rural areas getting aid and food from outside sources. The Cold War reinforced this dependency; one function of the Cold War was the increased forced dependency of these states by the superpowers through the vicious circle of aid and economic control.

As the states' institutions lost contact with the masses, so too did their ability to control or shape the economy and resources of their state lessen. The economies of these states went to 'hell in a hand basket,' thereby increasing their dependency on the outside world. In the Cold War dynamics, aid also deemed that trade in weapons was essential. Thus, there was the creation of city-states with the city-state army protecting the government and the people of the government rather than the people of the state. Thus, the government, the city, and the army became the state, while the masses become the nation or nations within a set of pre-determined boundaries where the state claimed control through its economic and military power. Many African states were ruled by power and not by the people. To the masses of the people, the nation or ethnic group to which they belonged was central. Their communal way of life protected them, fed them, and gave them a sense of belonging.

The power structure and its 'clientele' relationship becomes more important as the Cold War ends. The power brokers in government are divided as they are forced to look internally to maintain the lifestyle that was available to them through aid (financial and military) from their former Cold War 'allies.' Institutions and relationships traditionally established in class societies are not in place; thus, the state is without a nation and a population which should feed into this system.

For the majority of society, ethnicity was the core, the rural area was the core, the city and the state were foreign, and city and state institutions were the periphery. The situation of the state and its institutions as a periphery within the state had its sociological, physiographical, psychological images already in place for the majority of the peoplefrom the time of the formation of the state. Only a few states and their leaders realized this early in the post colonial history of the state. Those that did not have begun to realize it in the short period since the end of the Cold War. As a periphery, these states were important in the Cold War, particularly in the 1960's and 1970's when the Cold War moved out of the European theater and into the Third World. While this increased their importance, dependency on the outside world also increased and relations with their own people were weakened, perhaps irreparably (O'Loughlin , 1987).

Moreover as Welch (1986) points out, Africa does not have a good record on the creation of civilian governments, with only ten constitutional executive changes of government by constitutional means compared with sixty-five successful coups d'état between 1958 and 1985. Furthermore, almost all of the constitutional executives have been elected in one party systems and have remained in control unchallenged for decades. Richmond (1984) also notes that the ethnic compositions of the armed forces of many African states do not represent the ethnic microcosm of their societies a pattern which was also apparent in the security forces of the colonial period. Loyalty rather than any other factor has determined the composition of the security forces. This situation has been translated into the post-colonial state with little more than the transfer of power to the social elites in the name of independence.

Security forces in the past were chosen by the colonizer, often not from the largest ethnic groups but from the smallest ethnic groups, thereby avoiding arming the dominant ethnic groups. An element of a clientelist relationship existed between the state governing elites and the army, and by association between the state and some of the minor ethnic groups. The army in African states is a highly politicized institution, whereas in the Western World it is an apolitical institution with loyalties only to the sovereignty of the state. The army in Africa has a set of sectional interests which help to maintain and enhance the power of the 'clientele' relationship within the state. The military are not perceived to have the same role in independence movements in Africa as they had in the rest of the Third World. As a result, in much of Africa the initial leaders to emerge in post Colonial African states were the god-king leaders who had the ability to control and feed the needs of the old armed forces of the former colonizer.

AFRICAN STATES IN POST COLD WAR WORLD DISORDER

In the aftermath of the Cold War, processes of solidification established as part of the Cold War are beginning to 'thaw.' As a result, the physiographical, sociological, and psychological adjustments have to begin anew. Murphree (1988) noted than many neo-Marxist scholars dismissed ethnic desires as tribalism, claiming such desires were little more than "a manifestation of the proletariat's semi-peasant psychology which hampers the development of its class consciousness, the emergence and growth of its organizations and the dissemination of its ideology" (Murphree, 1988: 123).

Richmond (1984) however, postulated that there are certain links which can be established in the rise of ethnic nationalism withinpost-industrial society. The technological advances in the post-industrial period have resulted in the creation of the a global division of labor and increased power in the hands of large multinationals. These changes, in turn, give rise to the emergence of supranational states which threaten the sovereignty of older nation states. How does such a role play itself out in Africa?

The debate revolves about the concepts of political power, social control, and the role of ethnic groups. Political power is nominally exercised through control over coercive forces, but in doing so the state becomes the most supreme coercive power. The state, while normally created to protect its peoples and territorial boundaries, does use its powers to protect the ruling elites from any internal threats.

Wallerstein, Gutkind et. al. (1985) point out that the roots of the global economy can be traced back to the industrial revolution and the mercantilist era which sought to establish trade between industrial Europe and the rest of the world. This was initially achieved through Colonial domination and economic exploitation, usually backed by military control, in much of Africa, Asia and the Americas. Richmond (1984) notes the distinguishing feature of the global economy in the post-industrial era is the emergence of multi-national corporations whose capital investments take advantage of cheap labor supplies outside the already industrial countries. The dominant philosophy of the post-industrial era has been the justification of the actions of multinational corporations, corporations who owe national allegiance to no one, acknowledge no social obligations, and are concerned only with the creation of wealth. The dynamic aspect of the multinational corporation permeability has been the proliferation of arms and weapons technology throughout the world. While access to weapons was the prerogative of those who had the wherewithall to purchase them, the state no longer controls the flow of weapons into or out of a country. In the 1970's and 1980's patriotism gave way to ideological wars or regional wars which had some ideological input from the major superpowers.

The transition form nationalism to multiculturalism will not take place without a struggle between competing elites. In the past, the threat of nuclear war or ideological domination created a dependence by weaker states on larger and more powerful states. This dependency has been changed by the end of the Cold War and the lack of desire by former protectors to continue to subsidize weaker states or their ruling elites.

PAN-AFRICANISM, SPHERES OF INFLUENCE, AND THE GLOBAL ECONOMY

Given the present situation in Africa, there is a clear need for Pan-Africanism to assert itself as a philosophy or ideology so that African nations have a direction or a critical mass of thought as to where they are heading in the 21st century. Africa must realize that self help is important. Former Colonial colonies are in economic trouble themselves and are no longer willing to look sympathetically at Africa, if they ever did. In any case, attempts at helping African nations by former colonizers would no doubt be part of a dependency process. The Western world is starting to look at Africa as a 'Dark Continent' once again , and with the increase in violent activity in many African nations in the Post Cold War period, this is hardly surprising.

Pan-Africanism is therefore more important at this time, and the mistakes of past Pan-African policies should be forgotten or put down to intervention of disruptive external forces and seen as part of the Cold War conflict. We would suggest two directions on Pan-Africanism, neither of which will happen of their own. They need work and attention.

Firstly, Pan-Africanism must emerge as a philosophy of Africanism which can transcend the traditional ethnic, racial, ideological, and religious barriers. This may prove an increasingly difficult task as religion moves into the ideological vacuum left by the ending of the Cold War. The traditional religious North-sub-Saharan divide in Africa is ceasing with the expansion of Islam into Kenya, Uganda, Tanzania, Mozambique, and so on, making these areas more vulnerable to the religious violence which has increased in Africa and Third World areas of Asia. However, if these new ideological-religious conflicts are set to become the new pariah of African under-development, then they have to be addressed by African nations in a Pan-African setting as opposed to a national context, before the "belt of conflict" in Africa along the religious hinge states escalates into a continental conflict, a scenario not unlike the Wars of Religion which dominated and destroyed much of Europe in the medieval period.

Secondly, Pan-Africanism has to become a force with an economic development agenda, but an agenda which encourages greater interdependency between African states as opposed to the types of unions actively being proposed between former colonies and their colonizer.

Although granted that these unions may bring some short term benefits, they appear to reinforce the First World-Third World dependency problem, especially where the dominant partner is the First World partner who can dictate the means, processes, and trajectories of development. There is greater potential for such unions to be successful in certain parts of Africa and where certain colonizer relationships are strong and encouraging. The case in point might be the role of France in the attempts to economically unify the Magreb region, and possibly large areas of western Africa which have strong ties with France.

South of the former French colonial region there is not the same impetus for economic union. In addition, attempts at economic unions under the flag of Pan-Africanism failed before often leading to conflict. The idea of economic union under the flag of Pan-Africanism is not new. Having learned from prior mistakes and by adopting the federalist type system of the EEC or the North Americas in the NAFTA arrangement, a new attempt at such unions may be possible.

The failure of economic union under Pan-Africanism in the past was often blamed on the role of the 'god-king' rulers, who refused to allow any of their power to be taken over by outside forces or organizations. Again we see the individual maximizing behavior at work. In this new fragile Africa emerging from the side-effects of the Cold War, we see a demand by all peoples for representation in government in a multi-party system regardless of whether the country is homogeneous or heterogeneous in its ethnic composition. With the removal of one party systems and these 'god-king' rulers, the concept of economic unity may be greatly enhanced if violent upheaval can be avoided in the processes of change.

It would useful if certain countries in Africa took the lead on specific aspects of Pan-Africanism. From a geographic perspective, there are countries which could operate as spheres of influence because of their location and economic potential; they could drive Pan-African economic integration and interdependency. The Pan-African philosophy on transnational cooperation could then be translated into other aspects of African society, psychology, and politics. The region of Central Africa, including such countries as Gabon, Congo, Zaire, Uganda, Tanzania, Kenya, and Zambia, would make for an interesting economic block which could tie in to other economic blocs, based on South Africa in the South, Nigeria in West Africa, the Magreb in the North West, and Egypt in the North East.

The choice of Zaire, South Africa, Nigeria, the Magreb, and Egypt as the building blocs on which sets of economic trade blocs could be established is based on their economic potential, given the comparative advantages they hold in a variety of areas. The best cases in point are Zaire which accounts for over 15% of the hydroelectric potential of the entire continent given present technologies, a potential which may be much higher in the next decade. Similarly Egypt has comparative advantages in certain high technology products, while the Magreb and Nigeria have oil and mineral resources. Egypt and Nigeria, like Zaire, are subject to conflict within, yet remain within the inner political working of the UN system, a valuable asset if Africa is to move itself directly onto the world stage. This added political prestige can then possibly translate itself across the continent of Africa through the trade blocs established.

The creation of trade blocs would make it possible to operate on larger scales with markets generated within Africa as opposed to outside it. In addition, these blocs could integrate in a fashion as to avoid the exploitation of individual countries by the First World, and put African nations in a position to bid for and set prices on the world market. The global economy is regarded as the integration of all markets. However, up to now the mode and degree of integration has been determined by the First World, with the Third World left in a poor bargaining position. Economic integration and a philosophy of African unity in the global market would considerably enhance interest in African affairs by outside nations, possibly leading to greater aid in the development process.

CONCLUSIONS

Africa has an important role to play in the post Cold War world. However, it must be realized that within Africa a considerable adjustment will have to made in the process. Violent conflict and political upheaval may be part of this process, and outside involvement will undoubtedly decrease. Thus, there is a need for Pan-Africanism to reassert itself in a post Cold War Africa, with a new post Cold War and new post Colonial state philosophy on the direction African states must take in this new order. Africa must seek not only to develop but to put itself on the world's stage as a bloc and not have its desires and aspirations proxied for it by former colonial powers.

FOOTNOTES

1. It should be noted that political leaders, political scientists, political analysts, or political geographers have failed to actually agree on what is the nature of a 'new world order.' The authors concur that such a 'new order' may also bring chaos and conflict. In particular, the authors suggest that ethnic conflict may arise as superpower control is removed from much of the Third World. Ethnic issues created in colonial times that were not addressed in the march towards independence and during ideological conflicts will have to be confronted, some violently and some non-violently.

REFERENCES

Cox, M., (1990), "From the Truman Doctrine to the Second Superpower Détente: the Rise and Fall of the Cold War", *Journal of Peace Research*, 27, pp. 25-41.

Hogan, M., (1992), ed. The End of the Cold War: Its Meaning and Implications, Cambridge University Press, New York.

Hyden, G., (1973), No Shortcuts to Progress: African Development and Management in Perspective. Heinemann.

Hyden, G., (1983), "Problems and Prospects of State Coherence in Africa" in Rothchild, D., and Olorunsola, V., (eds) (1983) State versus Ethnic Claims; Africa Policy Dilemmas. Westview Press, pp. 647-84.

Mearsheimer, J.J, (1990), "Why we will soon miss the Cold War", *The Atlantic.* 266, pp. 35-50.

Murphree, M.W., (1988), "The Salience of Ethnicity in African States: A Zimbabwean Case Study," *Ethnic and Racial Studies* Vol. II, April 1988.

Myrdal, G., (1968), Asian Drama: An Inquiry into the Poverty of Nations, (Vol. 2) Pantheon and Twentieth Century Fund.

O'Loughlin, J., (1987), Superpower Competition and the Militarization of the Third World", *Journal of Geography,* 86, pp. 269-75.

Richmond, A.H., (1984), "Ethnic Nationalism and Postindustrialism," *Ethnic and Racial Studies*, Vol,. 7, pp. 4-18.

Rothchild, D., and Olorunsola, V., (eds) (1983), State versus Ethnic Claims; Africa Policy Dilemmas. Westview Press

van den Berghe, P.l., (1983), "Class, race, and ethnicity in Africa", *Ethnic and Racial Studies*, 6, pp. 221-325.

Wallerstein, I., and Gutkind, P.C.W., (1985) (eds), The Political Economy of Contemporary Africa. SAGE publications. Beverly Hills.

Young, C., (1976), The Politics of Cultural Pluralism. University of Wisconsin Press.